Chevrolet LUV Owners Workshop Manual

by J H Haynes
Member of the Guild of Motoring Writers
and Ian Coomber

Models covered:
All Series 1 thru 6
models. 110.8 cu in (1815 cc)

ISBN 0 85696 319 4

HAYNES PUBLISHING GROUP
SPARKFORD YEOVIL SOMERSET ENGLAND
distributed in the USA by
HAYNES PUBLICATIONS INC
861 LAWRENCE DRIVE
NEWBURY PARK
CALIFORNIA, 91320
USA

Acknowledgements

Thanks are due to General Motors (USA) for assistance in providing certain illustrations and technical information; Mike and John Fatz of Two Brothers Automotive in North Hollywood for the loan of the Chevy LUV pick-up used as the project vehicle for this manual, and the Champion Sparking Plug Company who supplied the illustrations showing the various spark plug conditions. The bodywork repair photographs used in this manual were provided by Lloyds Industries

Limited who supply 'Turtle Wax', 'Dupli-color Holts', and other Holts range products.

Special thanks are due to all of those people at Sparkford who helped in the production of this manual. Particularly, Brian Horsfall and Les Brazier who carried out the mechanical work and took the photographs respectively, John Rose who edited the text and Lee Saunders who planned the layout of each page.

About this manual

Its aims

The aim of this book is to help you to get the best value from your vehicle. It can do so in two ways. First it can help you decide what work must be done (even should you choose to get it done by a garage), the routine maintenance, and the diagnosis and of course action when random faults occur. However, it is hoped that you will also use the second and fuller purpose by tackling the work yourself. On the simpler jobs it may even be quicker than booking the vehicle into a garage and going there twice, to leave and collect it. Perhaps most important, considerable amounts of money can be saved by avoiding the costs a garage must charge to cover their labor and overheads.

The book has drawings and descriptions to show the function of the various components so that their layout can be understood. Then the tasks are described and photographed in a step-by-step sequence so that even a novice can cope with complicated work. Such a person is the very one to buy a vehicle needing repair yet be unable to afford garage costs.

The jobs are described assuming only normal tools are available, and not special tools. But a reasonable outfit of tools will be a worthwhile investment. Many special workshop tools produced by the makers merely speed the work, and in these cases guidance is given as how to do the job without them, the oft quoted example being the use of a large hose clip to compress the piston rings for insertion in the cylinder. But on a very few occasions when the special tool is essential to prevent damage to components, then its use is described. Though it might be possible to borrow the tool, such work may have to be entrusted to the official agent.

The manufacturer's official workshop manuals are written for their trained staff, and so assume special knowledge; detail is left out. This book is written for the owner, and so goes into detail.

Using the manual

The book is divided into twelve Chapters. Each Chapter is divided into numbered Sections which are headed in **bold type** between horizontal lines. Each Section consists of serially numbered paragraphs.

There are two types of illustration: (1) Figures which are numbered according to Chapter and sequence of occurrence in that Chapter. (2) Photographs which have a reference number on their caption. All photographs apply to the Chapter in which they occur so that the reference number pinpoints the pertinent Section and paragraph number.

Procedures, once described in the text, are not normally repeated. If it is necessary to refer to another Chapter the reference will be given.

When the left or right side of the vehicle is mentioned it is as if looking forward from the rear.

Great effort has been made to ensure that this book is complete and up-to-date. However, it should be noted that manufacturers continually modify their vehicles even in retrospect.

Whilst every care is taken to ensure that the information in this manual is correct, no liability can be accepted by the authors or publishers for loss, damage or injury caused by any errors in, or omissions from, the information given.

Contents

Chapter	Section	Page	Section	Page
Introductory sections	Buying spare parts	4	Lubrication chart	8
	General dimensions	4	Routine maintenance -	9
	Glossary	7	Tools and working facilities	14
	Jacking and spare wheel location	12		
1/Engine Series 1 to 4	Camshaft	24	Flywheel (driveplate)	29
	Connecting rods	27	Pistons	25
	Decarbonisation	29	Removal	19
	Fault diagnosis	49	Valve adjustment	37
Series 5 and 6	Camshaft	45	Flywheel (driveplate)	46
	Connecting rods	45	Pistons	49
	Decarbonisation	46	Removal	42
	Fault diagnosis	49	Valve adjustment	49
2/Cooling system	Antifreeze	53	Thermostat	54
	Fan/alternator	54	Radiator	54
	Fault diagnosis	55	Water pump	55
	Flushing - refilling	53		
3/Carburation, fuel, exhaust and emission control systems	Air cleaner	59	Fuel pump	69
	Carburetor	60	Manifolds and exhaust system	70
	Fault diagnosis	83 - 84	Fuel tank	67
	Fuel evaporative emission control system	73	Float level	43
4/Ignition system	Coil	95	Fault diagnosis	95
	Condenser	88	Ignition timing	95
	Contact breaker	88	Routine maintenance	86
	Distributor	89	Spark plug and HT leads	95
5/Clutch	Adjustment	98	Inspection - renovation	101
	Bleeding	98	Master cylinder	99
	Fault diagnosis	102	Release bearing	102
6/Part A Manual transmission	Clutch gear shaft	111	Transmission - removal	105
	Fault diagnosis	124	Transmission - reassembly	114
	Mainshaft - dismantling	110		
Part B Automatic transmission	Fault diagnosis	124	Shift linkage	122
	Fluid level	121	Throttle valve control	123
	Rear oil seal - renewal	124	Transmission - draining	122
7/Driveshaft	Dismantling and reassembly	125	Universal joints	125
	General description	125		
8/Rear axle	Axle housing	131	Fault diagnosis	132
	Axleshaft unit	129	General description	129
	Differential	131	Rear wheel bearing and seal	130
9/Braking system	Bleeding hydraulics	136	Disc pads	140
	Brake pedal adjustment	134	Fault diagnosis	146
	Disc calipers	140	Master cylinder	136
10/Electrical system	Alternator	150	Heater control	163
	Battery - charging	150	Ignition switch	157
	Bulbs	148	Starter motor	153
	Fault diagnosis	166	Voltage regulator	152
	Fuses	155	Windshield washer/wiper	160
	Headlamps	155		
11/Suspension and steering	Fault diagnosis	196	Steering linkage	190
	Front suspension	181	Steering wheel	190
	Hub and bearings	181	Torsion bar spring	185
	Shock absorber	186	Wheel alignment	181
12/Bodywork and fittings	Body repairs	198 - 199	Hood	208
	Bumpers	208	Maintenance	198 - 199
	Door locks	199 - 201	Windshield glass	204
Metric conversion tables				209 - 210
Index				211 - 214

Introduction to the Chevrolet LUV

This manual covers the Chevrolet LUV pick-up Truck Series 1 to 6. One basic body style has been used since the introduction in 1972 of the Chevrolet LUV (Light Utility Vehicle).

All models have a single overhead camshaft in-line engine of 110.8 cu in (1815 cc) capacity. The Series 1 to 4 engine remained basically unchanged up to the introduction of the Series 5 in 1976. The Series 5 engine differs in that it has a crossflow cylinder head, with hemispherical combustion chambers and the timing sprockets and chain layout have been considerably modified.

On Series 1 to 4 engines the distributor and oil pump were driven by a layshaft whilst on the Series 5 engine they are driven by a pinion gear in front of the timing sprocket on the crankshaft.

A dry single plate clutch transfers drive to the 4-speed all synchromesh gearbox. Series 5 and 6 models are available with 3-speed automatic transmission.

Drive to the rear axle is by a propeller shaft having a universal joint at each end to allow for the flexibility of axle movement under varying driving conditions. From the hypoid type differential unit, drive to the roadwheels is by semi-floating axle shafts.

Double acting shockabsorbers are fitted front and rear and the front suspension is of the independent type.

Series 1 to 4 models were fitted with drum brakes front and rear, whilst Series 5 and 6 models have disc front brakes. A servo unit is incorporated into all models and all brakes are self-adjusting.

Buying spare parts and vehicle identification numbers

Buying spare parts

Spare parts are available from many sources, for example GM garages, other garages and accessory shops, and motor factors. Our advice regarding spare parts is as follows:

Officially appointed GM garages - this is the best source of parts which are peculiar to your vehicle and otherwise not generally available (eg; complete cylinder heads, internal transmission components, badges, interior trim etc). It is also the only place at which you should buy parts if your vehicle is still under warranty; non-GM components may invalidate the warranty. To be sure of obtaining the correct parts, it will always be necessary to give the storeman your vehicle's engine and chassis number, and if possible, to take the old part along for positive identification. Remember that many parts are available on a factory exchange scheme - any parts returned should always be clean! It obviously makes good sense to go to the specialists on your car for this type of part for they are best equipped to supply you.

Other garages and accessory shops - These are often very good places to buy material and components needed for the maintenance of your vehicle (eg. oil filters, spark plugs, bulbs, fan belts, oils and greases, touch-up paint, filler paste etc). They also sell general accessories, usually have convenient opening hours, charge lower prices and can often be found not far from home.

Vehicle identification numbers

Modifications are a continuing and unpublicised process in vehicle manufacture quite apart from major model changes. Spare parts manuals and lists are compiled on a numerical basis, the individual vehicle numbers being essential to correct identification of the component required.

Chassis number. The chassis number is located on a plate attached to the left-side pillar and it also gives the date of production.

Engine number. The engine number is located between the distributor and the cylinder head on the cylinder block body.

Paint color code. The identification plate for the paint color code is located on the rear engine compartment panel.

The engine number above the distributor on the cylinder block

The paint color code identification plate in the engine compartment

The vehicle identification number (chassis number) on the left side rear pillar within the cab

CHEVROLET

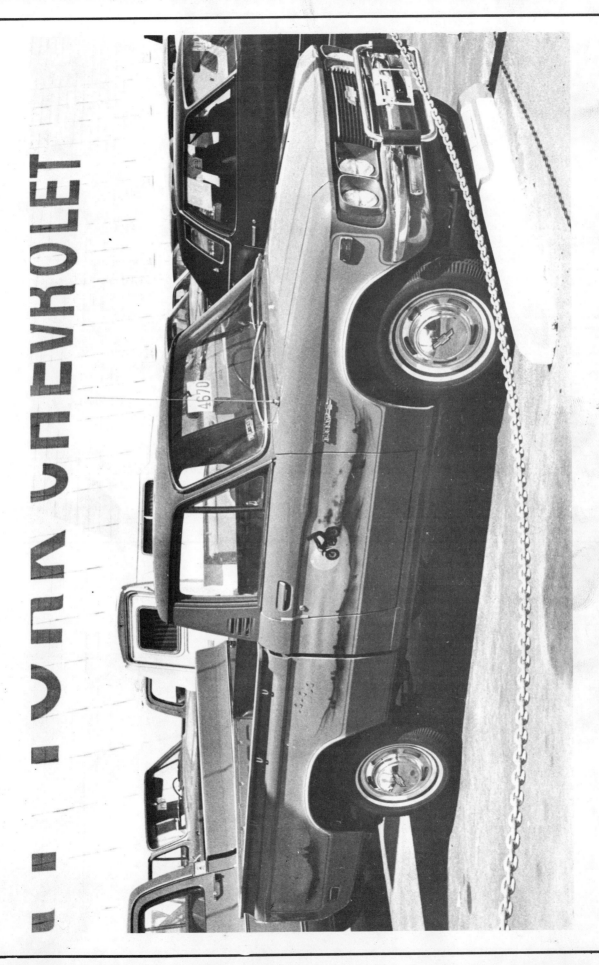

A neat looking Chevy LUV pick-up spotted on a Sales Lot in California

A Chevy LUV pick-up

Use of English

As this book has been written in England, it uses the appropriate English component names, phrases, and spelling. Some of these differ from those used in America. Normally, these cause no difficulty, but to make sure, a glossary is printed below. In ordering spare parts remember the parts list will probably use these words:

Glossary

English	American	English	American
Aerial	Antenna	Layshaft (of gearbox)	Counter shaft
Accelerator	Gas pedal	Leading shoe (of brake)	Primary shoe
Alternator	Generator (AC)	Locks	Latches
Anti-roll bar	Stabiliser or sway bar	Motorway	Freeway, turnpike etc.
Battery	Energizer	Number plate	Licence plate
Bodywork	Sheet metal	Paraffin	Kerosene
Bonnet (engine cover)	Hood	Petrol	Gasoline
Boot lid	Trunk lid	Petrol tank	Gas tank
Boot (luggage compartment)	Trunk	'Pinking'	'Pinging'
Bottom gear	1st gear	Propeller shaft	Driveshaft
Bulkhead	Firewall	Quarter light	Quarter window
Camfollower or tappet	Valve lifter or tappet	Retread	Recap
Carburettor	Carburetor	Reverse	Back-up
Catch	Latch	Rocker cover	Valve cover
Choke/venturi	Barrel	Roof rack	Car-top carrier
Circlip	Snap ring	Saloon	Sedan
Clearance	Lash	Seized	Frozen
Crownwheel	Ring gear (of differential)	Side indicator lights	Side marker lights
Disc (brake)	Rotor/disk	Side light	Parking light
Drop arm	Pitman arm	Silencer	Muffler
Drop head coupe	Convertible	Spanner	Wrench
Dynamo	Generator (DC)	Sill panel (beneath doors)	Rocker panel
Earth (electrical)	Ground	Split cotter (for valve spring cap)	Lock (for valve spring retainer)
Engineer's blue	Prussion blue	Split pin	Cotter pin
Estate car	Station wagon	Steering arm	Spindle arm
Exhaust manifold	Header	Sump	Oil pan
Fast back (Coupe)	Hard top	Tab washer	Tang; lock
Fault finding/diagnosis	Trouble shooting	Tailgate	Liftgate
Float chamber	Float bowl	Tappet	Valve lifter
Free-play	Lash	Thrust bearing	Throw-out bearing
Freewheel	Coast	Top gear	High
Gudgeon pin	Piston pin or wrist pin	Trackrod (of steering)	Tie-rod (or connecting rod)
Gearchange	Shift	Trailing shoe (of brake)	Secondary shoe
Gearbox	Transmission	Transmission	Whole drive line
Halfshaft	Axle-shaft	Tyre	Tire
Handbrake	Parking brake	Van	Panel wagon/van
Hood	Soft top	Vice	Vise
Hot spot	Heat riser	Wheel nut	Lug nut
Indicator	Turn signal	Windscreen	Windshield
Interior light	Dome lamp	Wing/mudguard	Fender

Miscellaneous points

An "Oil seal" is fitted to components lubricated by grease!

A "Damper" is a "Shock absorber", it damps out bouncing, and absorbs shocks of bump impact. Both names are correct, and both are used haphazardly.

Note that British drum brakes are different from the Bendix type that is common in America, so different descriptive names result. The shoe end furthest from the hydraulic wheel cylinder is on a pivot; interconnection between the shoes as on Bendix brakes is most uncommon. Therefore the phrase "Primary" or "Secondary" shoe does not apply. A shoe is said to be Leading or Trailing. A "Leading" shoe is one on which a point on the drum, as it rotates forward, reaches the shoe at the end worked by the hydraulic cylinder before the anchor end. The opposite is a trailing shoe, and this one has no self servo from the wrapping effect of the rotating drum.

Recommended lubricants

Component	Lubricant
1 Engine	SE engine oil SAE 10W-40
2 Transmission	
Manual	Engine oil
Automatic	Dexron ® II automatic fluid
3 Differential	GL-5 SAE 90
4 Steering box	GL-5 SAE 90
5 Brake and clutch system	Delco Supreme 11 or DOT-3
6 Wheel bearings	Grease GM Part No 1051344
Chassis lubrication	EP chassis grease

Note: *The above are general recommendations only. Different operating conditions require different lubricants. If in doubt as to the correct fluids, consult your driver's handbook or nearest GM dealer.*

Routine maintenance

Maintenance is essential for ensuring safety and desirable for the purpose of getting the best in terms of performance and economy from the vehicle. Over the years the need for periodic lubrication - oiling, greasing and so on - has been drastically reduced if not totally eliminated. This has unfortunately tended to lead some owners to think that because no such action is required, the items either no longer exist or will last forever. This is a serious delusion. It follows therefore that the largest initial element of maintenance is visual examination. This may lead to repairs or renewals.

In the maintenance summary, certain items are not applicable to all vehicles; as appropriate, these should be ignored.

Routine maintenance - all models

Every 250 miles (400 km) travelled, or weekly - whichever comes first

Check the engine oil level and top-up if necessary (photo).
Check the battery electrolyte level and top-up if necessary.
Check the windshield washer fluid level and top-up if necessary.
Check the tire pressures (when cold).
Examine the tires for wear and damage.
Check the brake and clutch reservoir fluid level and top-up if necessary.
Check the radiator coolant level and top-up if necessary.
Check that the brake operation is satisfactory.
Check the operation of all lights, instruments, warning devices, accessories, controls etc.
Check the cooling fan drivebelt adjustment.

Series 1 to 3 models

Every 3000 miles (5000 kms)

Lubricate the front suspension and steering linkages.
Drain and renew the engine oil. Check for leaks.
Check the tire pressures and their condition (including the spare).
Check that the wheel nuts are tight.
Check the brake lines and hoses for leakages and deterioration.
Check the brake master cylinder fluid level - top-up if required.
Check the clutch reservoir and top-up if required.
Inspect the battery terminal connections and also top-up with distilled water if required.
Check the coolant level and top-up if required. Check for leaks.
Inspect the exhaust system for signs of deterioration, leakage and secure mounting.
Check the engine idling and air fuel mixture - adjust if necessary.
Inspect the fuel lines for leakage, damage or poor connections.
Check the distributor contact breaker points - adjust if necessary.
Check the spark plugs condition and gap. Reset if necessary.

Every 6000 miles (9500 kms)

As per 3000 (5000 kms) miles plus the following:
Check the lubricant level in the rear axle and transmission - top-up as required.
Check propeller shaft flange bolts for tightness and the universal joints for wear.
Lubricate the parking brake pulleys and linkages - ensure that the cable is in good condition.

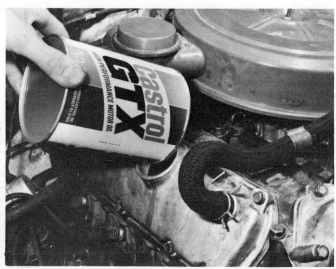

Topping up the engine oil

The engine oil filter

Raise the rear of the vehicle and check that the parking brake is in good working order.
Check the generator and air pump drivebelts for correct tension and condition - adjust/renew if required.
Check and lubricate the throttle linkages, the brake and clutch pedal springs and bushes.
Check and lubricate the hood and door latch hinges and latches.
Renew the engine oil filter (photo).
Check the throttle control linkage adjustment.
Check and adjust if necessary the ignition timing.

Every 12000 miles (19000 kms)

As per 6000 miles (9500 kms) plus the following:
Lubricate the front wheel bearings with wheel bearing grease.
Inspect the steering gear and check the lubricant level.
Inspect the brake linings and renew if required.
Check all electrical wiring, light bulbs and headlight alignment for malfunction and signs of deterioration - adjust and renew as required.
Drain the cooling system, flush and refill the system - check for leaks.
Lubricate the seat adjusters and seat track.
Remove the door trim panels and lubricate the window winder and door latch linkages.

Emission Control System
Carburetor/cylinder head
Check the carburetor and manifold retaining nuts for the correct torque specified.
Check the carburetor choke mechanism for correct adjustment and operation. Use a CO meter if available.
Check the cylinder head retaining bolts for correct torque specified.
Compression test each cylinder. If any cylinder registers less than 70% than the highest cylinder reading, the engine condition is suspect and should be repaired as required.
Check the valve clearances, and adjust if required.
Check the carburetor idle speed and adjust if required.

Distributor/timing
Renew the distributor points and condenser. Lubricate the cam.
Inspect the distributor cap and rotor and renew if worn or cracked.
Check the timing and advance mechanism, and adjust if required.

The recommended oil viscosity chart for the engine lubricant
Note: SAE 5W - 20 oils are not recommended for continued high speed driving.

Outside Temperature	Viscosity Lubricant To Be Used
BELOW 50°F	SAE 80
0° TO 90°F	SAE 90
ABOVE 50°F CONSISTENTLY	SAE 140

The recommended oil viscosity chart for the rear axle

Coasting richer system
Check the carburetor solenoid operation (see Chapter 3).

Fuel tank and supply lines
Inspect the fuel tank and supply lines for signs of leakage or damage.
Check that the fuel filler cap is correctly sealed. Renew as required.
Renew the fuel line filters.

Air cleaner
If vehicle operates in dusty conditions renew the air cleaner element.
Check the installation of the thermostat control and ensure that the hoses and ducting are securely connected. Test the check valve for correct operation.

Spark plugs
Renew the spark plugs and check the gaps.

Evaporation Control System (ECS)
Inspect all fuel and vapor lines/hoses to ensure good connections.
Remove the relief valve and check valve and test for correct operation. Renew as required.

Positive Crankcase Ventilation System (PCV)
Renew the PCV valve and ensure good connections.
Blow the hose out with compressed air.

Vacuum system and fittings
Inspect all fittings and connections for damage or deterioration. Renew as required.

Exhaust Gas Recirculation System (EGR)
Check the operation of the EGR valve. Run the engine at idle and open the throttle slightly. The valve should open and close on returning to idle.

Every 15000 miles (24000 kms)

Under extreme conditions of usage, such as heavy city traffic or very hot climatic conditions, drain the oil from the automatic transmission and replenish using the correct grade of lubricant.

Every 24000 miles (38500 kms)

Check the AIR system hoses and fittings and the mixture control valve operation. Renew as required.
Drain the transmission oil and renew with recommended grade.
Drain the rear axle oil and renew with recommended grade.
Renew the distributor cap and rotor.
Check the ignition HT cables and renew if needed.
Renew the air cleaner element.
Clean and repack the wheel bearings with the recommended grease.

Every 30000 miles (48000 kms)

Renew the automatic transmission fluid.

Every 36000 miles (58000 kms)

Drain and renew the steering gear lubricant with the recommended grade.

Series 4 and 5 models

Every 7500 miles (12000 kms) or 6 months

Chassis lubrication
Check and lubricate the front suspension and steering linkages.
Lubricate the parking brake pulley, cables and linkages.
Lubricate the hood latch and hinges, the tailgate latch and hinges.
Check condition of latches and hinges and adjust if required.

Lubricant and fluid levels
Check the brake master cylinder, clutch master cylinder, battery, rear axle, engine and transmission lubricant/fluid levels. Replenish as required.
A higher lubricant or fluid loss than normal in any of the above items is indicative of a malfunction, and should therefore be checked and rectified accordingly.

Propeller shaft
Ensure that the propeller shaft flange bolts are tightened to the correct torque - 18 - 20 lb f ft (2.4 - 2.7 kg fm).

Engine
Drain the engine oil and replenish with the correct grade.

Wheels and tires
Change the respective wheels and tires to alternative positions
Check the tires for wear, cuts or deterioration.
Check the wheel nuts for tightness. Torque to 60 - 80 lb f ft (8.2 - 11 kg fm).
If uneven tire wear is apparent, check with the tire wear diagram to ascertain the cause.

Exhaust system
Inspect the exhaust system for signs of leakage, deterioration and security. Repair or renew as required.

Suspension and Steering
Inspect the steering and suspension joints for signs of wear or lack of lubrication. Renew immediately any suspect components.

Brake lines and hoses
Clean and inspect the respective brake lines and hoses for any signs of cracks, chafing, leakage or general deterioration. Renew any suspect parts immediately.
On Series 5 models, inspect the disc pads on the front brakes - renew if required. Lubricate the caliper sliding parts.

General checks
Inspect the lap and shoulder safety belts, buckles and retractors for deterioration and efficient operation. Check that the anchorage points are secure.
Inspect the windshield wipers and fit new wiper blades if required.
Check the washer unit fluid level and ensure that the washer unit is fully operational.
Ensure that the parking brake is fully operational.
Check the side marker lights, headlamps, parking lights, indicators, back-up lights and hazard warning flashers.
Check the generator and air pump drivebelts for condition and tension.
Remove the spark plugs and clean and adjust the gaps.
Check the oil level in the rear axle and gearbox.

Every 15000 miles (24000 kms)

General
Service as per 7500 miles (12000 kms) plus the following:
Inspect the fan, generator and air pump drivebelts for signs of cracking, wear or deterioration. Check the tension and adjust if required.
Clean, inspect and lubricate the throttle and parking brake linkages and the brake and clutch pedal springs, bushes and pins.
Check the headlight alignment (see Chapter 10) and adjust if necessary.
Remove the rear brake drums and inspect the brake linings and wheel cylinders on each wheel.
Check the parking brake adjustment.
Steam clean or hose the underbody and chassis. Inspect for damage or signs of rust and repair as required.
Change the engine oil filter.
Drain and flush the cooling system. Replenish and check for leaks.
Check the steering gear lubricant - drain and renew lubricant every 37500 miles (60000 kms).

Emission control system

Timing
Adjust the carburetor idle speed and mixture - check with a CO meter if possible - see Chapter 3.
Check and adjust if required the engine timing and dwell.
Renew the distributor points and condenser, and inspect the distributor cap and rotor for signs of damage, wear or cracking. Renew as required.
Lubricate the cam.
Check and lubricate the distributor advance mechanism.

Carburetor/Cylinder head
Check the carburetor and manifold retaining nuts for tightness and tighten to the specified torque if required.
Check the choke adjustment and operation, in particular inspect the choke shaft which may be coated in petroleum gum or damaged.
Clean and repair/renew as required.

Fuel tank and fuel system
Check the fuel tank, fuel cap and supply lines for signs of leakage or damage. Ensure that the fuel cap is able to seal correctly.
Renew the fuel line.

Air cleaner
Inspect the thermostatically controlled air cleaner to ensure that all hoses, ducts and connections are in good condition. Check that the valve operates correctly.

Evaporation Control System
Inspect the fuel and vapor lines and hose connections.
Remove the relief and check valve and check that they are fully operational - renew damaged or worn parts as required.

Positive Crankcase Ventilation (PCV) system
Renew the PCV valve.
Inspect the hose and connections to ensure they are in good condition.
Blow the hose clean with compressed air, and if the hose is damaged or has deteriorated renew it.

Vacuum system and Air Injection Reactor (AIR) System
Inspect the fittings and connections for damage. If the hoses are cracked, worn or show signs of deterioration, renew them as required.

Valve clearance
Remove the cam cover to check the valve clearances.
Check that the camshaft carrier/rocker shaft bracket nuts are to the correct torque before checking the clearances. Adjust as required.

Spark plugs
Renew the spark plugs - check the clearances before assembly.
Check the HT cables and coil wires for condition - renew as required.

Air conditioning system
Inspect the air conditioning system hoses for secure connections and condition.
Inspect the refrigerant charge at sight glass (if fitted).
Renew the hoses or refrigerant if required. If any hoses show signs of deterioration they must be renewed by a GM Dealer. See Chapter . 10, Section 41.

Every 30000 miles (48000 kms)

Air cleaner
Remove and replace the engine air filter element, but do not use the vehicle with the filter removed - backfiring can occur causing a fire in the engine compartment.
Change the filter more frequently if vehicle operates in dusty areas.

Air Injector Reactor System
Check the hoses and fittings.
Check the mixture control valve operation and if defective renew.

Rear axle and Transmission
Drain and replenish the rear axle and transmission oils with the correct grade of lubricant.

Wheel bearings
Clean and repack the wheel bearings with the specified lubricant.

Cooling System
Drain, flush and refill the cooling system.
Renew any cracked or deteriorated hoses.
Have the filler cap pressure tested.

Spare wheel location

Jacking points

Jacking points: side/rear

Jacking points: front

Jacking points: rear

Chassis stand lift point

Tools and working facilities

Introduction

A selection of good tools is a fundamental requirement for anyone contemplating the maintenance and repair of a motor vehicle. For the owner who does not possess any, their purchase will prove a considerable expense, offsetting some of the savings made by doing-it-yourself. However, provided that the tools purchased are of good quality, they will last for many years and prove an extremely worthwhile investment.

To help the average owner to decide which tools are needed to carry out the various tasks detailed in this manual, we have compiled three lists of tools under the following headings: Maintenance and minor repair; Repair and overhaul; and Special. The newcomer to practical mechanics should start off with the 'Maintenance and minor repair' tool kit and confine himself to the simpler jobs around the vehicle. Then, as his confidence and experience grows, he can undertake more difficult tasks, buying extra tools as, and when, they are needed. In this way, a 'Maintenance and minor repair' tool kit can be built-up into a 'Repair and overhaul' tool kit over a considerable period of time without any major cash outlays. The experienced do-it-yourselfer will have a tool kit good enough for most repair and overhaul procedures and will add tools from the 'Special' category when he feels the expense is justified by the amount of use these tools will be put to.

It is obviously not possible to cover the subject of tools fully here. For those who wish to learn more about tools and their use there is a book entitled 'How to Choose and Use Car Tools' available from the publishers of this manual.

Maintenance and minor repair tool kit

The tools given in this list should be considered as a minimum requirement if routine maintenance, servicing and minor repair operations are to be undertaken. We recommend the purchase of combination spanners (ring one end, open-ended the other); although more expensive than open-ended ones, they do give the advantage of both types of spanner.

Combination spanners - 7/16, 1/2, 9/16, 5/8, 11/16, 3/4 AF
Combination spanners - 10, 11, 13, 14, 17 mm
Adjustable spanner - 9 inch
Engine sump/gearbox/rear axle drain plug key (where applicable)
Spark plug spanner (with rubber insert)
Spark plug gap adjustment tool
Set of feeler gauges
Brake adjuster spanner (where applicable)
Brake bleed nipple spanner
Screwdriver - 4 in. long x ¼ in. dia. (plain)
Screwdriver - 4 in. long x ¼ in. dia. (crosshead)
Combination pliers - 6 in.
Hacksaw, junior
Tire pump
Tire pressure gage
Grease gun (where applicable)
Oil can
Fine emery cloth (1 sheet)
Wire brush (small)
Funnel (medium size)

Repair and overhaul tool kit

These tools are virtually essential for anyone undertaking any major repairs to a motor vehicle, and are additional to those given in the Basic list. Included in this list is a comprehensive set of sockets. Although these are expensive they will be found invaluable as they are so versatile - particularly if various drives are included in the set. We recommend the ½ in. square-drive type, as this can be used with most proprietary torque wrenches. If you cannot affort a socket set, even bought piecemeal, then inexpensive tubular box spanners are a useful alternative.

The tools in this list will occasionally need to be supplemented by tools from the Special list.

Sockets (or box spanners) to cover range 6 to 27 mm
Reversible ratchet drive (for use with sockets)
Extension piece, 10 inch (for use with sockets)
Universal joint (for use with sockets)
Torque wrench (for use with sockets)
'Mole' wrench - 8 inch
Ball pein hammer
Soft-faced hammer, plastic or rubber
Screwdriver - 6 in. long x 5/16 in. dia. (plain)
Screwdriver - 2 in. long x 5/16 in. square (plain)
Screwdriver - 1½ in. long x ¼ in. dia. (crosshead)
Screwdriver - 3 in. long x 1/8 in. dia. (electricians)
Pliers - electricians side cutters
Pliers - needle nosed
Pliers - circlip (internal and external)
Cold chisel - ½ inch
Scriber (this can be made by grinding the end of a broken hacksaw blade)
Scraper (this can be made by flattening and sharpening one end of a piece of copper pipe)
Center punch
Pin punch
Hacksaw
Valve grinding tool
Steel rule/straight edge
Allen keys
Selection of files
Wire brush (large)
Axle stands
Jack (strong scissor or hydraulic type)

Special tools

The tools in this list are those which are not used regularly, are expensive to buy, or which need to be used in accordance with their manufacturers instructions. Unless relatively difficult mechanical jobs are undertaken frequently, it will not be economic to buy many of these tools. Where this is the case, you could consider clubbing together with friends (or a motorists club) to make a joint purchase, or borrowing the tools against a deposit from a local garage or tool hire specialist.

The following list contains only those tools and instruments freely available to the public, and not those special tools produced by the vehicle manufacturer specifically for its dealer network. You will find occasional references to these manufacturers special tools in the text of this manual. Generally, an alternative method of doing the job without the vehicle manufacturers special tool is given. However, sometimes there is no alternative to using them. Where this is the case and the relevant tool cannot be bought or borrowed you will have to entrust the work to a franchised garage.

> Valve spring compressor
> Piston ring compressor
> Ball joint separator
> Universal hub/bearing puller
> Impact screwdriver
> Micrometer and/or vernier gauge ·
> Carburetor flow balancing device (where applicable)
> Dial gage
> Stroboscopic timing light
> Dwell angle meter/tachometer
> Universal electrical multi-meter
> Cylinder compression gauge
> Lifting tackle
> Trolley jack
> Light with extension lead

Buying tools

For practically all tools, a tool factor is the best source since he will have a very comprehensive range compared with the average garage or accessory shop. Having said that, accessory shops often offer excellent quality tools at discount prices, so it pays to shop around.

Remember, you don't have to buy the most expensive items on the shelf, but it is always advisable to steer clear of the very cheap tools. There are plenty of good tools around, at reasonable prices, so ask the proprietor or manager of the shop for advice before making a purchase.

Care and maintenance of tools

Having purchased a reasonable tool kit, it is necessary to keep the tools in a clean and serviceable condition. After use, always wipe off any dirt, grease and metal particles using a clean, dry cloth, before putting the tools away. Never leave them lying around after they have been used. A simple tool rack on the garage or workshop wall, for items such as screwdrivers and pliers is a good idea. Store all normal spanners and sockets in a metal box. Any measuring instruments, gauges, meters, etc., must be carefully stored where they cannot be damaged or become rusty.

Take a little care when the tools are used. Hammer heads inevitably become marked and screwdrivers lose the keen edge on their blades from time-to-time. A little timely attention with emery cloth or a file will soon restore items like this to a good serviceable finish.

Working facilities

Not to be forgotten when discussing tools, is the workshop itself; if anything more than routine maintenance is to be carried out, some form of suitable working area becomes essential.

It is appreciated that many an owner mechanic is forced by circumstances to remove an engine or similar item, without the benefit of a garage or workshop. Having done this, any repairs should always be done under the cover of a roof.

Wherever possible, any dismantling should be done on a clean flat workbench or table at a suitable working height.

Any workbench needs a vice; one with a jaw opening of 4 in (100 mm) is suitable for most jobs. As mentioned previously, some clean dry storage space is also required for tools, as well as the lubricants, cleaning fluids, touch-up paints and so on which soon become necessary.

Another item which may be required, and which has a much more general usage, is an electric drill with a chuck capacity of at least 5/16 in. (8 mm). This, together with a good range of twist drills, is virtually essential for fitting accessories such as wing mirrors and reversing lights.

Last, but not least, always keep a supply of old newspapers and clean, lint-free rags available, and try to keep any working area as clean as possible.

Spanner jaw gap comparison table

Jaw gap (in)	Spanner size
0.250	1/4 in. AF
0.275	7 mm AF
0.312	5/16 in. AF
0.315	8 mm AF
0.340	11/32 in. AF 1/8 in. Whitworth
0.354	9 mm AF
0.375	3/8 in. AF
0.393	10 mm AF
0.433	11 mm AF
0.437	7/16 in. AF
0.445	3/16 in. Whitworth 1/4 in. BSF
0.472	12 mm AF
0.500	1/2 in. AF
0.512	13 mm AF
0.525	1/4 in. Whitworth/5/16 in. BSF
0.551	14 mm AF
0.562	9/16 in. AF
0.590	15 mm AF
0.600	5/16 in. Whitworth/3/8 in. BSF
0.625	5/8 in. AF
0.629	16 mm AF
0.669	17 mm AF
0.687	11/16 in. AF
0.708	18 mm AF
0.710	3/8 in. Whitworth/7/16 in. BSF
0.748	19 mm AF
0.750	3/4 in. AF
0.812	13/16 in. AF
0.820	7/16 in. Whitworth/1/2 in. BSF
0.866	22 mm AF
0.875	7/8 in. AF
0.920	1/2 in. Whitworth/9/16 in. BSF
0.937	15/16 in. AF
0.944	24 mm AF
1.000	1 in. AF
1.010	9/16 in. Whitworth/5/8 in. BSF
1.023	26 mm AF
1.062	1 1/16 in. AF/27 mm AF
1.100	5/8 in. Whitworth/11/16 in. BSF
1.125	1 1/8 in. AF
1.181	30 mm AF
1.200	11/16 in. Whitworth/3/4 in. BSF
1.250	1 1/4 in. AF
1.259	32 mm AF
1.300	3/4 in. Whitworth/7/8 in. BSF
1.312	1 5/16 in. AF
1.390	13/16 in. Whitworth/15/16 in. BSF
1.417	36 mm AF
1.437	1 7/16 in. AF
1.480	7/8 in. Whitworth/1 in. BSF
1.500	1 1/2 in. AF
1.574	40 mm AF/15/16 in. Whitworth
1.614	41 mm AF
1.625	1 5/8 in. AF
1.670	1 in. Whitworth/1 1/8 in. BSF
1.687	1 11/16 in. AF
1.811	46 mm AF
1.812	1 13/16 in. AF
1.860	1 1/8 in. Whitworth/1 1/4 in. BSF
1.875	1 7/8 in. AF
1.968	50 mm AF
2.000	2 in. AF
2.050	1 1/4 in. Whitworth/1 3/8 in. BSF
2.165	55 mm AF
2.362	60 mm AF

Chapter 1 Part A: Engine - Series 1 to 4

Contents

Ancillary components - removal 8	General ancillary items - reassembly 44
Camshaft carrier - installation 42	General description 1
Camshaft - examination and renovation 28	Layshaft - examination and renovation 29
Camshaft - removal 17	Lubrication system - description 22
Clutch and flywheel - removal 15	Major operations possible with the engine installed 2
Connecting rods and connecting rod/big-end bearings -	Major operations requiring engine removal 3
examination and renovation 25	Methods and equipment for engine removal 4
Crankshaft and main bearings - examination and	Oil pan (sump) - installation 39
renovation 24	Oil pan (sump) - removal 11
Crankshaft and main bearings - reassembly 35	Oil pump - examination 33
Crankshaft and main bearings - removal 21	Oil pump - installation 38
Cylinder bores - examination and renovation 26	Oil pump - removal 12
Cylinder head and valves - servicing and decarbonising 31	Piston pin (gudgeon pin) - removal 20
Cylinder head - installation 41	Piston rings - removal 19
Cylinder head - removal 10	Pistons and connecting rods - removal 18
End plates, layshaft and primary timing sprocket - assembly ... 37	Pistons and rings - examination and renovation 40
Engine/Transmission - installation 46	Pistons, rings and connecting rods - reassembly and
Engine and Transmission - removal 6	installation 36
Engine dismantling - general 7	Primary timing sprocket and layshaft - removal 14
Engine - initial start-up after overhaul 47	Secondary timing sprocket - installation 43
Engine reassembly - general 34	Timing case - removal 13
Engine - removal 5	Timing chain, sprockets and camshaft - removal 9
Examination and renovation - general 23	Timing chain, sprockets and chain tensioners - examination and
Flywheel and ring gear - inspection and renovation 32	renovation 30
Flywheel, crankshaft pulley and oil filter - installation 39	Valve clearances - adjustment 45
Front and rear plates - removal 16	

Specifications

Engine	4-cylinder, 4-stroke in-line, ohc, water cooled
Firing order	1, 3, 4, 2
Combustion chambers type	Wedge
Bore	3.31 in
Stroke	3.23 in
Piston displacement	110.8 cu in
Compression ratio	8.2 : 1
Compression pressure	163.56 psi @ 300 rpm
Compression pressure maximum variance	8.53 psi
Maximum output	75 AP @ 5000 rpm (SAE net)
Maximum torque	88 ft lb @ 3000 rpm

Engine weight-dry
Dry   ... ...   342 lb
With oil/coolant ...   .   355 lb

Exhaust gas control   ... ...   Air Injection Reactor system (AIR) (Federal)
Exhaust Gas Recirculation (EGR) (California)

Cylinder head
Inlet valves open at   ... ...   31° BTDC
  close at   ... ...   67° ATDC
Exhaust valves open at ...   .   59° BTDC
  close at   ... ...   23° ATDC
Valve clearance (between rocker and cam) at low temperature
  inlet   ... ...   0.004 in
  exhaust   ... ...   0.006 in
Valve head diameter
  inlet   ... ...   1.69 in
  exhaust   ... ...   1.30 in
Valve stem to guide clearance
  inlet (standard)   ... ...   0.0016 in
   maximum wear allowance   ... ...   0.0079 in
  exhaust (standard) ...   .   0.0020 in
   maximum wear allowance   ... ...   0.0098 in
Valve spring tension
  outer spring at length of 1.58 in   ... ...   47.4 lb nominal
   wear limit   ... ...   41.8 lb
   maximum deviation from vertical   ... ...   0.08 in
  inner spring at length of 1.50 in   ... ...   17.8 lb nominal
   wear limit   ... ...   15.4 lb
   maximum deviation from vertical   ... ...   0.08 in

Camshaft
Camshaft
  nominal height of cam   ... ...   1.534 in
  minimum height   ... ...   1.514 in
Camshaft journals
  nominal diameter   ... ...   1.89 in
  minimum diameter allowance   ... ...   1.87 in
  minimum wear allowance   ... ...   0.002 in
Camshaft endplay
  standard   ... ...   0.032 in
  maximum end play allowance   ... ...   0.008 in
Camshaft journal to bearing clearance
  standard   ... ...   0.0024 in
  maximum wear allowance ...   .   0.0059 in
Layshaft end play
  standard   ... ...   0.0032 in
  maximum wear allowance ...   .   0.008 in
Layshaft clearance between journal and bearing
  journal outside diameter   ... ...   1.772 in nominal
  maximum wear allowance ...   .   1.756 in
  maximum uneven wear allowance ...   .   0.002 in
  journal to bearing clearance (standard)   ... ...   0.0024 in

Pistons
Type   ... ...   Trunk (no T slot)
Material ...   .   LO-EX
Number of rings
  compression   2
  oil control   1
Piston to cylinder wall clearance   ... ...   0.0018 to 0.0026 in
Piston size
Standard:
  Grade 'A'   ... ...   3.3049 to 3.3053 in
  Grade 'B'   ... ...   3.3053 to 3.3057 in
  Grade 'C'   ... ...   3.3507 to 3.3061 in
  Grade 'D'   ... ...   3.3061 to 3.3065 in
Oversize pistons
  Standard   to cylinder diameter   ... ...   3.3071 to 3.3087 in
  0.005 in oversize to cylinder diameter   ... ...   3.3120 to 3.3136 in
  0.010 in oversize to cylinder diameter   ... ...   3.3169 to 3.3185 in
  0.020 in oversize to cylinder diameter   ... ...   3.3268 to 3.3283 in
  0.030 in oversize to cylinder diameter   ... ...   3.3366 to 3.3382 in
  0.040 in oversize to cylinder diameter   ... ...   3.3465 to 3.3480 in
  0.050 in oversize to cylinder diameter   ... ...   3.3563 to 3.3579 in
  0.060 in oversize to cylinder diameter   ... ...   3.3661 to 3.3677 in

Piston ring gap

1st compression ring	...	...	...	...	...	...	...	...	0.008 to 0.016 in
2nd compression ring	...	...	...	...	...	...	...	...	0.008 to 0.016 in
Oil ring	...	...	...	...	...	...	...	...	0.039 to 0.012 in

Piston ring to groove clearance

standard compression rings	...	...	...	...	...	...	...	0.0012 to 0.0028 in
maximum limit	...	...	...	...	...	...	...	0.012 in
Oil control ring	...	...	...	...	...	...	...	0.0008 to 0.0024 in
maximum limit	...	...	...	...	...	...	...	0.006 in

Gudgeon pin

nominal outside diameter	...	...	...	...	...	...	...	0.87 in
maximum wear allowance	...	...	...	...	...	...	...	0.8650 in

Connecting rods end play

Connecting rod to crankpin

standard	...	...	...	...	...	...	...	...	0.011 in
maximum wear allowance	...	...	...	...	...	...	...	0.014 in
Connecting rod to piston boss	...	...	...	...	...	...	...	0.069 in

Gudgeon pin to connecting rod small end bush clearance

standard	...	...	...	...	...	...	...	...	0.00024 in
maximum wear allowance	...	...	...	...	...	...	...	0.002 in
Connecting rod small end bush inside diameter (after reaming)				...	...	0.8662 to 0.8665 in

Crankshaft

									Journal outside diameter	Crankpin outside diameter
Standard	...	...	...	...	...	...	...	...	2.2016 to 2.2022 in	1.9262 to 1.9268 in
−0.010	...	...	...	...	...	...	...	...	2.1917 to 2.1923 in	1.9163 to 1.9169 in
−0.020	...	...	...	...	...	...	...	...	2.1819 to 2.1825 in	1.9065 to 1.9071 in
−0.030	...	...	...	...	...	...	...	...	2.1720 to 2.1726 in	1.8967 to 1.8972 in
−0.040	...	...	...	...	...	...	...	...	2.1622 to 2.1628 in	1.8868 to 1.8874 in
−0.050	...	...	...	...	...	...	...	...	2.1524 to 2.1529 in	1.8770 to 1.8776 in

Crankshaft end float

standard setting	...	...	...	...	...	...	...	0.0059 in
maximum allowance	...	...	...	...	...	...	...	0.012 in

Torque settings

									lb f ft	kg f m
Cylinder head bolts										
Series 1 - initial	...	...	...	...	...	...	...	...	43	5.9
Final	...	...	...	...	...	...	...	...	58	8.0
Series 2 to 4 - initial	...	...	...	...	...	...	...	43	5.9
Final - as specified	...	...	...	...	...	...	70	9.6
Crankshaft main bearing cap bolt	...	...	...	...	...	...	72	9.9
Crankcase bolts (Series 1)	...	...	...	...	...	...	...	15	2.0
Camshaft sprocket retaining nut	...	...	...	...	...	...	33	4.5
Connecting rod big-end bolts	...	...	...	...	...	...	...	43	5.9
Camshaft carrier mounting bolts	...	...	...	...	...	...	15	2.0
Layshaft sprocket retaining nut	...	...	...	...	...	...	33	4.5
Layshaft thrust plate bolts										
Series 1	...	...	...	...	...	...	...	...	6	0.8
Series 2 to 4	...	...	...	...	...	...	...	...	9	1.2
Flywheel retaining bolt -										
Series 1	...	...	...	...	...	...	...	...	36	4.9
Series 2 to 4	...	...	...	...	...	...	...	...	69	9.5

---

1 General description

The engine is of the four cylinder in-line type, the valves being operated by an overhead camshaft.

Both the crankcase (cylinder block) and cylinder head are manufactured in cast aluminium alloy. To increase rigidity, the crankshaft is supported by five main bearings which also enable the engine to operate smoothly under its varied operating conditions and prolong the life of the crankshaft bearings and allied components.

Both the crankshaft main bearings and the connecting rod 'big-end' bearings are of the shell type. The connecting rod small ends are fitted with bushes reamed to suit the piston pin (gudgeon pin) size.

In the cylinder head the valve system incorporates double valve springs unequally pitched to minimize valve bounce at high engine revolutions.

Wedge type combustion chambers are used.

The engine components are lubricated by means of a trochoid type oil pump driven from the engine layshaft (auxilary shaft). A full flow oil filter is fitted so that oil, delivered from the pump, is filtered prior to being forced into circulation to the various components.

The engine cooling system incorporates a radiator, thermostat, cooling fan and connecting pipes and hoses.

Special notes

Special precautions must be taken when handling the refrigerant lines of the air conditioning system (when fitted), and these are as follows:

a) *Flexible hose lines must not be bent to a radius of less than 4 inches (101.6 mm).*

b) *Flexible hose lines must be located at least 2½ inches (63.5 mm) from the exhaust manifold when refitted.*

Fig. 1.1, Sectional drawing of the engine

5.7a Disconnect the carburetor control cable

Fig. 1.2. Remove the air filter unit

c) *All metal tubing lines must be free of kinks and must therefore be handled with care.*
d) **Do not disconnect any of the air conditioning supply lines.**
e) *Do not weld or apply heat in the vicinity of the air conditioning lines.*

2 Major operations possible with the engine installed

The following major tasks can be achieved with the engine installed in the vehicle. The degree of difficulty varies according to the tools, lifting tackle and personal mechanical experience.

a) *The removal and installation of the cylinder head.*
b) *The removal and installation of the camshaft and bearings.*
c) *The removal and installation of the engine mountings.*
d) *The removal and installation of the flywheel.*
e) *The removal and installation of the clutch pilot bearing.*
f) *The removal and installation of the gear case and seal.*
g) *The removal and installation of the timing chains and sprockets.*
h) *The removal and installation of the oil and water pumps.*
i) *The removal and installation of the oil pan (sump).*
j) *The removal and installation of the pistons and connecting rods.*
k) *The removal and installation of the connecting rod bearings.*

3 Major operations requiring engine removal

The only items which cannot be removed and installed without the engine being removed are the crankshaft and main bearings.

4 Methods and equipment for engine removal

1   The engine can either be removed complete with the transmission, or the two units can be removed separately. If the transmission is to be removed, it is preferable to remove it while still coupled to the engine.
2   Essential equipment includes a suitable jack or support(s) so that the vehicle can be raised whilst working underneath, and a hoist or lifting tackle capable of taking the engine (and transmission, if applicable) weight. If the lifting tackle demands a reduction of weight, such items as the cylinder head, manifolds and engine ancillaries can be removed before lifting out the engine, provided that a suitable sling can be used for lifting purposes. If an inspection pit is available some problems associated with jacking will be alleviated, but at some time during the engine removal procedure a jack will be required beneath the transmission (a trolley jack is very useful for this application).

5 Engine - removal

1   Prior to commencing work it is necessary to drive the vehicle over an inspection pit, onto ramps or jack it up for access to the exhaust and transmission.
2   Remove the hood (bonnet) as described in Chapter 12.
3   Detach the ground cable from its battery terminal.
4   Drain the cooling system and remove the radiator as described in Chapter 2.
5   Drain the engine oil into a suitable container (and transmission if the gearbox is to be removed also).
6   Disconnect the hoses from the air cleaner and unscrew the air cleaner retaining clamp. Remove the air cleaner unit from the carburetor.
7   Disconnect the carburetor control cable (photo) and the fuel supply hoses. Disconnect the carburetor wiring (photo).
8   Unscrew the exhaust pipe to manifold flange retaining nuts and disconnect the pipe from the manifold.
9   Detach the connecting wires from the generator and starter unit. Remove the starter motor retaining bolts and withdraw the starter motor (if removing engine only).

5.7b Disconnect the carburetor wiring from the multi plug connector

5.8 Unscrew the exhaust pipe to manifold nuts

5.12 The ground cable and chain tensioner oil feed pipe

6.3 Remove the gearshift lever

Fig. 1.3. Remove the gearshift lever

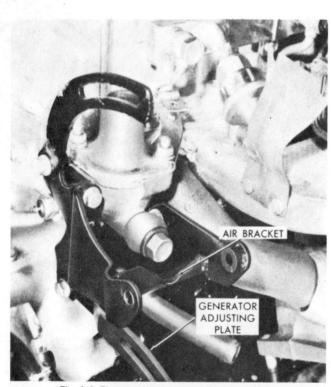

AIR BRACKET

GENERATOR ADJUSTING PLATE

Fig. 1.4. Remove the air pump adjustment plates

6.7 Removing the engine and transmission units. Note the angle of tilt and take care not to damage surrounding bodywork or fittings when lifting

8.8 Remove the generator retaining bolts and note the hose clip attached to the lower bolt at the rear

10 Detach the heater hose from the fender side and the vacuum hose.

11 On the right-hand engine side, detach the distributor high tension cables and the ground cable from the cylinder head cover to dashboard on the cylinder head cover side. Detach the distributor ground cable three retaining clips on the engine unit.

12 Disconnect the thermometer unit and oil pressure unit cords, and detach the ground cable from the timing gear case on the engine side (photo).

13 Detach the check and relief valve hoses.

14 Locate the lifting sling into the engine hangers and slightly lift the engine. Undo and remove the rear and front engine mountings.

15 Place a jack under the gearbox to support it and then undo and withdraw the respective engine to clutch housing retaining bolts.

16 Check that all of the surrounding engine to body connections and fittings are disconnected.

17 Carefully draw the engine forwards, away from the transmission, taking care that the engine weight is not transferred to the transmission input shaft (manual transmission), then lift the engine upwards and away from the vehicle.

18 It may be necessary to detach and remove the fan and pulley and also the crankshaft drive pulley to allow the engine extra forward movements in order to clear the transmission input shaft, and prevent damage to the matrix just forward of the radiator position. Take care not to let the engine sway or damage accessories, wiring or vehicle paintwork during removal.

19 With the engine removed, do not attempt to move the vehicle with the transmission installed unless the transmission is supported by a suitable means from the vehicle frame.

6 Engine and transmission - removal

Follow the instructions given in Section 5, paragraphs 1 to 13 and then proceed as follows:

1 Undo the clutch slave cylinder retaining bolts and detach the cylinder unit. Disconnect the exhaust pipe bracket from the clutch housing.

2 Withdraw the speedo drive cable from the transmission unit and detach the transmission to body ground cable.

3 From inside the cab, lift the gearshift lever boot clear of the transmission tunnel and unscrew the two gearshift lever retaining bolts (Fig. 1.3). Remove the lever (photo).

4 Detach the propeller shaft from the differential unit end (see Chapter 7) and withdraw the propeller shaft from the transmission unit. Insert a plug into the end of the transmission extension housing to prevent oil spillage.

5 On some models, it will be necessary to remove the gearbox rear mounting plate and crossmember to facilitate the gearbox downwards movement during removal. Support the gearbox with a jack and then remove the two bolts on top of the crossmember and two at the front.

6 Locate the lifting sling into the engine hangers and slightly lift the engine. Undo and remove the rear and front engine mountings.

7 Check that the surrounding engine and gearbox fittings and accessories are detached, lift the engine and transmission unit forwards and upwards (at an approximate angle of 60°). Take care not to let the engine and transmission unit sway or damage the surrounding accessories and paintwork (photo).

8 Transfer the engine and transmission to a suitable clean work area so that the engine and transmission ancillaries can be detached as necessary.

7 Engine dismantling - general

1 It is best to mount the engine on a dismantling stand but if one is not available, then stand the engine on a strong bench so as to be at a comfortable working height. Failing this, the engine can be stripped down on the floor.

2 During the dismantling process the greatest care should be taken to keep the exposed parts free from dirt. As an aid to achieving this, it is sound advice to thoroughly clean down the outside of the engine,

removing all traces of oil and congealed dirt.

3 Use kerosene or a good grease solvent. The latter compound will make the job much easier, as, after the solvent has been applied and allowed to stand for a time, a vigorous jet of water will wash off the solvent and all the grease and filth. If the dirt is thick and deeply embedded, work the solvent into it with a wire brush.

4 Finally wipe down the exterior of the engine with a rag and only then, when it is quite clean should the dismantling process begin. As the engine is stripped, clean each part in a bath of kerosene.

5 Never immerse parts with oilways in kerosene, (eg. the crankshaft) but to clean, wipe down carefully with a kerosene dampened rag. Oilways can be cleaned out with wire. If an air-line is present all parts can be blown dry and the oilways blown through as an added precaution.

6 Re-use of old engine gaskets is false economy and can give rise to oil and water leaks, if nothing worse. To avoid the possibility of trouble after the engine has been reassembled always use new gaskets throughout

7 Do not throw the old gaskets away as it sometimes happens that an immediate replacement cannot be found and the old gasket is then very useful as a template for making up a replacement. Hang up the old gaskets as they are removed on a suitable hook or nail.

8 To strip the engine it is best to work from the top down. The oil pan provides a firm base on which the engine can be supported in an upright position. When the stage where the oil pan must be removed is reached, the engine can be turned on its side and all other work carried out with it in this position.

9 Wherever possible install nuts, bolts and washers fingertight from wherever they were removed. This helps avoid later loss and muddle. If they cannot be installed then lay them out in such a fashion that it is clear from where they came.

8 Ancillary components - removal

1 If you are stripping the engine completely or preparing to install a reconditioned unit, all the ancillaries must be removed first. If you are going to obtain a reconditioned 'short' motor (block, crankshaft, pistons and connecting rods) then obviously the cam box, cylinder head and associated parts will need retention for installing to the new engine. It is advisable to check just what you will get with a reconditioned unit as changes are made from time to time.

2 If the transmission is attached, unscrew the retaining bolts from the clutch housing and separate the engine and gearbox units.

3 Unscrew the oil feed pipe joint bolt and remove the pipe.

4 Detach the respective hoses and cables from the engine, taking note of their respective positions for reassembly. Attach identity labels to ensure correct refitting.

5 Unscrew the distributor retaining bolt and mark the distributor bowl and engine in line with the rotor segment to ensure correct reassembly (see Chapter 4). Disconnect the vacuum line and withdraw the distributor from the engine.

6 Unscrew the oil filter retaining bolts and remove the filter. Withdraw the engine oil dipstick.

7 Slacken the air pump adjustment bolt and mounting bolt. Pivot the air pump and remove the drive belt, then remove the bolts to withdraw the pump unit.

8 Slacken the generator adjustment bolt and mounting bolt, pivot the generator and remove the drive belt, then remove the bolts to withdraw the generator (photo).

9 If it has not already been removed during the engine removal, undo the four securing bolts and remove the fan, spacer and fan pulley.

10 The air pump brackets are now removed after unscrewing the retaining bolts. Also remove the air pump and generator adjustment plates as in Fig. 1.4.

11 Disconnect the air cleaner bracket and air duct.

12 From the carburetor, unclip the throttle return spring and then unscrew the four nuts retaining the carburetor to the manifold. Remove the carburetor unit, and also the heat insulator and heat protector.

13 Unscrew the air injection nozzle joint bolt in the air manifold and remove the nozzle from the manifold. Slacken the air injection sleeve nut, unscrew the two retaining bolts from the air manifold bracket and remove the air manifold.

8.9 Remove the fan, spacer and pulley

Fig. 1.5. Unscrew the retaining bolts to remove the front cover

Fig. 1.6. Unscrew the timing sprocket retaining bolt

Fig. 1.7. The locating dowel

Fig. 1.8. Slacken the air injection nozzle sleeve nuts

Fig. 1.9. Method of removing the secondary timing sprockets

14 From the crankshaft pulley unscrew the retaining bolt. To stop the crankshaft from turning, wedge the flywheel ring gear with a piece of wood. Remove the bolt and pulley.

15 Unscrew the four bolts retaining the water pump and remove the pump unit.

9 Timing chain, sprockets and camshaft - removal

1   Undo and remove the screws retaining the camshaft timing sprocket front cover and remove the cover (Fig. 1.5.)

2   From the secondary chain tensioner plug remove the oil line. Withdraw the tensioner plug and tensioner spring.

3   Unscrew the timing sprocket retaining bolt and plate washer (Fig. 1.6) and then unscrew and remove the two damper bolts from the front of the cylinder head which retain the upper secondary timing chain.

4   Slacken the lower timing chain damper bolts and then remove the timing sprocket from the camshaft with the chain. The timing sprocket can now be carefully removed from the chain, but ensure that the timing sprocket pin does not fall out. It must be noted that when the camshaft is removed from the timing sprocket, the pin should be positioned at the top. Mark the pin position on the timing sprocket before dismantling.

5   Locate the chain with a suitable piece of wire or cord, and then unscrew the securing bolts and remove the camshaft cover.

6   The camshaft carrier bolts can now be unscrewed in an alternate and progressive manner. This is essential as the camshaft carrier is tensioned by the valve springs and therefore the tension must be evenly distributed and reduced to all of the carrier bolts. On removal of the bolts the camshaft carrier and cam can be withdrawn, but take care not to misplace the camshaft carrier locating dowel (Fig. 1.7).

7   Slacken each of the air injection nozzle sleeve nuts and rotate the nozzles 180° to remove them (Fig. 1.8).

8   Unscrew the timing gear cover retaining bolts and detach the cover. Unscrew the secondary timing sprocket securing bolt and remove the sprocket from the layshaft. This is easily achieved by locating and tightening alternatively two suitable bolts into the timing sprocket threaded holes as in Fig. 1.9.

9   On removal of the sprocket, extract the chain from the top and then remove the secondary chain tensioners from the cylinder head. Remove the bolts from the sprocket.

10 Cylinder head - removal

1   Undo and remove the timing gear case to cylinder head retaining bolts and then using an extension bar wrench progressively unscrew the cylinder head retaining bolts in the sequence shown in Fig. 1.10.

2   Having removed the cylinder head bolts the cylinder head can now be detached from the block.

3   The thermostat housing and air pump bracket can now be removed and also the inlet and exhaust manifolds from the head.

11 Oil pan (sump) and crankcase - removal

1   Invert the cylinder block and place on a clean flat surface.

2   Unscrew and remove the oil pan securing bolts in the sequence shown in Fig. 1.11.

3   The oil pan can now be removed. If it is reluctant to be separated from the base of the block, lightly tap it with a wooden or hide mallet.

4   On Series 1 models the crankcase is removed by unscrewing the 18 retaining bolts and prised from the cylinder block using a screwdriver.

12 Oil pump - removal

1   Unscrew the oil pipe connecting nut from the cylinder block.

2   Unscrew and remove the two oil pump body retaining bolts and withdraw the oil pump unit (photo).

13 Timing case - removal

1   Unscrew the timing case retaining bolts.

2   Remove the access plug and then unscrew the inner timing case securing bolt as in photo.

3   With a screwdriver, apply pressure to the cut-away sections of the timing case outer rim and prise the case from the block.

14 Primary timing sprocket and layshaft - removal

1   Unscrew the primary chain tensioner securing nuts (Fig. 1.12) and carefully remove the tensioner, ensuring that the shoe is not dislodged by the spring tension.

2   Remove the timing sprockets and chain. To do this, insert screw rods alternately and evenly into the layshaft sprocket holes.

3   The layshaft can now be withdrawn from the cylinder block after removing the two thrust plate to layshaft bolts. Take care not to dislodge the layshaft bearings during removal.

15 Clutch/flywheel - removal

1   Mark the relative positions of the clutch unit to the flywheel to ensure that they are reassembled in the exact position.

12.2 Removing the oil pump and feed pipe

Fig. 1.10. Cylinder head bolt removal and tightening sequence

13.2 The access plug removed and wrench to remove the inner securing bolt

2   Slacken the clutch cover to flywheel securing bolts evenly one turn at a time to release the spring tension.
3   Supporting the clutch pressure plate, unscrew fully the securing bolts and remove the clutch unit.
4   Bend the flywheel retaining bolt locking tabs over. Earlier engines had four retaining bolts with two locking tabs (photo), whilst the later engines have six with three locking tabs.
5   Undo the retaining bolts and remove the flywheel.

16 Front and rear plates - removal

1   Unscrew the retaining bolts and remove the front plate by tapping lightly with a mallet.
2   Unscrew the retaining bolts and remove the rear plate by tapping with a mallet.

17 Camshaft - removal

1   Unscrew the thrust plate retaining bolts from their position on the front of the camshaft carrier, as in Fig. 1.13.
2   With the bolts removed, detach the thrust plate and withdraw the camshaft from the front of the engine.

18 Pistons/connecting rods - removal

1   Stand the block on end with the flywheel side down.
2   Examine the respective big-end bearing caps and connecting rods. They should be match-marked from 1 to 4 from the front of the engine. If they are not, numerically dot punch the caps and rods at adjacent points, noting which side of the engine the numbers or punch marks face so that they can be installed in their original relative positions.
3   Unbolt number 1 big-end (connecting rod bearing) cap and remove it.
4   Before removing the pistons and connecting rods, carefully remove the ridge of carbon at the top of the cylinder bores with a scraper or emery cloth.
5   Using a wooden hammer handle, carefully tap the piston and connecting rod assembly upwards and out of the bore, taking care not to score the cylinder wall with the connecting rod as it passes through.
6   It is unlikely that the original shell bearings will be used again but should this be the case, retain them in exact order, identifying them in sequence with the connecting rod and cap sections.
7   Extract the remaining pistons and rods in the same manner.

Fig. 1.11. The oil pan (sump) retaining bolt removal and tightening sequence

Fig. 1.12. Unscrew the primary chain tensioner securing nuts

15.4 The early flywheel showing four retaining bolts and locking tabs

Fig. 1.13. Unscrew the thrust plate nuts

Fig. 1.14. Method of removing the piston pin

19 Piston rings - removal

1   Each ring should be sprung open just sufficiently to permit it to ride over the lands of the piston body, but take care not to scratch the land outer surfaces with the ends of the rings. Broken rings congealed in their grooves with carbon can be carefully extracted using a hooked tool. An old hacksaw blade ground to shape is ideal, but take care not to damage the ring lands and grooves.
2   If a piston ring expander tool is not available and the 2nd compression and oil control rings are out of their grooves, it is helpful to cut three ¼ in (6 mm) wide strips of tin and slip them under the ring at equidistant points.
3   Using a twisting motion, this method of removal prevents the ring dropping into the empty groove(s) as it is being removed from the piston. Always remove the rings over the top of the piston.

20 Piston pin (gudgeon pin) - removal

1   The piston pins are an interference fit in the pistons and finger pressure fit in the connecting rod small end bush.
2   With a pair of snap-ring pliers remove the snap-rings from the piston.
3   Immerse the piston into hot water and heat to approximately 158 to 212°F (70° to 100°C)..
4   Locate the connecting rod in a vise as in Fig. 1.14 and using a soft drift, drive the pin from the piston and connecting rod.
5   Ensure that each piston and piston pin are kept with its respective connecting rod, and note which way round the piston is fitted on the connecting rod.

21 Crankshaft and main bearings - removal

1   Position the cylinder block with the crankshaft side upwards.
2   Unscrew the crankshaft rear oil seal retaining bolts and remove the seal and housing and note direction of seal.

3   Examine the main bearing caps for numbers and directional fitting arrows. If they are not marked, dot punch them in order from the front.
4   Unbolt and remove each of the bearing caps, and note that the number 3 journal incorporates the thrust washers.
5   The crankshaft can now be lifted from the cylinder block. If the original shell bearings are to be used again, which is unlikely, retain them in exact order identifying them in relation to the respective crankcase and cap sections.

22 Lubrication system - description

The engine lubricating oil is drawn from the oil pan (sump) by a trochoid type oil pump which is fitted with a filter. From the pump the oil is forced into a disposable element type full flow filter. The oil is then transferred by force to the various engine bearings and components via oil galleries and feed pipes.

At normal operating temperature the trochoid oil pump will deliver 4.57 gallons of SAE30 oil per minute at a pump speed of 1400 rpm. The system is developed to supply oil at a pressure of 57lbs ft per square inch.

The oil pressure relief valve is incorporated into the oil filter mounting and pressure unit body (Fig. 1.16). The opening pressure of the relief valve is 61 to 67 lbs per square inch. The overflow valve opening pressure is 11 to 17 lbs per square inch.

23 Examination and renovation - general

1   With the engine stripped, and all components thoroughly cleaned, it is now time to examine everything for wear and damage. Parts and assemblies should be checked and, where possible, renovated or otherwise renewed as described in the following Sections.
2   Oilseals and gaskets must always be renewed. Oilseals can be prised out using a screwdriver or in the case of the timing gear case oilseal, it can be drifted out via the two holes as shown in the photo. Refit the seals by tapping in with a wooden block (Fig. 1.18).

Fig. 1.15. Remove the rear oil seal

Fig. 1.16. The lubrication system

OIL FILTER

PRESSURE UNIT

RELIEF VALVE

Fig. 1.17. The oil filter and mounting showing the pressure relief and pressure unit removed

23.2 Remove the gearcase oil seal

Fig. 1.18. Replacing an oil seal using a wooden block

PLASTIC GAGE

Fig. 1.19. Compare the plastigage strip with the index to calculate the clearance

3 Clean and inspect all casings for signs of damage and cracks. Renew if required. Clean all old gaskets and sealing compound from the mating surfaces.
4 If for any reason paper gaskets are not available, they can be made by smearing the surface to be sealed with engineers marking blue and a suitable sheet of gasket paper is then pressed carefully against the surface. The gasket can then be cut out round the blue marking left on the paper. A set of hole punches are useful if an extensive amount of gaskets are to be cut.
5 This system is especially useful when only one gasket is required as it saves buying a complete set.

24 Crankshaft and main bearings - examination and renovation

1 Examine the crankpin and main journal surfaces for signs of scoring or scratches. Check the ovality of the crankpins at different positions with a micrometer. If out of round by more than the specified amount, the crankpin will have to be reground. It will also have to be reground if there are any scores or scratches present. Also check the journals in the same fashion.
2 If it is necessary to regrind the crankshaft and fit new bearings your local garage or engineering works will be able to decide how much metal to grind off and the size of new bearing shells, required.
3 Full details of crankshaft regrinding tolerances and bearing undersizes are given in Specifications.
4 The main bearing clearances may be established by using a strip of Plastigage between the crankshaft journals and the main bearing/shell caps. Tighten the bearing cap bolts to a torque of 72 lb f ft (9.9 kg fm). Remove the cap and compare the flattened Plastigage strip with the index provided. The clearance should be compared with the tolerances in the Specifications. **Note:** Do not rotate the crankshaft with plastigage installed.
5 Temporarily install the crankshaft to the crankcase having positioned the other halves of the shell main bearings in their locations. Install the No. 3 main bearing cap only, complete with shell bearing and tighten the securing bolts to between 72 lb f ft (9.9 kg fm) torque. Using a feeler gauge, check the end-play by pushing and pulling the crankshaft. Where the end-play is outside the specified tolerance, the center bearing shells will have to be renewed (photo).
6 Finally examine the clutch pilot bearing (bush) which is located in the center of the flywheel mounting flange at the rear end of the crankshaft. If it is worn, renew it by tapping a thread in it and screwing in a bolt. Carefully press in the new bush so that it is fully located.

25 Connecting rods and connecting rod (big-end) bearings - examination and renovation

1 Big-end bearing failure is indicated by a knocking from within the crankcase and a slight drop in oil pressure.
2 Examine the bearing surfaces for pitting and scoring. Renew the shells in accordance with the sizes specified in Specifications. Where the crankshaft has been reground, the correct undersize shell bearings will be supplied by the repairer.
3 Should there be any suspicion that a connecting rod is bent or twisted or the small end bush no longer provides an interference fit for the gudgeon pin then the complete connecting rod assembly should be exchanged for a reconditioned one but ensure that the comparative weight of the two rods is equal.
4 Measurement of the big-end bearing clearances may be carried out in a similar manner to that described for the main bearings in the previous Section. The running clearances are given in Specifications.
5 Finally check the big-end thrust clearance which should be between 0.008 and 0.013 in (0.2 and 0.3 mm).

26 Cylinder bores - examination and renovation

1 The cylinder bores must be examined for taper, ovality, scoring and scratches. Start by carefully examining the top of the cylinder bores. If they are at all worn, a very slight ridge will be found on the thrust side.

This marks the top of the piston ring travel. The owner will have a good indication of the bore wear prior to dismantling the engine, or removing the cylinder head. Excessive oil consumption accompanied by blue smoke from the exhaust is a sure sign of worn cylinder bores and piston rings.
2 Measure the bore diameter just under the ridge with a micrometer and compare it with the diameter at the bottom of the bore, which is not subject to wear. If the difference between the two measurements is more than 0.008 in (0.2 mm) then it will be necessary to install special pistons and rings, or to have the cylinders rebored and install oversize pistons.
3 The standard clearance between a piston and the cylinder walls is between 0.0018 and 0.0026 in (0.045 and 0.066 mm). The easiest way to check this is to insert the piston into its bore with a feeler blade 0.001 in (0.04 mm) in thickness inserted between it and the cylinder wall. Attach the feeler blade to a spring balance and note the force required to extract the blade while pulling vertically upwards. This should be between 1.1 and 2.2 lbs.
4 Where less than specified force is required to withdraw the feeler blade, then remedial action must be taken. Oversize pistons are available as listed in Specifications.
5 These are accurately machined to just below the indicated measurements so as to provide correct running clearances in bores bored out to the exact oversize dimensions.
6 If the bores are slightly worn but not so badly worn as to justify reboring them, then special oil control rings and pistons can be installed, which will restore compression and stop the engine burning oil. Several different types are available and the manufacturer's instructions concerning their installation must be followed closely.
7 If new pistons are being installed and the bores have not been reground, it is essential to slightly roughen the hard glaze on the sides of the bores with fine glass paper so that the new piston rings will have a chance to bed in properly.

27 Pistons and piston rings - examination and renovation

1 Where new pistons have been supplied to match the rebore diameter, new sets of piston rings will also be provided but it is worthwhile checking the ring clearances, as described in the following paragraphs.
2 If the original pistons are being used, carefully remove the piston rings as described in Section 19.
3 Clean the grooves and rings free from carbon, taking care not to scratch the aluminium surfaces of the pistons.
4 If new rings are being fitted to old pistons (cylinders not rebored) then order the top compression ring to be stepped to prevent it impinging on the 'wear ring' which will almost certainly have been formed at the top of the cylinder bore.
5 Before installing the rings to the pistons, push each ring in turn down its cylinder bore (use an inverted piston to do this to keep the ring square) and then measure the ring end gap. The gaps must be as given in the Specifications and should be measured with a feeler blade.
6 The piston rings should now be tested in their respective grooves for side clearance. The clearances must be as listed in the Specifications.
7 Piston ring end gaps can be increased by rubbing them carefully with carborundum stone.
8 Where necessary, a piston ring which is slightly tight in its groove may be rubbed down holding it perfectly squarely on a carborundum or a sheet of fine emery cloth laid on a piece of plate glass. Excessive tightness can only be rectified by having the grooves machined out.

28 Camshaft - examination and renovation

1 Clean and inspect the camshaft lobes and journals for signs of wear or pitting. If these are readily apparent then the camshaft must be renewed.
2 Slight score marks on the cams can be removed by carefully and lightly rubbing down with a very fine emery cloth or oil stone.
3 Measure with a micrometer the outside diameter of the camshaft journals and cam profiles. Check them against the dimensions quoted in the Specifications and if necessary renew the camshaft.
4 To measure the camshaft end play, install the thrust plate into position. If outside the specified limits, renew the thrust plate.

31.5a The rocker arm and springs showing the location of the springs

31.5b Unclip the spring ...

31.5c ... remove the rocker arm and ...

31.5d ... the rocker guide

31.7a Compress the valve spring and remove the collets ...

31.7b ... and withdraw the springs and seats

31.11 Remove the valve

33.3 Remove the filter pan to gain access to the four bolts retaining the case to the pump

Fig. 1.20. Depress the rocker spring (1) and remove from rocker spring (2). Detach the rocker arm (3) and extract the rocker guide (4)

29 Layshaft - examination and renovation

1   Clean and carefully inspect the layshaft journals and oil pump drive gear for signs of wear, and renew the shaft if necessary.
2   Check the layshaft end play by fitting the thrust plate and timing sprockets to the layshaft and tighten the retaining bolts to 33 lb f ft (4.5 kg f m).
3   Move the thrust plate fully towards the timing sprocket and measure the distance between the end of the journal and the thrust plate. Renew the thrust plate if the clearance is beyond that specified.
4   Inspect the clearance between the bearing and journal and if beyond that specified, renew either the layshaft or the bearing.
5   If the bearing is being renewed it is a job best left to your local Chevrolet dealer who has the necessary tool for removing the bearing.

30 Timing chain, sprockets and chain tensioners - examination and renovation

1   If the timing sprockets show signs of excess wear or damage they must be renewed.
2   Lay the timing chain out straight and pull on it with a force of 40 ft. lbs. Now measure the length 40 links (at random) from the pin centers. The standard length is 15 inches and the maximum allowance for wear is 15.16 in. If the chain has stretched beyond this length it must be renewed.
3   Inspect the primary and secondary chain tensioners and shoes. Renew the tensioners if they show signs of wear or damage and if the tension spring is broken or distorted it must be renewed.
4   Inspect the primary and secondary chain side dampers for signs of wear or damage and renew if required.

31 Cylinder head and valves - servicing and decarbonising

1   With the cylinder head removed, use a blunt scraper to remove all traces of carbon deposits from the combustion spaces and ports. Remember that the cylinder head is aluminium alloy and can be damaged easily during the decarbonising operations. Scrape the cylinder head free from scale or old pieces of gasket or jointing compound. Clean the cylinder head by washing it in kerosene and take particular care to pull a piece of rag through the ports and cylinder head bolt holes. Any dirt remaining in these recesses may well drop onto the gasket and cylinder block mating surfaces as the cylinder head is lowered into position and could lead to a gasket leak after reassembly is complete.
2   With the cylinder head clean, test for distortion if a history of coolant leakage has been apparent. Carry out this test using a straight edge and feeler gauges or a piece of plate glass. If the surface shows any warping in excess of 0.0079 in (0.2 mm) then the cylinder head will have to be resurfaced which is a job for a specialist engineering company.
3   Clean the pistons and top of the cylinder bores. If the pistons are still in the block then it is essential that great care is taken to ensure that no carbon gets into the cylinder bores as this could scratch the cylinder walls or cause damage to the piston and rings. To ensure this does not happen, first turn the crankshaft so that two of the pistons are at the top of their bores. Stuff rag into the other two bores or seal them off with paper and masking tape. The waterways should also be covered with small pieces of masking tape to prevent particles of carbon entering the cooling system and damaging the water pump.
4   Before scraping the carbon from the piston crowns, press grease into the gap between the cylinder walls and the two pistons which are to be worked on. With a blunt scraper carefully scrape away the carbon from the piston crown, taking great care not to scratch the aluminum. Also scrape away the carbon from the surrounding lip of the cylinder wall. When all carbon has been removed, scrape away the grease which will be contaminated with carbon particles, taking care not to press any into the bores. To assist prevention of carbon build-up the piston crown can be polished with a metal polish. Remove the rags or masking tape from the other two cylinders and turn the crankshaft so that the two pistons which were at the bottom are now at the top. Place rag or masking tape in the cylinders which have been decarbonised and proceed as just described.

5   The rocker arms can be removed from the cylinder head by the following method, refer to Fig. 1.20. Depress the rocker spring (1) and remove the arm from the adjuster ball (2). Detach the rocker arm (photo) (3), and extract the rocker guide (4).
6   On removal, the rockers must be kept in their correct sequence unless they are badly worn and are to be renewed.
7   With a valve spring compressor, compress each valve in turn until the two halves of the collets can be removed (photo). Release the compressor and remove the inner and outer springs and spring seats (retaining caps) (photo).
8   If, when the valve spring compressor is screwed down, the valve spring retaining cap refuses to free to expose the split collet, do not continue to screw down the compressor as there is a likelihood of damage occuring.
9   Gently tap the top of the tool directly over the cap with a light hammer. This will free the cap. To avoid the compressor jumping off the valve spring retaining cap when it is tapped, hold the compressor firmly in position with one hand.
10 When the valve springs are being compressed ensure that the valve spring compressor screw contacts the center of the valve head.
11 Remove the valve (photo). Examine the heads of the valves for pitting and burning, especially the heads of the exhaust valves. The valve seatings should be examined at the same time. If the pitting on valve and seat is very slight the marks can be removed by grinding the seats and valve together with coarse, and then fine, valve grinding paste.
12 Where bad pitting has occured to the valve seats it will be necessary to recut them and fit new valves. If the valves seats are so worn that they cannot be recut, then it will be necessary to fit new valve seat inserts. These latter two jobs should be entrusted to the local Chevrolet agent or engineering works. In practice it is very seldom that the seats are so badly worn that they require renewal. Normally, it is the valve that is too badly worn for replacement, and the owner can easily purchase a new set of valves and match them to the seats by valve grinding.
13 Valve grinding is carried out as follows:
    Smear a trace of coarse carborundum paste on the seat face and apply a suction grinder tool to the valve head. With a semi-rotary motion, grind the valve head to its seat, lifting the valve occasionally to redistribute the grinding paste. When a dull matt even surface finish is produced on both the valve seat and the valve, wipe off the paste and repeat the process with fine carborundum paste, lifting and turning the valve to redistribute the paste as before. A light spring placed under the valve head will greatly ease this operation. When a smooth unbroken ring of light grey matt finish is produced, on both valve and valve seat faces, the grinding operation is complete.
14 Scrape away all carbon from the valve head and the valve stem. Carefully clean away every trace of grinding compound, taking great care to leave none in the ports or in the valve guides. Clean the valves and the valve seats with a kerosene soaked rag then with a clean rag, and finally, if an air-line is available, blow the valves, valve guides and valve ports clean.
15 Test each valve in its guide for wear. After a considerable mileage, the valve guide bore may wear oval. This can be tested by inserting a new valve in the guide and moving it from side to side. If the tip of the valve stem deflects by about 0.0080 in (0.2 mm) inlet or 0.010 (0.25 mm) exhaust then it must be assumed that the tolerance between the stem and guide is greater than the permitted maximum.
16 If replacement valve guides are to be fitted this is a job best left to your local GM dealer or auto engineer, who will have the correct tool for removal and refitting of the guide.
17 The pivot should not be removed from the head unless it is being renewed. When fitting a new pivot, tighten it to a torque of 90 lb f ft (12.4 kg f m).

32 Flywheel and ring gear - inspection and renovation

1   If the teeth on the flywheel starter ring are badly worn or some are missing, it will be necessary to renew the ring gear.
2   This can be achieved by splitting the ring with a cold chisel, but the greatest care must be taken not to damage the flywheel during this process.
3   To fit the new ring heat it evenly with an oxy-acetylene flame until the ring has expanded sufficiently to allow it to be located on the

Fig. 1.21. The oil pump component parts

2	Pinion	7	Case
3	Pin	8	Screen
4	Bolt, lockwasher, plain washer	9	Bolt, lockwasher
5	Pipe assembly	10	Body
6	Rotor set	11	Cover

33.4 The rotor and vanes cleaned for inspection

35.2 Insert the main bearing shells into position

flywheel. Allow the ring gear to cool naturally, and it will contract and should be a tight and permanent fit on the flywheel.

4　Care must be taken to ensure that the ring is not overheated or the temper of the ring will be lost.

5　Inspect the flywheel for signs of cracks or damage and renew if necessary. Check also the thickness of the friction face which is 1.46 in standard hub with a maximum wear limit of 1.42 in.

33 Oil pump - examination and renovation

1　The oil pump drive gear is located on its shaft by a taper pin. At the other end of the shaft the drive rotor in the oil pump is located with a pin.

2　Remove the oil pump shaft drive gear to obtain access to the pin on the oil pump drive rotor.

3　The oil pump rotors are accessible on removing the filter pan and four bolts retaining the case to the pump (photo).

4　Clean the components of the pump and inspect for signs of excessive wear (photo).

5　Inspect the rotor and lobes. Any deep score marks or pittings will necessitate renewal of the pump.

6　With a feeler gauge measure the clearance between the tip of the rotor and vane. The normal clearance is 0.0012 to 0.0059 in and any wear beyond these limits necessitates renewal of the pump, rotor or vane (Fig. 1.21.).

7　Measure the clearance between the vane and pump body inner wall. Renew the pump body or vane if the clearance exceeds 0.008 to 0.011 in.

8　Check the clearance between the rotor, vane and pump body cover as in Fig. 1.23 using a straight edge rule and feeler gauge. A clearance beyond 0.006 in means the pump must be renewed.

9　With a micrometer measure the pump rotor shaft diameter and the inside diameter of the rotor shaft bore in the body. If the clearance exceeds 0.008 in renew the pump.

Fig. 1.22. Insert feeler gauge between rotor and vane tip

Fig. 1.23. Method to check the rotor, vane and pump body clearance using straight edge and feeler gauge

34 Engine reassembly - general

1   To ensure maximum life with minimum trouble from a rebuilt engine, not only must every part be correctly assembled, but everything must be spotlessly clean, all the oilways must be clear, locking washers and spring washers must always be fitted where indicated and all bearings and other working surfaces must be thoroughly lubricated during assembly. Before assembly begins, renew any bolts or studs whose threads are in any way damaged; whenever possible use new spring washers and cotter pins.

2   Apart from your normal tools, a supply of lint-free cloths, an oil can filled with engine oil (an empty washing-up fluid plastic bottle thoroughly clean and washed out will invariably do just as well), a supply of new spring washers, a set of new gaskets and a torque wrench should be collected together.

3   Carefully check the specified clearances of components during reassembly, and where given tighten all nuts and bolts to the recommended torque values.

35 Crankshaft and main bearings - reassembly

1   Invert the cylinder block and ensure that it is perfectly clean and that the oil ways are clear.

2   Insert the main bearing shells into their seats (photo) and lubricate them with clean engine oil.

3   On Series 1 engines locate the seal into its groove in the rear end of the block and cut off any protruding seal flush with the end cap mating face (photo). Insert the seal into the rear main bearing cap groove and cut off flush any protruding seal, see Fig. 1.24.

4   Place the crankshaft carefully into position in the block (photo), and then install the thrust bearings into their location on both sides of the No. 3 journal as in Fig. 1.27. The thrust bearing smooth face is positioned towards the crankshaft on later models. On Series 1 engines the smooth face is towards the crankcase.

5   Place the bearing shells into their caps and lubricate them with oil. Place them in position. The marking on the back face of the caps point to the front of the engine. No. 1 bearing cap differs in contour from the other caps. Nos. 2 and 3 caps are marked with an 'A' on the back face as in Fig. 1.25..

6   Alternatively tighten the bearing caps starting at number 3, to a torque of 72 lb f ft (9.9 kg f m). (photo).

7   With all the bearing caps tightened, rotate the crankshaft to ensure that it turns smoothly and does not drag. Check the crankshaft and play which should be 0.0059 in (photo). If on Series 1 engines the crankshaft is tight in rotation, recheck the location of the rear oil seal. The crankshaft on this engine series should be able to turn freely under a torque loading of 15 to 22 lb f ft (2 to 3 kg f m).

8   On Series 2 to 4 models the rear oil seal is now positioned in its retainer. The seal is an interference fit in the retainer and can be inserted by locating squarely on the retainer and tapped into position using a wooden block as in Fig. 1.18.

9   Grease the lips of the oil seal and position the gasket to cylinder block, smearing a jointing compound over the two faces. Align the dowel rods and holes and fit the oil seal and retainer, securing with the bolts and washers.

36 Pistons, rings and connecting rods - reassembly and installation

1   Position the cylinder block with the flywheel end downwards.

2   To assemble the respective pistons to their connecting rods, heat the piston to 158° to 212°F (70° to 100°C), the piston can be suspended in a bowl of hot water to achieve this. Fit a snapring into a piston pin bore groove and then align the connecting rod small end bore with the piston pin bore.

3   Press the piston pin, using finger pressure, into the piston and through the small end and locate the pin against the previously inserted snapring (photo).

The piston and connecting rod must be assembled with the cylinder number mark on the righthand side of the groove in the front of the piston crown.

4   Assemble the rings to the pistons. The rings must be fitted with their markings NPR or TOP facing upwards. Use a ring expander for fitting if available or alternatively reverse the dismantling procedure

Fig. 1.24. Series 1 models rear oil seal location

A   must be free from projection and depression
B   cut off excess seal
C   cut off excess seal

With the seal correctly located the crankshaft can be rotated using a torque of 15 to 22 ft. lbs. (2.0 to 3.0 kg fm).

Fig. 1.25. The respective main bearing caps

Fig. 1.26. Using a ring expander to fit the piston rings

35.3 Insert and trim off excess rear seal into recess in rear main of block and cap (Series I models)

35.4 Place the crankshaft carefully into position

35.5 Position the main bearing caps

35.6 Tighten the main bearing caps to the recommended torque

35.7 Check the crankshaft end play with a feeler gauge

36.3 Insert the piston pin, pressing it flush against the snap ring

36.8 Locate the respective connecting rods, caps and bearing shells prior to assembly

36.9 Use a ring compressor to fit the pistons and compress the rings

36.12a Fit the big end (connecting rod) bearing and cap ...

36.12b ... but ensure that the identification numbers are adjacent to each other

36.13 Tighten the connecting rod end cap bolts to the specified torque

37.2 The front end plate bolted into position

Fig. 1.27. Insert the thrust bearings

Fig. 1.28. Align the sprockets with the timing marks adjacent

37.4 The layshaft thrust plate bolted
in position

37.6a Refit the timing chain tensioner.
Note the timing marks

37.6b Refit the water pump and gasket

5   When all the rings are assembled onto the pistons, rotate each top
compression ring so that its gap faces the front of the piston and then
rotate and position the 2nd compression and oil ring gaps at 120°
intervals.
6   Rotate the crankshaft to the TDC position.
7   Lubricate with clean engine oil the bore of the first piston to
be fitted and also lubricate the piston and rings.
8   Position the connecting rod and big-end cap bearing shells into
position (photo) and lubricate them.
9   Compress the piston rings with a suitable compressor and locate in
the cylinder bore (photo).
10 Carefully tap the piston crown with a wooden hammer handle and
insert the piston into its cylinder.
11 Engage the connecting rod with the crankshaft when the crankpin
is at its lowest point of rotation and travel. Lubricate the exposed
part of the crankpin.
12 Install the big-end cap (photo) complete with shell bearing ensuring
that the numbers are adjacent in their sequence (photo).
13 Tighten the big-end bolts to the specified torque figure of 43 lb f ft
(5.9 kg fm) (photo) and then check the connecting rod end play which
should be 0.0079 to 0.0130 in (0.2 to 0.3 mm).
14 Repeat the operations to install the remaining three pistons/
connecting rod assemblies.

37 End plates layshaft and primary timing sprocket - assembly

1   Relocate the rear plate to the cylinder block and secure with bolts
2   Smear the front plate gasket with jointing compound and refit the
front plate. Secure with bolts, (photo).
3   Rotate the crankshaft to position number 1 and 4 pistons at TDC
(top dead centre). To check that TDC position is correct, position the
timing cover over the dowels and place the crankshaft pulley in position.
The TDC mark should align with the timing pointer.
4   Lubricate the layshaft and insert it into position. Locate the thrust
plate on the layshaft and tighten the securing bolts to a torque of
9 lb f ft (1.2 kg f m), on Series 2 to 4. Series 1 models tighten to 6 lb f ft
(0.8 kg f m) (photo).
5   Insert the crankshaft and layshaft primary timing sprockets into
position in their drive chain and ensure that the timing marks (Fig. 1.28)
are adjacent to each other as shown. When fitting the primary sprocket
to the layshaft the timing mark on the layshaft timing mark must
align with that of the crankshaft sprocket.
Note: The layshaft keyway is not the timing mark. The layshaft keyway
and sprocket are aligned and then the layshaft is turned and the sprocket
positions for timing set by lightly tapping each sprocket alternately.
Support the layshaft from within the crankcase to prevent it
turning when locating the sprockets.
6   Refit the primary chain tensioner (photo), and install the
water pump and gasket (photo).

38 Oil pump - installation

1   With the marks on the timing sprockets aligned, fit the oil pump into
position (photo) with the groove in the end of the pump drive pinion
at a right-angle to the layshaft, and the oil pump rotor slot towards the
rear of the cylinder block.

Fig. 1.29. Fit the oil pan/cylinder block rubber gasket

2   The oil pump drive pinion must mesh with the helical drive gear on the layshaft.
3   Insert the pump retaining bolts and tighten.
4   Reconnect the oil pipe from the pump to the cylinder block, and tighten the pipe nut.

39 Crankcase oil pan (sump) - installation

Series 1

1   Apply a liberal quantity of jointing compound to the sealing gaskets. Insert the gaskets into position in the No. 1 and 5 main bearing caps. The gaskets must fit fully with no end clearances.
2   Fit the crankcase and insert the retaining bolts. Tighten to 15 lb f ft torque (2.0 kg f m).

Series 2 to 4

3   Smear a liberal quantity of jointing compound to the front and rear portions of the jointing face and install the rubber gasket as in Fig. 1.29.
4   Reposition the oil pan and gasket, and locate the retaining bolts and nuts.
5   Tighten the retaining bolts and nuts evenly in the sequence shown in Fig. 1.30 to a torque of 50 in^2 lbs (3.5 Hg/cm^2).

40 Flywheel/Crankshaft pulley/Oil filter - installation

1   Locate the flywheel onto the crankshaft and fit the lock plates and retaining bolts.
2   Tighten the bolts to a torque of 36 lb f ft (4.9 kg f m) on Series 1 models, and 69 lb f ft (9.5 kg f m) on Series 2 to 4.
3   Lock the bolts by bending over the lock plate tabs. Reassemble the clutch unit as described in Chapter 5.
4   Refit the under cover to the rear plate.
5   Lubricate with oil the face of the crankshaft pulley to oil seal face and refit the pulley onto the shaft.
6   Secure the pulley with bolt and lock washer.
7   Refit the oil filter unit (photo). If the pressure unit or oil pressure relief valve have been removed they must be installed to the filter unit but ensure that the respective components are perfectly clean.

41 Cylinder head - installation

1   Ensure that the cylinder block and gear case upper faces are parallel using a straight edge as in Fig. 1.31. The gearcase must be relocated or renewed if the distributor is in access of 0.007 in (0.17 mm).

Fig. 1.30. The oil pan retaining nuts/bolts tightening sequence

38.1 Relocate the oil pump - observe the instructions in paragraphs 1 and 2

38.4 Reconnect the oil pipe

39.3 The oil pan gasket in position

40.7 Refit the oil filter unit using a new sealing gasket

41.3 The cylinder head gasket in position

41.6 Tighten the cylinder head bolts to the torque specified - see paragraph No. 6.

41.7 Locate and tighten the timing case bolts

41.8 Relocate the air injection nozzles but do not tighten

43.2 Align the camshaft shaft and thrust plate

43.5 Locate the timing chain onto the timing sprocket

43.6 The layshaft timing sprocket located and with the timing mark at the 2 o'clock position

43.7 The camshaft timing sprocket located with the timing mark at approximately 12 o'clock position (exact position if correct 6° 20')

44.2 The thermostat housing, air pump bracket and generator adjuster plate

44.3 Fit the heater hose nipple

Fig. 1.31. Check cylinder block and gear case upper faces for alignment using a straight edge

Fig. 1.32. The cylinder head bolt tightening sequence

Fig. 1.33. The cam carrier in position showing the PVC hose clips and air manifold bracket locations

44.5 Locate the generator

44.6 Attach the air nozzles to the air manifold and tighten securely

44.7 The inlet and exhaust manifolds refitted

44.9 The secondary chain tensioner oil pipe location

44.10 Refit the air pump

45.1 The crankshaft pulley and timing case pointer indicating top dead center (TDC)

2   Fit the secondary chain tensioner with its thick shoe side facing up.

3   Ensure that the cylinder head and cylinder block mating surfaces are perfectly clean and position the cylinder head gasket in position on the block with the side marked 'TOP' uppermost (photo).

4   Locate the 'O' rings into the oil ports and place the gear case to cylinder head gasket in position on the gear case.

5   Carefully place the cylinder head into position and insert the retaining bolts. Refer to Figure 1.32 and tighten all of the bolts in the sequence shown to a torque figure of 43 lb f ft (5.9 kg f m). Then loosen them.

6   On Series 1 models retighten the bolts to 58 lb f ft (8.01 kg f m) and on Series 2 to 4 further tighten the bolts marked 1, 2, 3 and 6 to 70 lb f ft (9.6 kg f m) and the remaining 6 bolts to a torque figure of 60 lb f ft (8.2 kg f m) (photo).

7   The timing gear case retaining bolts are now tightened (photo).

8   Relocate the air injection nozzles but do not fully tighten (photo).

42 Camshaft carrier - installation

1   Align the camshaft thrust plate mark with the corresponding alignment mark on the camshaft.

2   Fit the 'O' rings to the camshaft carrier and install in position, but do not fully tighten the dowel retaining bolts. The longest bolt is installed in the dowel position.

3   Insert the camshaft carrier mounting bolts and tighten in progression alternately to 15 lb f ft torque (2.0 kg f m).

4   It should be noted that the camshaft carrier mounting bolts also retain two parts of the air manifold bracket and the PVC hose clips (Fig. 1.33).

5   Reconnect the air injection nozzle to the air manifold and tighten.

43 Secondary timing sprocket - installation

1   Rotate the crankshaft and position number 4 piston to its top dead centre (TDC) on compression stroke.

2   Ensure that the alignment marks on the camshaft and thrust plate are in alignment (photo). If they are not aligned, position the camshaft sprocket on the camshaft and fit the pin into the camshaft sprocket. Now turn the crankshaft and align the marks.

3   Remove the camshaft sprocket and reposition the number four piston to TDC position on compression stroke. If to make adjustment the crankshaft was turned in the reverse direction, the final adjustment must be made in the normal direction to align the relative marks, and the chain must be tensioned (in direction of rotation).

4   It is essential that the camshaft timing sprocket and the mating surface on the camshaft are perfectly clean. This is necessary as the drive torque from the camshaft to sprocket is by means of frictional contact.

5   The timing chain is now inserted through the aperture in the top and the layshaft timing sprocket located into it (photo). The punched timing mark on the sprocket must align with the key on the layshaft.

6   When installed the sprocket punch mark must be approximately at the 2 o'clock position (photo).

7   Insert the camshaft sprocket into the chain with its punch mark at the 12 o'clock position, and fit the sprocket to the camshaft (photo).

8   The camshaft timing sprocket position must be adjusted in relation to the camshaft. The punch mark on the sprocket must be up when the timing chain drive side is tensioned. To tension for adjustment, apply pressure to the tensioner shoe thru the plug hole in the secondary chain tensioner.

9   Correctly installed, the camshaft sprocket punch mark will be at a position of 6° 20' from the top center, (in direction of rotation).

10 Insert the locating pin into the hole in the camshaft flange which aligns with a sprocket hole.

11 Tighten the layshaft retaining bolt to a torque of 33 lb f ft (4.5 kg f m).

12 Fit the camshaft sprocket plate washer and tighten the retaining bolt to 33 lb f ft (4.5 kg f m).

13 Prior to fitting the gearcase front cover and camshaft carrier cover ensure that the alignment marks on the sprockets are correct then fit the covers.

44 Generaly ancillary items - reassembly

1   Fit the secondary chain tensioner.

2   Fit the thermostat housing, the air pump bracket, adjusting plate and also the generator adjustment plate (photo).

3   Fit the heater hose joint nipple and locate the air cleaner bracket and air duct into position (photo).

4   Insert the distributor into its location and ensure that with the No. 4 piston on TDC (compression stroke) that the scribed marks on the distributor bowl aligns with the rotor segment.

5   Refit the generator but do not fully tighten the adjustment bolts (photo).

6   Reconnect the air injection nozzles to the air manifold and ensure they are firmly tightened.

7   Refit the inlet and exhaust manifolds using new gaskets (photo).

8   Refit the carburetor heat protector, heat insulator, and then the carburetor unit.

9   Reconnect the secondary drain tensioner oil pipe (photo).

10 Refit the air pump (photo) and then install the spacer fan pulley and fan.

11 Refit the fan belt and air pump drive belts and tension both to a deflection of 0.4 in.

12 Attach the distributor primary cable and meter unit cable.

45 Valve clearances - adjustment

1   Rotate the crankshaft so that No. 1 or No. 4 piston is on top dead center (TDC) on compression stroke. In this position the timing marks on the gear case and crankshaft pulley are in alignment (photo).

2   The valve clearances are now adjusted with a feeler gauge in the following manner.

3   Slacken the locknut and insert the feeler gauge between the rocker arm and cam (photo). Turn the rocker arm adjustment screw to take up the clearance and lock in position by retightening the locknut.

4   The correct clearances are:

   Inlet – 0.004 in (0.101 mm) at low temperature
   Exhaust – 0.006 in (0.152 mm) at low temperature

5   Refit the camshaft side cover.

6   Refit the respective hoses to their connections ensuring that they are in good condition and also their securing clips. Position the hoses so that they are not in contact with adjoining components.

46 Engine/transmission - installation

1   Whether the engine is to be installed on its own, or together with the transmission, the procedure is basically the reverse of the removal procedure.

45.3 Method of checking valve clearance

2   Raise the engine (and transmission, where appropriate), using a hoist, and lower it into position in the vehicle engine bay. A jack will be required to support the transmission until the rear support is installed if the transmission is connected to the engine.

3   Install the engine and transmission mounts.

4   Where applicable, install the starter motor and the flywheel housing bolts.

5   Install the exhaust pipe.

6   Install the oil filter (where applicable).

7   Connect the electrical, earth, fuel and air lines to the engine.

8   Install the carburetor controls and linkages.

9   Connect the heater and emission control hoses.

10 Install the fan, radiator and hoses.

11 If applicable, connect the gearshift lever, speedometer drive cable and propeller shaft.

12 Top-up the engine oil and coolant (and transmission oil, where applicable) (photo).

13 Install the air cleaner.

---

47 Engine - initial start-up after overhaul

1   Make sure that the battery is fully charged and that all lubricants, coolant and fuel are replenished.

2   If the fuel system has been dismantled it will require several revolutions of the engine on the starter motor to pump the petrol up to the carburetor on models fitted with a mechanical fuel pump.

3   As soon as the engine fires and runs, keep it going at a fast idle only, (no faster) and bring it up the normal working temperature.

4   As the engine warms up there will be odd smells and some smoke from parts getting hot and burning off oil deposits. The signs to look for are leaks of water or oil which will be obvious if serious. Check also the exhaust pipe and manifold connections, as these do not always 'find' their exact gas tight position until the warmth and vibration have acted on them, and it is almost certain that they will need tightening further. This should be done of course, with the engine stopped.

5   When normal running temperature has been reached adjust the engine idling speed as described in Chapter 3.

6   Stop the engine and wait a few minutes to see if any lubricant or coolant is dripping out when the engine is stationary.

7   Road test the car to check that the timing is correct and that the engine is giving the necessary smoothness and power. Do not race the engine - if new bearings and/or pistons have been fitted it should be treated as a new engine and run in at a reduced speed.

Chapter 1 Part B: Engine - Series 5 and 6

Contents

Ancillary components - removal 51
Cam cover - removal 52
Camshaft - examination and renovation 69
Connecting rods and connecting rod
bearings - examination and renovation 66
Crankshaft and main bearings 62
Crankshaft and main bearings - examination and
renovation 65
Cylinder bores - examination and renovation 67
Cylinder head and valves - servicing and decarbonising 71
Cylinder head - assembly and installation 76
Cylinder head - removal 53
Engine and transmission - removal 49
Engine and transmission - installation 79
Engine dismantling - general 50
Engine - final assembly after major overhaul 78
Engine - reassembly 75
Engine reassembly - general 74
Engine - removal 48

Examination and renovation - general 64
Flywheel and ring gear - servicing 72
Front cover - removal 58
General description 47
Initial start-up after major overhaul 80
Inlet and exhaust manifolds - removal 55
Lubrication system - description 63
Oil pan (sump) - removal 56
Oil pump - examination and renovation 73
Oil pump - removal 57
Pistons and connecting rods - removal 60
Pistons and rings - examination and renovation 68
Rear main oil seal 61
Rocker arms/valves and springs - removal 54
Timing chain, pinion gear, sprockets and chain adjuster/
tensioner and guides - examination and renovation 70
Timing chain, pinion gear, sprockets and chain adjuster/
tensioner and guides - removal 59
Valve clearance - adjustment 77

Specifications

Engine type	... ...	4-cylinder, 4-stroke in-line, ohc, water cooled
Firing order	... ...	1, 3, 4, 2
Combustion chamber type	... ...	Hemispherical
Bore	... ...	3.31 in
Stroke	... ...	3.23 in
Piston displacement	... ...	110.8 cu in
Compression ratio	... ...	8.5
Compression pressure	... ...	170.64 psi @ 300 rpm
Maximum compression pressure variance	... ...	8.53 psi
Maximum output	... ...	80 HP @ 4,800 rpm
Maximum torque	... ...	95 ft lb @ 3,000 rpm
Engine weight		
Dry	316 lb
With oil/coolant	334 lb
Lubrication method	... ...	Forced circulation

Oil pump

Type	Trochoid
Oil pressure @ 2,800 rpm	56 to 71 psi @ 122°F
Drive rotor to driven rotor clearance	0.0005 to 0.0059 in
Maximum permissible clearance	0.0079 in
Driven rotor to inner pump body wall clearance	0.0063 to 0.0087 in
Maximum permissible clearance	0.0098 in
Drive rotor/driven rotor to oil pump cover clearance	0.0012 to 0.0035 in
Maximum permissible clearance	0.0079 in
Drive shaft O/D to pump cover bore I/D clearance	0.0028 to 0.0043 in
Maximum permissible clearance	0.0098 in
Maximum oil capacity	5.7
Oil pan capacity	Maximum 5.3 liq/qt
Oil filter type	Full-flow paper (cartridge type)
Oil pressure switch actuation pressure	4.27 - 7.11 psi
Relief valve opening pressure	56.88 - 71.10 psi
Overflow valve opening pressure	11.38 - 17.06 psi

Cylinder head

Inlet valves	
open at	21° BTDC
close at	65° ATDC
Exhaust valves	
open at	55° BBDC
close at	20° ATDC
Valve clearance (between rocker and cam) - at low temperature	
inlet	0.006 in
exhaust	0.010 in
Valve head diameter	
inlet	1.67 in
exhaust	1.34 in
Valve spring free height	
outer spring nominal height	1.8465 in
limit for use	1.7874 in
Inner spring nominal height	1.7835 in
limit for use	1.7244 in
Valve spring tension	
outer spring compressed to 1.614 in (standard)	32.2 to 37.0 lbs
limit for use	30.9 lbs
inner spring compressed to 1.516 in (standard)	18.7 to 21.5 lbs
limit for use	16.5 lbs
Maximum valve spring inclination allowance	0.0787 in
Camshaft	
nominal height	1.4508 in
minimum height	1.4311 in
Camshaft journals	
nominal diameter	1.3362 to 1.3368 in
minimum wear allowance	0.0020 in
minimum diameter allowance	1.3307 in
Camshaft run out	
nominal	0.0020 in
maximum run out allowance	0.0038 in
Camshaft end play	
standard	0.0020 to 0.0059 in
maximum end play allowance	0.0078 in
Camshaft journal diameter	1.3362 to 1.3370 in
Camshaft bearing inside diameter	1.3386 to 1.3398 in
Standard camshaft journal/bearing clearance	0.0016 to 0.0035 in
Maximum journal to bearing clearance allowance	0.0059 in
Rockers and shaft	
nominal shaft diameter	0.8071 in
maximum wear allowance	0.8012 in
maximum shaft run out	0.0079 in
rocker arm shaft diameter to rocker arm inside diameter maximum	
clearance allowable	0.0078 in

Pistons

Type	Track (No T slot)
Number of rings	
compression	2
oil	1

Standard size

'A' grade	3.3049 to 3.3053 in
'B' grade	3.3053 to 3.3057 in
'C' grade	3.3057 to 3.3061 in
'D' grade	3.3061 to 3.3065 in
0.020 in oversize A, B	3.3246 to 3.3254 in
0.040 in oversize A, B	3.3443 to 3.3451 in
Piston ring gaps in bore	
1st compression	0.008 to 0.016 in
2nd compression	0.008 to 0.016 in
oil control	0.008 to 0.035
Maximum limit for use 1st, 2nd and oil control	0.059 in

Crankshaft

nominal	2.205 in
wear limit	0.002 in or more
limit for use	2.1555 in
Crankpin diameter	
nominal	1.929 in
wear limit	0.002 in or more
limit for use	1.8799 in
Crankshaft journal diameter	
standard bearing size	2.2016 to 2.2022 in
0.010 in undersize	2.1917 to 2.1923 in
0.020 in undersize	2.1819 to 2.1825 in
Crankpin diameter	
standard	1.9262 to 1.9268 in
0.010 in undersize	1.9163 to 1.9169 in
0.020 in undersize	1.9065 to 1.9071 in
Cylinder bore grades (Stamped on cylinder block upper face)	
'A' grade	3.3071 to 3.3075 in
'B' grade	3.3075 to 3.3079 in
'C' grade	3.3079 to 3.3083 in
'D' grade	3.3083 to 3.3087 in
Crankshaft end play	
crankshaft to thrust bearing clearance	0.0024 to 0.0094 in
maximum allowance	0.0117 in

Torque wrench settings

	lb f ft	kg f m
Cylinder head bolts		
initial	61	8.4
final	72	9.9
Main bearing cap bolts	72	9.9
Connecting rod bearing cap bolts	33	4.5
Flywheel bolts	69	9.5
Rocker arm shaft bracket nuts	16	2.2
Camshaft sprocket bolt	58	8.0

47 General description

The engine is a four-cylinder in-line type, the valve being operated by overhead camshaft.

The aluminum alloy cylinder head has hemispherical combustion chambers with inclined valves, transversely opposed giving a crossflow head design for maximum efficiency.

The camshaft is located in five main bearings. The bearing caps are incorporated in the rocker arm shaft brackets which in turn are bolted to the cylinder head.

A double rocker arm shaft is used to operate the valves, the inlet and exhaust valves being operated independently. The camshaft, operated by the timing chain, actuates the rocker arms to open and close the valves. The valves have double return springs to improve the valve performance at high engine speeds.

The timing chain, driven from the crankshaft pulley, is adjusted by means of an automatic tensioner and mechanical adjuster.

The engine lubricant is circulated by means of a trochoid type oil pump and a full flow oil filter with disposable cartridge element is also fitted.

The cooling system is of the pressurised circulation type incorporating an impeller type water pump and wax-pellet type thermostat.

A comprehensive emission control system is fitted comprising the following:

Fig. 1.34. Sectional view of the Series 5 and 6 engines

a) *Positive Crankcase Ventilation System (PCV).*
b) *Evaporative Control System (ECS).*
c) *Air Injection Reactor System (AIR).*
d) *Coasting Richer System (CRS).*
e) *Exhaust Gas Recirculation System (EGR).*
f) *Controlled Combustion System (CCS).*
g) *Oxidizing Catalytic Converter (OCS) (California only).*
h) *Over Temperature Control System (OTC) (California only).*

The carburetor fitted is a Stromberg down-draft two barrel type incorporating an electric automatic choke system.

48 Engine - removal

1   Before commencing work, drive the vehicle over an inspection pit, onto ramps or jack it up, for access to the exhaust and transmission.
2   Remove the hood (bonnet) as described in Chapter 12.
3   Detach the ground cable from the battery terminal.
4   Drain the cooling system as described in Chapter 2 and remove the radiator. Remove the fan blade unit.
5   Drain the engine oil into a suitable container (and transmission if gearbox is to be removed).
6   Remove the air cleaner unit by detaching:

a) *The Positive Crankcase Ventilation System (PCV) hose from the cam cover.*
b) *The Evaporative Control System (ECS) hose from the air cleaner unit body.*
c) *The Air Injection Reactor System (AIR) hose from the thermosensor to inlet manifold.*
d) *Undo the air cleaner unit clamping bolt, lift the cleaner unit sufficiently to detach the Controlled Combustion System (CCS) hose from the thermosensor to inlet manifold.*

Now remove the air cleaner unit.
7   Detach the Controlled Combustion System hose and also the manifold cover.
8   Disconnect the generator wires, the cylinder block to frame ground cable, the coil high tension cable and the back-up lamp switch and top/third switch wires to the connector at the rear of the engine.
9   Disconnect the exhaust downpipe to manifold connection.
10 Disconnect the following hoses:

a) *The heater hoses at heater core tubes.*
b) *The carburetor fuel hoses.*
c) *The inlet manifold vacuum hose.*
d) *The Evaporative Control System hose from the oil pan.*
e) *The radiator hoses.*

11 Detach the accelerator cable from the carburetor.
12 Disconnect the wires from the thermosensor unit, the distributor and the oil pressure switch.
13 From the carburetor, disconnect the leads to the solenoid valve and the auto choke at the connector.
14 From underneath remove the clutch return spring and then the slave cylinder retaining bolts. Detach the slave cylinder and suspend out of the way - tie to the frame with cord or wire.
15 Unscrew the retaining bolts and remove the starter motor.
16 Unscrew the bellhousing bolts and remove the flywheel splash shield.
17 Support the transmission with a jack.
18 Locate the engine lifting sling into position and slightly lift the engine.
19 Unscrew and remove the engine mounting nuts.
20 Before lifting the engine from the vehicle, check that all fittings and attachments are free and where possible, tied back out of the way.
21 Pull the engine forward and upwards to clear the transmission and tilting the engine upwards at the front lift the engine clear.

49 Engine and transmission - removal

Manual transmission
1   To remove the engine and manual transmission as a unit, follow the instructions given in Part 'A' of this Chapter, Section 6.

Automatic transmission
2   Slacken the throttle valve cable adjusting nuts, withdraw the cotter pin and joint pin from the carburetor level. Detach the control cable (Fig. 6.38).
3   Disconnect the transmission oil level gauge.
4   From underneath, remove the lower converter housing dust cover.
5   Detach the control rod from the shift lever by removing the cotter pin (Fig. 6.38).
6   Disconnect the exhaust pipe bracket.
7   Slacken the oil cooler pipe retaining nuts (on the right-hand side), detach the pipe location clips and place the pipes towards the body sides.
8   Remove the speedo cable from the transmission.
9   Unscrew and remove the three nuts and bolts retaining the frame bracket to the transmission rear mounting.
10 Lift the engine and transmission accordingly to remove the four bolts securing the frame bracket and crossmember. Remove the rear mounting.
11 The engine and transmission units can now be removed from the vehicle. Take care not to damage the transmission oil cooler pipes and surrounding fittings.

50 Engine dismantling - general

Refer to Part 'A', Section 7.

51 Ancillary components - removal

1   Refer to the procedures given in paragraphs 1, 2 and 4 in Section 8, and in addition remove the oil filter.
2   Remove the clutch unit as in Chapter 5.
3   To remove the flywheel bend over the lock tabs and remove the retaining bolts.
4   Remove the rear plate.

52 Cam cover - removal

1   Remove the air cleaner unit (see Chapter 3).
2   Detach the HT cables from the cam cover brackets.
3   Unscrew and remove the four cam cover securing nuts and washers.
4   Remove the cover.

53 Cylinder head - removal

1   Remove the cam cover as described in the previous Section.
2   Detach the Exhaust Gas Return (EGR) pipe clamp bolt from the cylinder head at the rear.
3   If engine is still in the vehicle, disconnect the exhaust manifold to downpipe connection and drain the cooling system (see Chapter 2). Detach the heater hoses from the inlet manifold and rear of the cylinder head. Remove the sparking plugs, all electrical wiring connections to the cylinder head (noting their respective positions), the vacuum lines and sparking plug cables.
4   Turn the engine to position the No. 1 piston at TDC (firing position). Lift off the distributor cap and mark the rotor to housing relative position. Remove the distributor (see Chapter 4).
5   Depress and turn the automatic timing chain adjuster slide pin 90° clockwise (Fig. 1.35) to lock the chain adjuster.
6   Unscrew and remove the camshaft timing sprocket retaining bolt. Remove the sprocket from the camshaft, but do not remove the sprocket from the chain - retain it on the damper and tensioner.
7   Detach the air injector reactor (AIR) hose and the check valve from the exhaust manifold.
8   Unscrew and remove the cylinder head to timing cover bolts.
9   Using an extension bar wrench unscrew and remove the cylinder head bolts. Progressively unscrew the bolts in reverse sequence, starting with the outer bolts (Fig. 1.37).
10 The cylinder head and manifolds can now be lifted clear. The help of an assistant will be useful at this point.
11 Remove the cylinder head to the workbench for cleaning and inspection/dismantling.

54 Rocker arm/valves and springs - removal

1 With the cam cover removed, slacken each rocker arm shaft bracket nut, in sequence, a little at a time, Start with the outer brackets (Fig. 1.36).
2 Remove the nuts from the brackets.
3 Remove the spring from the rocker arm shaft and dismantle the rocker arm brackets and arms, keeping in sequence of removal.
4 The valves can be removed from the cylinder head by the following method. Compress each spring in turn with a valve spring compressor until the spring retainers can be removed. If available, use special spring compressor J-26513 (Fig. 1.37). Release the compressor and remove the spring and spring retainer.
5 If, when the valve spring compressor is screwed down, the valve spring retaining cap refuses to free, do not continue to screw down on the compressor as there is a likelihood of damaging it.
6 Gently tap the top of the tool directly over the cap with a light hammer. This will free the cap. To avoid the compressor jumping off the valve spring retaining cap when it is tapped, hold the compressor firmly in position with one hand.
7 Slide the rubber oil control seal off the top of each valve stem and then drop out each valve through the combustion chamber.
8 It is essential that the valves are kept in their correct sequence unless they are so badly worn that they are to be renewed.

55 Inlet/exhaust manifolds - removal

Inlet manifold
1 If the engine is still in the vehicle, disconnect the following:

   a) The EGR pipe clamp bolt from the rear of the cylinder head.
   b) The EGR pipe from the inlet and exhaust manifolds.
   c) The EGR valve from the lower side of the inlet manifold complete with bracket.
   d) Drain the cooling system (Chapter 2) and disconnect the radiator top hose at the water outlet and the heater hose from the manifold upper side.
   e) Detach the accelerator linkage, vacuum lines and the electrical connections from the carburetor. Disconnect the fuel feed line to the carburetor.

2 Unscrew the manifold securing nuts and remove the manifold/carburetor from the studs and position on cam cover temporarily. Detach the lower heater hoses and then remove the manifold and carburetor unit.
3 From the manifold disconnect the carburetor, the temperature sender switch and vacuum fittings.

Exhaust manifold
4 If the engine is still in vehicle, follow instructions 1a and b for inlet manifold removal and detach the exhaust pipe to manifold connection.
5 Unscrew the manifold shield bolts and detach the shield.
6 Detach the heat stove hose from the air cleaner unit and remove the heat stove.
7 Unscrew and remove the exhaust manifold to cylinder head retaining nuts. Remove the manifold and clean off any gasket material from the manifold or head flanges.

56 Oil pan - removal

1 If engine is still in vehicle, drain the oil into a suitable container and detach the front splash shield.
2 Remove the front crossmember. Detach the relay rod from the idler arm and lower relay rod.
3 Remove the bellhousing brace from the left-hand side and disconnect the vacuum line from the oil pan.
4 Remove the bolts and detach the oil pan and gasket.

57 Oil pump - removal

1 The oil pump can be removed with the engine in place in the vehicle or out of it as required.
2 To remove it in the vehicle, remove the cam cover, the distributor unit and oil pan as described in Sections 52, 53 and 56, respectively.
3 Unscrew and remove the oil pick up tube to block bolt and detach the tube from the pump (Fig. 1.38).
4 Unscrew the pump unit mounting bolts and withdraw the pump unit.
5 Detach the rubber hose and relief valve assembly from the pump unit.

Fig. 1.36. The rocker arm assemblies

Fig. 1.35. The locking timing chain adjuster positions

Fig. 1.37. Using the special valve spring compressor J-26513 to compress the valve springs

Fig. 1.38. Remove the oil pump pick up tube

Fig. 1.39. Remove the crankshaft timing sprocket using a puller

Fig. 1.40. The timing chain tensioner, guide and adjuster and inset the oil jet position

OIL PAN

Fig. 1.41. The engine lubrication system

58 Front cover - removal

1   Remove the cylinder head as given in Section 53 and the oil pan, see Section 56.
2   Detach the oil pick up tube from the oil pump.
3   Remove the generator and air conditioning drive belts and fan unit.
4   Unscrew and remove the crankshaft pulley center bolt and remove the pulley and harmonic balancer unit.
5   Undo the air pump mounting bolts, hinge the pump towards the engine and remove the drive belt.
6   On vehicles fitted with air conditioning, undo the mounting bolts and remove the compressor and brackets.
7   Remove the distributor as described in Chapter 4.
8   Unscrew and remove the front cover retaining bolts.
9   Remove the front cover, carefully tapping with a soft faced mallet if it sticks.

59 Timing chain, pinion gear, sprockets and chain adjusters, tensioner and guides - removal

1   With the front cover removed, see previous Section, remove the timing chain from the lower timing sprocket and the camshaft sprocket.
2   Withdraw the pinion gear and timing sprocket using a puller as in Fig. 1.39. If available use special puller J-25031.
3   Refer to Fig. 1.40 and 'E' clip on the automatic chain adjuster.
4   Remove the 'E' clip and the chain tensioner.
5   Remove the guide bolts and withdraw the guide and oil jet.

60 Pistons and connecting rods - removal

1   If the engine is in the vehicle, remove the cylinder head and oil pan as described in Sections 53 and 56.
2   Remove the pistons and connecting rods in the same manner as described in Part A, Section 18.

61 Rear main oil seal - removal

1   This can be removed from the vehicle, with the engine installed providing that the oil pan and transmission are removed. Refer to Section 56 and Chapter 6, respectively for the relevant removal instructions.
2   On manual transmission models detach the clutch cover and pressure plate assembly.
3   With the battery ground cable disconnected, remove the starter motor unit.
4   Bend over the bolt locking tabs and remove the flywheel bolts. Remove the flywheel and cover.
5   Unscrew the main seal retainer bolts and remove the seal and retainer. Prise the seal from the container assuming it is to be renewed.

62 Crankshaft and main bearings - removal

1   Rotate the crankshaft and position it vertically to the top of the cylinder block.
2   Unscrew the crankshaft main bearing cap bolts in sequence. Start from the end caps.
3   Before removal note the respective positions of the caps. The arrow mark on the rear face of each cap points to the front of the engine and each journal and cap number are in alignment.
4   On removing the caps, lay them out in sequence with their respective bearing shells ready for cleaning and inspection.
5   Remove the crankshaft and thrust bearings from the cylinder block.

63 Lubrication system - description

The pressurised circulation type lubrication system consists of a Trochoid type oil pump, a full flow oil filter with cartridge element, and the various front cover/cylinder block/cylinder head oilways for supplying oil to the engine components.

Oil is drawn from the oil pan by the oil pump and is fed to the full flow oil filter. From the filter the oil is forced into the oil gallery then onto the crankshaft journals via the oil ports. The number 3 crankshaft oil port has a diversion port which feeds oil to the cylinder head. This then lubricates the rocker assemblies via oilways in the inlet and exhaust valve rocker shafts.

The camshaft is lubricated from an oil well in the upper cylinder head face.

The timing sprockets and chain are lubricated by oil which is delivered from the number 1 crankshaft journal oil port which delivers the oil to the oil jet on the timing chain guide.

A relief valve is incorporated in the oil pump and under excess pressure the valve opens and allows excess oil to be diverted back into the oil pan.

The oil filter body contains an overflow valve in order that a difference of oil pressure on each side of the filter maintains the specified level. When the overflow valve opens the oil is by-passed direct to vital engine parts.

64 Examination and renovation - general

Refer to Section 23.

65 Crankshaft and main bearings - examination and renovation

Refer to the procedure given in Section 24 but where reference to Specifications are concerned refer to those given at the start of Part B for the Series 5 and 6 models.

66 Connecting rods and connecting rod (big end) bearings - examination and renovation

Refer to Section 25, and the Specifications in Part B.

67 Cylinder bores - examination and renovation

Refer to the procedure given in Section 26 and the Specifications in Part B.

68 Pistons and rings - examination and renovation

Refer to the procedure given in Section 27 and the Specifications in Part B.

69 Camshaft - examination and renovation

Refer to the procedures given in Section 28 and the Specifications in Part B.

70 Timing chain, pinion gear, sprockets and chain adjuster and tensioner - examination and renovation

1   Check the timing chain sprockets for signs of excessive wear or damage. Renew if required.
2   Inspect the timing chain for excessive wear or damage. Refer to Fig. 1.42 and calculate the distance (L) with the chain stretched to a tension of 22 lbs (9.9 kg). If distance (L) exceeds 15.16 inches (38.4 cm) the chain must be renewed.
3   Check the automatic chain adjuster pin, arm, wedge and rack teeth of the locking plate. If worn or damaged, renew.
4   Check the chain adjuster and renew if required.
5   Inspect the chain guide and oil jet. If worn or damaged, renew.

Fig. 1.42. Check the timing chain for wear - see Sec. 70, paragraph 2

---

71 Cylinder head and valves - servicing and decarbonising

Refer to the procedures given in Section 31 and the Specifications in Part B. Note the following differences:

Maximum valve stem to guide allowable clearance
                    0.1298 in (3.27 mm)   inlet
                    0.0097 in (0.23 mm)   exhaust

---

72 Flywheel and ring gear - servicing

Refer to the procedures given in Section 32 but note that the minimum friction face thickness of the flywheel is 1.22 in (3.1 cm).

---

73 Oil pump - examination and renovation

1   Thoroughly clean and dry the pump unit.
2   Insert a feeler gauge between the drive rotor and driven rotor. The maximum allowable clearance is 0.0079 in (0.19 mm). If the clearance exceeds this tolerance or the respective parts are damaged or scored, renew the pump unit.
3   Insert the feeler gauge between the driven rotor and pump body inner wall. The maximum allowable clearance is 0.0098 in (0.25 mm). Renew the pump unit if the clearance exceeds this tolerance or if damaged or badly pitted or scored.
4   Insert a feeler gauge between the drive rotor and driven rotor end faces and a straight edge placed across the pump body end faces (Fig. 1.43). If the clearance exceeds 0.0079 in (0.19 mm) or the faces are damaged in any way, renew the pump unit.
5   Measure the driveshaft outside diameter and the driveshaft bore diameter. If the clearance exceeds 0.0098 in (0.25 mm) renew the pump.
6   Inspect the oil pump rubber hose and renew if damaged or deterioration is apparent.
7   Inspect the relief valve and spring. If worn, weak or damaged, renew the oil pump unit.
8   Inspect the oil pump body, cover and drive gear for signs of wear, cracks or damage. If apparent, renew the oil pump unit.

---

74 Engine reassembly - general

Refer to Section 34.

---

75 Engine - reassembly

1   In general, the engine reassembly is a reversal of the dismantling process. The crankshaft, piston and connecting rod assembly procedures are basically the same as those given in Part A for the Series 1 to 4 models, although the clearance and torque tightening specifications may differ. Careful reference should therefore be made to the Specifications quoted in Part B during assembly.
2   The following instructions are the principle assembly details which differ to those in Part A and where special care must be taken.
3   Lubricate all crankshaft journals, main bearings and connecting rod bearings with clean engine oil as the respective components are assembled. Also lubricate the pistons, rings and cylinder bores in the same manner.

4   Insert the crankshaft thrust bearing with the oil groove face turned outwards (Fig. 1.44).
5   Fit the crankshaft bearing caps with the marking arrow on the rear face of each cap pointing to the front of the engine, and the corresponding cap and journal numbers aligned.
6   Half tighten the main bearing cap bolts in the sequence 3 - 4 - 2 - 5 - 1. Then fully tighten the bolts to 72 lb f ft (9.9 kg fm) torque and ensure that the crankshaft rotates freely.
7   When fitting the piston rings, ensure that they are positioned with their gaps located as shown in Fig. 1.45.
8   When fitting the piston and connecting rods, ensure that the face of the connecting rod with the cylinder number mark is located on the starter motor side with the piston facing the front (Fig. 1.46). Tighten the connecting rod cap bolts to 33 lb f ft (4.5 kg fm). Rotate the crankshaft to ensure that it turns without binding.
9   Torque the flywheel retaining bolts to 69 lb f ft (9.4 kg fm) and lock by bending over the lock tabs.
10 Refit the timing sprocket and pinion gear with the grooved side to the front cover.
11 When refitting the timing chain align the mark plate on the chain with the crankshaft timing sprocket mark. The mark plate is on the front side of the chain with the greater number of links between mark plates on the chain guide side. The crankshaft sprocket is fitted with the marked side forward and the triangular mark in alignment with the chain mark plate (Fig. 1.47).
12 Ensure that the camshaft sprocket and timing chain are in mesh until the sprocket is fitted to the camshaft.
13 When fitting the front cover, the oil pump drive gear punch mark must be aligned with the oil filter side of the cover. The dowel pin center and the alignment mark on the oil pump casing must be in line as in Fig. 1.48.
14 Before fitting the cover, ensure that the no. 1 and 4 pistons are at TDC, then install the cover engaging the pinion gear with the oil pump drive gear, and check that the oil pump drive gear punch mark faces the rear side. This can be seen through the front cover to cylinder block clearance as in Fig. 1.49.
15 The oil pump shaft end slit must be parallel to the front cylinder block face but with the offset forward (Fig. 1.50).
16 When installing the oil pump, align the notch on the crankshaft pulley with the 'O' marking on the front cover. If the cylinder head is in position, also align the camshaft and number 1 rocker arm marks. This is to ensure that the number 4 piston is on TDC on compression stroke.
17 Insert the driven rotor with the alignment mark in line with the drive rotor mark as in Fig. 1.51.
18 The oil pump unit is installed so that the drive gear and pinion gear are engaged. The drive gear alignment mark faces rearwards and at an angle of about 20° clockwise from the crankshaft line as in Fig. 1.52. The oil relief valve, pump cover, oil pipe and hose can then be refitted. When refitting the oil pan, a thin coating of Permatex No. 2 or equivalent should be applied to the positions indicated by the arrows in Fig. 1.53.

Fig. 1.43. Measuring the rotor to pump cover clearance with a feeler gauge and straight edge

Fig. 1.44. Installing the thrust bearing

Fig. 1.45. The correct piston ring positions prior to assembly

Fig. 1.46. The piston in position showing the front mark

Fig. 1.47. The timing chain position showing the alignment marks

Fig. 1.48. The oil pump alignment position

Fig. 1.49. Check the oil pump drive gear punch mark

Fig. 1.50. The correct oil pump shaft alignment position

Fig. 1.51. Align the drive and driven rotors punch marks

Fig. 1.52. Insert the oil pump

Fig. 1.53. The sealer positions on the oil pan gasket surface

Fig. 1.54. The cylinder head bolt tightening sequence

Fig. 1.55. The rocker arm and camshaft alignment marks

76 Cylinder head - assembly and installation

1 Position the head gasket over the dowel pins with the 'TOP' side upwards.
2 Insert each valve into its respective guide, applying a little engine oil to the stems.
3 Reassemble the respective valves, springs, retainers and seals to the cylinder head using the valve spring compressor. Ensure that each retainer is fully seated in the valve stem groove.
4 Place the cylinder head into position on the cylinder block and fit the retaining bolts. Retain the camshaft sprocket and chain with a piece of wire or rod. Tighten the head bolts progressively in sequence (Fig. 1.54), to 61 lb f ft (8.4 kg fm), then further tighten to 72 lb f ft (9.9 kg fm).
5 Lubricate the camshaft and place it into position.
6 Install the rocker arm shafts and note that the longer shaft is fitted to the exhaust valve side.
7 Fit the rocker arm shaft brackets and rocker arms to the shafts with the cylinder number marked on the bracket upper faces pointing forwards.
8 The mark on the number 1 rocker arm shaft bracket must align with that of the inlet and exhaust valve side rocker arm shafts.
9 When the rocker arm shaft stud holes are in line with the rocker arm shaft bracket stud holes, ensure that the number 1 rocker arm shaft bracket is longer on the exhaust side as can be seen by the amount of projection.
10 Insert the rocker arm springs into position between the shaft bracket and rocker arm. Ensure that the rocker arm shaft is turned upwards as indicated by the punch marks (see Fig. 1.55) and then install the rocker arm shaft bracket assembly onto the head studs.
11 Now align the camshaft and number 1 rocker arm shaft bracket marks, and then tighten the rocker arm shaft bracket nuts to 16 lb f ft (2.2 kg fm).
12 To prevent damaging the rocker arm springs, retain them with an adjustable wrench when tightening the bracket stud nuts.
13 Align the camshaft sprocket with the pin on the camshaft and assemble the sprocket to the shaft, but do not remove the sprocket from the chain. Retain the sprocket with bolt and washer and refit the half moon seal in the front of the head. Torque the retaining bolt to 58 lb f ft (8.0 kg fm).
14 Reset the automatic adjuster with a screwdriver by rotating the slide pin 90° counter clockwise, and check the timing chain tension.
15 To check the valve timing the rotor and mark on the distributor housing must be aligned with the number 1 piston at TDC on firing position. The crankshaft pulley timing mark must align with the 'O' mark on the front cover.

77 Valve clearance - adjustment

1 To check and reset the valve clearances follow the procedure given in Section 45, paragraphs 1 to 4, but note that the valve clearances are as follows:

Inlet valves	0.006 in (0.152 mm)	at low
Exhaust valves	0.010 in (0.254 mm)	temperature

2 Refit the cam cover and attach the HT cables to the cam cover brackets.

78 Engine - final assembly after major overhaul

1 Fit the inlet manifold gasket over the studs and reverse the inlet manifold removal sequence as given in Section 55. Tighten the manifold retaining nuts progressively from the inner studs outwards.
2 Reconnect the hoses to the inlet manifold with the PCU hose to the upper left side, the hot idle hose compensation hose on the upper right and the air vacuum hose on the lower side.
3 Fit the exhaust manifold gasket into position over the studs and reverse the manifold removal sequence given in Section 55. Tighten the retaining nuts working from the inside-out in a progressive manner.
4 Refit the crankshaft pulley and harmonic balancer. Tighten the retaining bolt and washer to a torque of 87 lb f ft (12.027 kg fm).
5 Refit the flywheel splash shield.
6 Re-install the starter motor if engine and transmission are being refitted.

79 Engine/transmission - installation

1 Locate lifting slings to the engine and lift and lower into position in the vehicle, taking care not to damage the surrounding fittings.
2 With the engine transmission in position, refit the engine mounting nuts and then refit the respective ancillary components in the reverse order of removal given in Section 51.
3 When all hoses, wires and attachments are refitted, refill the engine cooling system and check for leaks.
4 Refill the engine/transmission oil.
5 On manual transmission models check the clutch pedal free play.
6 Adjust the fan belt and air pump drivebelts for tension.

80 Initial start-up after major overhaul

Follow the instructions given in Section 47.

81 Fault diagnosis - engine

Symptom	Reasons	Remedy
Engine fails to turn over when starter control operated		
No current at starter motor	Flat or defective battery	Charge or renew battery. Push start car.
	Loose battery leads	Tighten both terminals and earth ends of earth leads.
	Defective starter solenoid or broken wiring	Run a wire direct from the battery to the starter motor or by-pass the solenoid.
	Engine earth strap disconnected	Check and retighten strap.
Current at starter motor	Jammed starter motor drive pinion	Place car in gear and rock to and fro.
	Defective starter motor	Remove and recondition.
Engine turns over but will not start		
No spark at spark plug	Ignition damp or wet	Wipe dry the distributor cap and ignition leads.
	Ignition leads to spark plugs loose	Check and tighten at both spark plug and distributor cap ends.
	Earthed or disconnected low tension leads	Check the wiring on the coil and to the distributor.

Symptom	Reasons	Remedy
	Dirty, incorrectly set, or pitted contact breaker points	Clean, file smooth, and adjust.
	Faulty condenser	Check contact breaker points for arcing, remove and install new.
	Defective ignition switch	By-pass switch with wire.
	Ignition leads connected wrong way round	Remove and refit leads to spark plugs in correct order.
	Faulty coil	Remove and install new coil.
	Contact breaker point spring earthed or broken	Check spring is not touching metal part of distributor. Check insulator washers are correctly placed. Renew points if the spring is broken.
No fuel at carburetor float chamber or at jets	No petrol in petrol tank	Refill tank!
	Vapor lock in fuel line (in hot conditions or at high altitude)	Blow into petrol tank, allow engine to cool, or apply a cold wet rag to the fuel line.
	Blocked float chamber needle valve	Remove, clean and refit.
	Fuel pump filter blocked	Remove, clean and refit
	Choked or blocked carburetor jets	Dismantle and clean.
	Faulty fuel pump	Remove, overhaul and refit
Engine stalls and will not start Excess of petrol in cylinder or carburetor flooding	Too much choke allowing too rich a mixture to wet plugs	Remove and dry spark plugs or with wide open throttle, push start the car.
	Float damaged or leaking or needle not sealing	Remove, examine, clean and refit float and needle valve as necessary.
	Float damaged or	
	Float lever incorrectly adjusted	Remove and adjust correctly.
No spark at spark plug	Ignition failure - sudden	Check over low and high tension circuits for breaks in wiring.
	Ignition failure - misfiring precludes total stoppage	Check contact breaker points, clean and adjust. Renew condenser if faulty.
	Ignition failure - in severe rain or after traversing water splash	Dry out ignition leads and distributor cap.
No fuel at jets	No petrol in petrol tank	Refill tank!
	Sudden obstruction in carburetor	Check jets, filter, and needle valve in float chamber for blockage.
	Water in fuel system	Drain tank and blow out fuel lines.
Engine misfires or idles unevenly Intermittent spark at spark plug	Ignition leads loose	Check and tighten as necessary at spark plug and distributor cap ends.
	Battery leads loose on terminals	Check and tighten terminal leads.
	Battery earth strap loose on body attachment point	Check and tighten earth lead to body attachment point.
Intermittent sparking at spark plug	Engine earth lead loose	Tighten lead.
	Low tension leads to coil loose	Check and tighten leads if found loose.
	Dirty, or incorrectly gapped plugs	Remove, clean and regap.
	Dirty, incorrectly set, or pitted contact breaker points	Clean, file smooth and adjust.
	Tracking across inside or distributor cover	Remove and install new cover.
	Ignition too retarded	Check and adjust ignition timing.
	Faulty coil	Remove and install new coil.
Fuel shortage at engine	Mixture too weak	Check jets, float chamber needle valve, and filter for obstruction. Clean as necessary.
	Carburetor incorrectly adjusted	Remove and overhaul carburetor.
	Air leak in carburetor	Remove and overhaul carburetor.
	Air leak at inlet manifold to cylinder head, or inlet manifold to carburetor	Test by pouring oil along joints. Bubbles indicate leak. Renew manifold gasket as appropriate.
Lack of power and poor compression Mechanical wear	Incorrect valve clearances	Adjust rocker arms to take up wear.
	Burnt out exhaust valves	Remove cylinder head and renew defective valves.
	Sticking or leaking valves	Remove cylinder head, clean, check and renew valves as necessary.
	Weak or broken valve springs	Check and renew as necessary.
	Worn valve guides or stems	Renew valve guides and valves.
	Worn pistons and piston rings	Dismantle engine, renew pistons and rings.

Symptom	Reason	Remedy
Fuel/air mixture leaking from cylinder	Burnt out exhaust valves	Remove cylinder head, renew defective valves.
	Sticking or leaking valves	Remove cylinder head, clean, check, and renew valves as necessary.
	Worn valve guides and stems	Remove cylinder head and renew valves and valve guides.
	Weak or broken valve springs	Remove cylinder head, renew defective springs.
	Blown cylinder head gasket (accompanied by increase in noise)	Remove cylinder head and install new gasket.
	Worn pistons and piston rings	Dismantle engine, renew pistons and rings.
	Worn or scored cylinder bores	Dismantle engine, rebore, renew pistons and rings.
Incorrect adjustments	Ignition timing wrongly set. Too advanced or retarded	Check and reset.
	Contact breaker points incorrectly gapped	Check and reset contact breaker points.
	Incorrect valve clearances	Check and reset rocker arm to valve stem gap.
	Incorrectly set spark plugs	Remove, clean and regap.
	Carburation too rich or too weak	Tune carburetor for optimum performance.
Carburation and ignition faults	Dirty contact breaker points	Remove, clean and refit.
	Fuel filters blocked causing poor top end performance through fuel starvation	Dismantle, inspect, clean and refit all fuel filters.
	Distributor automatic balance weights or vacuum advance and retard mechanisms not functioning correctly	Overhaul distributor.
	Faulty fuel pump giving top end fuel starvation	Remove, overhaul, or install exchange reconditioned fuel pump.
Excessive oil consumption	Excessively worn valve stems and valve guides	Remove cylinder head and fit new valves and valve guides.
	Worn piston rings	Install oil control rings to existing pistons or purchase new pistons.
	Worn pistons and cylinder bores	Install new pistons and rings, rebore cylinders.
	Excessive piston ring gap allowing blow-up	Install new piston rings and set gap correctly.
	Piston oil return holes choked	Decarbonise engine and pistons.
Oil being lost due to leaks	Leaking oil filter gasket	Inspect and install new gasket if necessary.
	Leaking rocker cover gasket	Inspect and install new gasket as necessary.
	Leaking timing gear cover gasket	Inspect and install new gasket as necessary.
	Leaking sump gasket	Inspect and install new gasket as necessary.
	Loose sump plug	Tighten and install new gasket as necessary.
Unusual noises from engine Excessive clearances due to mechanical wear	Worn valve gear (noisy tapping from rocker box)	Inspect and renew rocker shaft, rocker arms, and ball pins as necessary.
	Worn big-end bearing (regular heavy knocking)	Drop sump, if bearings broken up clean out oil pump and oilways, install new bearings. If bearings not broken but worn install bearing shells.
	Worn timing chain and sprockets (rattling from front of engine)	Remove timing cover, install new timing sprockets and timing chain.
	Worn main bearings (rumbling and vibration)	Drop sump, remove crankshaft, if bearing worn but not broken up, renew. If broken up strip oil pump and clean out oilways.
	Worn crankshaft (knocking, rumbling and vibration)	Regrind crankshaft, install new main and big-end bearings.

Chapter 2 Cooling system

Contents

Antifreeze and rust inhibitors 6	Fault diagnosis - cooling system 11
Cooling system - draining 3	General description 1
Cooling system - filling 5	Radiator - removal and installation 8
Cooling system - flushing 4	Thermostat - removal, testing and installation 9
Cooling system - routine maintenance 2	Water pump - removal and installation 10
Fan/alternator drivebelt - tension adjustment 7	

Specifications

System type	Pressurized circulation with pump assistance
Radiator type	Flat tubes with corrugated fins
Cap pressure valve opening pressure	15 psi
Vacuum valve opening pressure	0.6 - 0.7 psi
Radiator leakage test specified pressure	28.4 psi

Coolant capacity

Series 1 to 4	1.5 US gallons
Series 5 and 6	1.6 US gallons

Water pump

Type	Centrifugal impeller
Delivery volume at 3000 rpm	13.2 gal/min or more (Series 1 to 4)
Delivery volume at 6000 rpm (68°F water temperature)	42.3 gal/min (Series 5)
Seal type	Mechanical
Bearing type	Ball bearing
Pump pulley ratio	1.10 (1.8 with A/C)
Number of impellers	6
Impeller diameter	2.756 in

Cooling fan

Number of blades	4
Series 5 and 6 with A/C	7
Cooling fan diameter -	
Series 1 to 4	12.6 inch
Series 5 and 6	13 in without A/C
Series 5 and 6	15.4 in with A/C
Fan belt deflection	0.4 in

Thermostat

Type	Wax pellet
Valve opening temperature	177° - 182°F (80° - 83°C)
Valve lift 203°F (96°C)	0.32 inches or more

1 General description

The cooling system comprises the radiator, top and bottom water hoses, the water pump, cylinder block and head water jackets and a thermostat. The radiator cap has a pressure relief valve.

The principle of the system is that cold water in the bottom of the radiator circulates upwards through the lower radiator hose to the water pump, where the pump impeller pushes the water round the cylinder block and head through the various cast-in passages to cool the cylinder bores, combustion surfaces and valve seats. When sufficient heat has been absorbed by the cooling water, the engine has reached an efficient working temperature, the water moves from the cylinder head past the now open thermostat into the top radiator hose and into the radiator header tank.

The water then travels down the radiator tubes where is is rapidly cooled by the in-rush of air, when the vehicle is in forwards motion. A multi-bladed fan, mounted on the water pump pulley, assists this cooling action. The water, now cooled, reaches the bottom of the radiator and the cycle is repeated.

When the engine is cold the thermostat remains closed until the coolant reaches a pre-determined temperature (see Specifications); this assists rapid warming-up.

2 Cooling system - routine maintenance

1 The cooling system requires very little routine maintenance but in view of its important nature, this maintenance must not be neglected.
2 The maintenance intervals are given in the Routine Maintenance Section at the beginning of this manual.
3 Apart from regular checking of the coolant level, and inspection for leaks and deterioration of hose connections, the only other items of major importance are the use of antifreeze solutions or rust inhibitors suitable for aluminium engines, and renewal of the coolant. These items are covered separately in this Chapter.
4 It must be remembered that the cooling system is pressurized. This means that when the engine is hot, the coolant will be at a temperature in excess of 212°F (100°C). Great care must therefore be taken if the radiator pressure cap has to be removed when the engine is hot since steam and boiling water will be ejected. If possible, let the engine cool down before removing the pressure cap. If this is not possible, place a cloth on the cap and turn it slowly counter-clockwise to the first notch. Keep it in this position until all the steam has escaped then turn it further until it can be removed.

3 Cooling system - draining

1 Park the vehicle on level ground. If the coolant is to be re-used, place a suitable clean container under the drain taps or plug for its collection.

Radiator
Heater (Option)
Thermostat
Cylinder Head
Water Pump
Cylinder Body

Fig. 2.1. The cooling system circulation

2 Remove the radiator cap. If the engine is hot see paragraph 4 of the previous Section.
3 Open the radiator and engine drain taps/plugs and drain off all of the coolant.
4 When coolant ceases to flow from the drain taps, probe them with a stiff wire to ensure that no sediment is blocking the drain orifices.
5 On completion refer to Section 4 or 5 as applicable.

4 Cooling system - flushing

1 With the passage of time deposits can build up in an engine which will lead to engine overheating and possibly serious damage.
2 It is a good policy, whenever the cooling system is drained, to flush the system with cold water from a hosepipe. This can conveniently be done by leaving a hosepipe in the radiator filler orifice for about 15 minutes while water is allowed to run thru. This will usually be sufficient to clear any sediment which may be present.
3 If there appears to be a restriction, first try reverse flushing; this is the application of the hose to the drain orifices and forcing water back thru the radiator tubes and out of the filler.
4 If the radiator flow is restricted by something other than loose sediment, then no amount of flushing will shift it and it is then that a proprietary chemical cleaner, suitable for aluminium engines, is needed. Use this according to the directions and make sure that the residue is fully flushed out afterwards. If leaks develop after using a chemical cleaner, a proprietary radiator sealer may cure them, but the signs are that the radiator has suffered considerable chemical corrosion and that the metal is obviously getting very thin in places.

5 Cooling system - filling

1 When draining (and flushing if applicable) has been accomplished, close the drain taps and top-up the cooling system with water which contains the correct proportion of antifreeze or inhibitor (see Section 6). Ensure that the heater water valve is open to prevent airlocks from occurring in the heater matrix.
2 When the radiator is full, run the engine for 5 to 10 minutes at a fast idle. As the water circulates and the thermostat opens, the coolant level will be seen to fall. Top-up the radiator to about halfway up the fill elbow, install the cap, then run the engine for a few more minutes and check carefully for wear leaks.
3 Allow the system to cool, then recheck the coolant level. Top-up if necessary so that, with the engine idling, the coolant is withing 1½ in of the top of the filler neck and then refit the radiator cap.

6 Antifreeze and rust inhibitors

1 Tap water alone should not be used in an aluminium engine except in an emergency. If it has to be used, it should be drained off at the earliest opportunity and the correct coolant mixture used instead.
2 Generally speaking, the basis of the coolant mixture can be tap water, except where this has a high alkali content or is exceptionally hard. If these conditions exist, clean rainwater or distilled water should be used.
3 Antifreeze must be of a type suitable for use with aluminium engines (ethylene glycol based antifreeze is suitable) and many proprietary products will be available for use. The fact that all products tend to be expensive should not deter you from using them, since they are a good insurance against freezing and corrosion.
4 The following table gives suitable concentrations of antifreeze. Do not use concentrations in excess of 55% except where protection to below −35°F (−37°C) is required as there is a possibility of overheating in very hot weather.

Coolant freezing water point	Mixture percentage (volume)		Specific gravity of mixture at 68°F (20°C)
	Anti-freeze	Water	
−4°F (−20°C)	35	65	1.051
−49°F (−45°C)	55	45	1.078

Fig. 2.2. The drive belt layout and their adjustment

8.3 Lift the radiator clear taking care not to damage the core

Fig. 2.3. Loosen but do not remove the bolt arrowed

5 Antifreeze mixtures are normally suitable for use for a period of two years (even so-called permanent antifreeze) after which they should be discarded and a fresh mixture used.
6 Antifreeze normally contains suitable corrosion inhibitors for protection of the engine. However, if antifreeze is not used for some reason, the vehicle manufacturers market suitable inhibitors which will give satisfactory protection to the engine. Any inhibitors which are used must be mixed in accordance with the instructions on the container.

7 Fan/alternator drivebelt - tension adjustment

1 In order that the engine cooling and alternator charge rate are efficient, the drivebelt tension must be correct.
2 To check the belt tension, apply thumb pressure to the belt at its midway point of its longest run between pulleys.
3 If the distance between the pulleys is 13 to 16 inches, the belt deflection should be ½ inch. If the distance between the pulleys is 7 to 10 inches the belt deflection must be ¼ inch.
4 If adjustment is required, loosen the alternator mounting bolts and pivot bolt and move the alternator as necessary. Avoid prying against the side of the alternator or irreparable damage may result.
5 Tighten the bolts after adjustment has been made, then recheck the tension. After running the vehicle for about 150 miles (250 km), recheck the belt tension and adjust if necessary.

8 Radiator - removal and installation

1 Drain the cooling system - refer to Section 3 if necessary.
2 Loosen the hose clamps and then disconnect the top and bottom hoses.
3 Undo and remove the four radiator retaining bolts, then lift the radiator clear of the vehicle taking care not to damage the core (photo).
4 Installation is a direct reversal of removal but be sure to shut the drain tap before refilling with coolant. After filling check the hose connections for any signs of leakage.

9 Thermostat - removal, testing and installation

Series 1 to 4
1 Drain the radiator by means of the drain tap. Any coolant to be re-used may be drained into a suitable clean container.
2 Undo the top hose clamp from the engine connection.
3 Disconnect the outlet pipe to remove the thermostat.
4 To test whether the unit is serviceable, suspend the thermostat on a piece of string in a pan of water being heated. Using a thermometer, with reference to the opening and closing temperature in Specifications, its operation may be checked. The thermostat should be renewed if it is stuck open or closed or if it fails to operate at the special temperature. The operation of the thermostat is not instantaneous and sufficient time must be allowed for the movement during test. Never install a faulty unit - leave it out if no replacement is available immediately.
5 Installation of the thermostat is the reverse of the removal procedure, but be sure to check for leaks when fully reassembled and the engine is running.

Series 5 and 6
6 Drain the radiator as described in Section 3.
7 Detach the crankshaft ventilation hose, the emission control system hose, the air hose and the controlled combustion system hose from the hot idle compensator to the inlet manifold.
8 Unscrew the two air cleaner attachment bolts and slacken the clamp bolt.
9 Remove the air cleaner from the carburetor and disconnect the controlled combustion hose from the thermosenser to the inlet manifold from the air cleaner. Remove the air cleaner unit.
10 Unscrew and remove the two outlet pipe attachment bolts and withdraw the outlet pipe and water hose. The thermostat can now be removed from the inlet manifold.
11 To test the thermostat refer to paragraph 4 of this Section.
12 Refitting is a direct reversal of removal but be certain to renew any defective hoses or clips. On refilling the system check for leaks.

10 Water pump - removal and installation

Series 1 to 4

1 Detach the battery ground cable.

2 Drain the cooling system as described in Section 3.

3 Remove the raditator and shroud assembly.

4 Disconnect the generator and the air pump drivebelts by slackening their respective adjustment bolts.

5 Disconnect the fan with pulley and spacer.

6 The water pump unit can now be removed from the engine complete with gasket. When disconnecting the water pump, the bolt to the rear of the timing gear cover (Fig. 2.3) must be loosened but not removed.

7 The heater hose and radiator bottom hose can now be detached from the water pump.

8 Installation of the water pump is a direct reversal of removal but always fit a new gasket to the pump. Readjust the generator and air pump belts on reassembly and finally check for leaks when the system has been refilled.

Series 5 and 6

9 Disconnect the ground cable from the battery and drain the cooling system as described in Section 3.

10 On models without air conditioning equipment, undo and remove the four nuts securing the engine fan and detach the fan. On models with air conditioning equipment fitted, unscrew the generator and air pump mounting bolts and remove the drive belts. Detach the engine fan and pulley by unscrewing the four retaining bolts. Unscrew the four fan set plate and pulley attachment bolts to remove the set plate and pulley.

11 The water pump can now be removed by unscrewing the six retaining bolts.

12 Installation is a direct reversal of removal but be certain to readjust the generator and air pump drivebelts and when the system has been refilled, check for any signs of leakage.

11 Fault diagnosis - cooling system

Symptom	Reason/s	Remedy
Loss of coolant	Leak in system	Examine all hoses, hose connections, drain taps and the radiator and the heater for signs of leakage when the engine is cold, then when hot and under pressure. Tighten clips, renew hoses and repair radiator as necessary.
	Defective radiator pressure	Examine cap for defective seal and renew if necessary.
	Overheating causing too rapid evaporation due to excessive pressure in system	Check reasons for overheating.
	Blown cylinder head gasket causing excess pressure in cooling system forcing coolant out	Remove cylinder head for examination.
	Cracked block or head due to freezing	Strip engine and examine. Repair as required.
Overheating	Insufficient coolant in system	Top up.
	Water pump not turning properly due to slack fan belt	Tighten fan belt.
	Kinked or collapsed water hoses causing restriction to circulation of coolant	Renew hose as required.
	Faulty thermostat (not opening properly)	Check and renew as necessary.
	Engine out of tune	Check ignition setting and carburetor adjustments.
	Blocked radiator either internally or externally	Flush out cooling system and clean out cooling fins.
	Cylinder head gaskets blown forcing coolant out of system	Remove head and renew gasket.
	New engine not run-in	Adjust engine speed until run-in.
Engine running too cool	Missing or faulty thermostat	Check and renew as necessary.

Chapter 3 Carburetion; fuel, exhaust and emission control systems

Contents

Air cleaner (Series 1 to 4) - removal and installation 2
Air cleaner (Series 5) - removal and installation 3
Automatic temperature controlled air cleaner - testing 4
Carburetor (DCP-340 Series 4 and 5 models) - dismantling and reassembly ... 12
Carburetor (DCP-340 Series 4 models) - idle adjustment ... 14
Carburetor (DCP-340 Series 5 models) - idle adjustment 15
Carburetor (DCP-340 Series 4 and 5 models) - linkage adjustment... 13
Carburetor (DRJ-340 Series 1 and 2 models) - dismantling and reassembly 6
Carburetor (DRJ-340 Series 1 and 2 models) - idle adjustment ... 8
Carburetor (DRJ-340 Series 1 and 2 models) - linkage adjustment... 7
Carburetor - Types DRJ-340 (Series 1 and 2), DRJ-340 4C (Series 3) and DCP-340 (Series 4) - removal and installation 5
Carburetor (DRJ-340 4C Series 3 models) - dismantling and reassembly 9
Carburetor (DRJ-340 4C Series 3 models) - idle adjustment ... 11
Carburetor (DRJ-340 4C Series 3 models) - linkage adjustment ... 10

Crankcase emission control - description and maintenance ... 25
Electric automatic choke - adjustment 17
Electric automatic choke - general 16
Emission control system - description 23
Evaporative emission control system - description and maintenance 26
Exhaust emission control system - component description and maintenance 24
Exhaust system - removal and installation 27
Fuel filter element - removal and installation 22
Fuel pump (electro magnetic) - removal and installation ... 20
Fuel pump (mechanical) - dismantling, inspection and reassembly 19
Fuel pump (mechanical) Series 1 to 3 models - removal and installation 18
Fuel tank - removal and installation 21
General description 1

Specifications

Carburetor
Type ...	...	...	...	...	...	...	...	...	Two barrel downdraft
Series 1 and 2 models ...	...	...	...	...	...	...	...	DRJ-340
Series 3 model ...	...	...	...	...	...	...	...	DRJ-340 4C
Series 4 and 5 models ...	...	...	...	...	...	...	...	DCP-340

	Series 1	Series 2	Series 3	Series 4	Series 5
Inner air horn diameter	2.95 in	2.95 in	2.95 in	2.95 in	2.95 in
Fuel pressure	3.13 lb/in^2	4.55 lb/in^2	4.55 lb/in^2	4.55 lb/in^2	3.56 lb/in^2
Outlet diameter					
Primary	1.18 in	1.18 in	1.18 in	1.18 in	1.18 in
Secondary	1.35 in	1.35 in	1.34 in	1.34 in	1.34 in
Venturi diameter					
Large					
Primary	0.91 in	0.91 in	0.91 in	0.91 in	0.91 in
Secondary	1.14 in	1.14 in	1.14 in	1.14 in	1.14 in
Small					
Primary	0.32 in	0.32 in	—	—	—
Secondary	0.35 in	0.35 in	—	—	—
Main jet					
Primary	0.043 in	0.045 in	No. 115		
Secondary	0.061 in	0.061 in	No. 115		
Series 4					
Primary	No. 100 (f)/No. 112 (C)				
Secondary	No. 155				

Series 5 and 6
    Primary ... ...   No. 103 (f)/No. 114 (C)
    Secondary ... ...   No. 170 (f)/No. 160 (C)

Slow jet
Series 1 and 2
    Primary ... ...   0.020 in
    Secondary ... ...   0.032 in
Series 3 ... ...   No. 50
Series 4
    Primary ... ...   No. 70
    Secondary ... ...   No. 80
Series 5 and 6
    Primary ... ...   No. 50 (f)/No. 45 (C)
    Secondary ... ...   No. 100

Power jet
Series 1 and 2 ... ...   0.016 in
Series 3 ... ...   No. 40
Series 4 ... ...   No. 45 (f)/ No. 40 (C)
Series 5 and 6 ... ...   No. 40 (f)

Main air bleed	Primary	Secondary
Series 1	0.022 in	0.020 in
Series 2	0.026 in	0.020 in
Series 3	No. 65	No. 70
Series 4	No. 65	No. 60
Series 5 and 6	No. 50 (f)/No. 80 (C)	No. 50

Slow air bleed	Primary	Secondary
Series 1	0.063 in	0.039 in
Series 2	0.059 in	0.039 in
Series 3	No. 150	No. 100
Series 4	No. 120 (f)/No. 130 (C)	No. 100
Series 5	No. 160 (f)/No. 140 (C)	No. 70

	Series 1	Series 2	Series 3	Series 4	Series 5
Coasting jet	0.017 in	0.017 in	No. 43	No. 43	No. 60 (f; MT)/ No. 67 (C)
Coasting air bleed	0.098 in	0.098 in	No. 290	No. 290	No. 290
Vacuum jet					1.5 (Series 6)
Idle port	0.07 in	0.07 in	0.07 in	0.07 in	0.07 in
Accelerator - pump nozzle diameter	0.02 in	0.02 in	0.02 in	0.02 in	0.02 in
Accelerator - pump delivery (1 stroke)	0.026 in^3	0.026 in^3	0.026 in^3	0.026 in^3	0.026 in^3
Power valve opening pressure	5.12 in Hg	5.12 in Hg	5.12 in Hg	6.3 in Hg	6.3 in Hg
Throttle valve opening angle (check valve closed) .	17°	18.5°	17.5°	17°	17°
Diaphragm spring (set force)	0.64 lbs	0.64 lbs	0.64 lbs	0.64 lbs	0.80 lbs
Engine speed at which diaphragm opens (engine fully loaded)	50°	50°	50°	50°	47°
Main nozzle inside diameter					
Primary	0.091 in	0.091 in	0.091 in	0.091 in	0.091 in
Secondary	0.098 in	0.098 in	0.098 in	0.098 in	0.098 in
Throttle valve closing angle					
Primary	10°	10°	10°	10°	10°
Secondary	20°	20°	20°	20°	20°

Emission control
Air pump type ... ...   ECP200 - 12 (Series 1 and 2)
                                                     ECP200 - 12A (Series 1 and 4)

Construction ... ...   Positive displacement type

Number of vanes   2

Inlet diameter	0.748 in
Outlet diameter	0.748 in
Theoretical delivery	11.29 cu in
Maximum speed	6000 rpm Series 1 to 4 7000 rpm Series 5
Relief valve opening pressure	6.12 lb/in^2 Series 1 to 3 5.3 lb/in^2 Series 4 2.84 - 4.98 lb/in^2 Series 5
Check valve type	CV27 - 12
Mixture control valve type	AV54 - 11

Automatic temperature controlled air cleaner
Sensor

1 118.4°F	2.756 in Hg
2 100.4°F	6.693 in Hg

Vacuum motor

1 Starting negative pressure	2.756 in Hg
2 With rod lifted 0.236 in	6.693 in Hg

Idle valve opening and compensator: closing temperature ...	122° - 140°F - Series 1 to 3 122° - 149°F - Series 4
Series 5 and 6	Oxidizing catalytic converter system
Converter size	16.98 x 8.98 x 3.5 in
Converter volume	160 cu in
Converter (with catalyst) weight	18 lbs
Catalyst dimension	Pellet 1/8 in min - 1/4 in max

Over temperature control system

Warning system operating temperature	Over 1830°F (at converter)
Engine speed sensor	'On' over engine speed of 1600 rpm

Exhaust gas recirculation (EGR) system
EGR valve operating negative pressure

Starting	3.5 in Hg
Fully opening	8 in Hg
Thermal vacuum valve opening temperature	Over 180° - 126°F

Controlled combustion system
Thermo sensor operating temperature

Starting	100°F
Fully opening	111°F
Idle compensator operating temperature	115° - 126°F

Evaporating control system
Check and relief valve operating pressure

Check valve open	1.0 - 1.4 in Hg
Relief valve open	0.2 - 0.6 in Hg

Fig. 3.1. The fuel system layout (Series V)

1 General description

All models are equipped with a rear mounted fuel tank, a fuel filter and, on Series 1 to 3 models, a mechanically operated fuel pump. On Series 4 and 5 the fuel pump is of an electric magnetic type.

A two-barrel downdraft carburetor is fitted to all models although the type depends on the year and model.

The carburetors incorporate emission control features and are fitted with a renewable element type of fuel filter, and on some models the air cleaner has an automatic temperature-control unit fitted.

The general information on the emission control equipment is detailed in the appropriate Section in this Chapter.

Fig. 3.2. Lift the air cleaner unit from the carburetor then disconnect the remaining hoses

2 Air cleaner (Series 1 to 4) - removal and installation

1   The air cleaner fitted to all Series 1 to 4 models is a wet paper element type. The air cleaner unit is fitted with an automatic intake air temperature control system and a hot idle compensator.
2   To remove the cleaner unit, first unscrew the wing nut and detach the rubber hoses on the cover. Also remove the rubber hose from the vacuum motor.
3   Unscrew the air cleaner cover bracket bolts.
4   Detach the hot air hose from the hot air duct, and the air pump hose from the cleaner. Also detach the vacuum hose from the joint nipple side of the inlet manifold.
5   Slacken the air cleaner to carburetor retaining bolt and separate the cleaner unit body from the carburetor (photo). Now disconnect the PVC hose from the camshaft cover, and the rubber hoses from the check and relief valves. The air cleaner unit can now be removed.
6   Installation is a reversal of removal but ensure that all hose connections are good.

3 Air cleaner (Series 5 and 6 models) - removal and installation

1   Refer to Fig. 3.3 and disconnect the PVC hose from the cylinder head cover and the ECS hose from the air cleaner unit.

2.5 Lift the air cleaner from the carburetor and disconnect the hoses

2 Detach the air hose from the air pump and unscrew the retaining bolts from the air cleaner. Loosen the clamp bolts.

3 Lift the air cleaner sufficiently to disconnect the CCS vacuum hose. Remove the air cleaner unit.

4 Installation is the reverse of removal but ensure that the respective hose connections are good.

4 Automatic temperature - controlled air cleaner - testing

1 The principle of the automatic air intake temperature control system is basically that the hot air switch valve is operated by the vacuum motor. The motor operates under vacuum pressure and is controlled by the thermo-sensor. Therefore in accordance with the engine operating conditions and the ambient air temperature, the hot air switching valve maintains the air intake temperature at a constant level.

Vacuum motor and hot air switching valve - checking

2 Connect the vacuum motor inlet pipe hose direct to the inlet manifold nipple. View thru the air intake side of the air cleaner and when the vacuum pressure is nearly zero, check that the hot air switching valve is fully closed.

Start and run the engine at idle speed and check that the air switch valve operates instantly, shutting off the fresh air intake. Check that the hot air switching valve closes instantly and smoothly.

Thermo-sensor - checking

3 Remove the air cleaner as previously described, and detach the thermo couple thermometer from the sensor. Refit the cover and refit the air cleaner unit to the carburetor. Allow the engine to cool and then restart it.

Viewing thru the air intake of the air cleaner check that the hot air switching valve starts to move towards the fresh air intake.

When the valve starts to operate, note the thermo couple thermometer reading. Check again several times and note the mean reading. Any deviation between $100^{\circ}F$ to $111^{\circ}F$ indicates that the thermo sensor unit is faulty and must be renewed.

Hot idle compensator

4 Connect a thermocouple thermometer as when tesing the thermo-sensor. Run the engine at idle speed with the air cleaner cover detached so that the idle compensator is supplied with hot air.

As soon as the hot idle compensator starts to operate, note the thermometer reading. The hot idle compensator starts to operate when the sound of outside air intake is audible. If the hot idle compensator actuates between $115^{\circ}F$ and $126^{\circ}F$ it is in good order. If the reading is outside of these figures then it must be renewed.

5 Carburetor - Types DRJ-340 (Series 1 and 2) DRJ-340 4C (Series 3) and DCP-340 (Series 4) - removal and installation

1 Unscrew the air cleaner wing nut and detach the rubber hoses from the air cleaner cover. The rubber hose must also be disconnected from the vacuum motor.

2 Unscrew and remove the air cleaner bracket bolts. Detach the air cleaner cover and lift out the air cleaner filter element.

3 Detach the hot air hose from the hot air duct, and the air hose to the air pump from the air cleaner. The vacuum hose must be disconnected from the inlet manifold at the joint nipple side.

4 The air cleaner to carburetor bolt is now loosened, lift the air cleaner from the carburetor, and then detach the PVC hose to the camshaft cover and the hoses to the relief valve and check valve. The air cleaner body can now be lifted clear.

5 Detach the choke control cable on Series 1 to 2. On Series 3 and 4 models detach the signal passage rubber pipe from the Exhaust Gas Recirculation valve (on California models only).

6 Disconnect the anti-dieselling solenoid lead from its connection.

7 Disconnect the accelerator return spring and operating cable.

8 Disconnect the carburetor fuel supply pipe (photo) and on Series 4 models, the check valve from the air manifold.

9 Unscrew the four carburetor retaining nuts and remove with lockwashers. Carefully lift the carburetor from the manifold.

10 When installing the carburetor, reverse the removal sequence but note the following.

Ensure that the carburetor manifold flanges are perfectly clean. Always use a new gasket. Reset the choke and throttle adjustments and check that all hose connections are good particularly those of the emission control. When the engine is restarted, check for fuel leaks.

6 Carburetor (DRJ-340 - Series 1 and 2 models) - dismantling and reassembly

Refer to Figures 3.5 and 3.6

1 Clean off the outside of the carburetor and remove to the workbench. When dismantling or assembling the various components always use the correct tools and lay the parts out on a clean area in the sequence of removal.

2 Commence dismantling by disconnecting the accelerator pump lever as in Fig. 3.7.

3 Undo the retaining screws and remove the throttle switch and bracket unit in Fig. 3.8.

4 Disconnect and remove the throttle return spring. Then undo the retaining screws and remove the diaphragm return spring (photo). Detach the choke chamber unit complete with choke cable bracket and disconnect the connection rod (Fig. 3.9).

5 Unscrew the float chamber to throttle chamber retaining bolts - one bolt/screw to the upper section and three to the lower.

They must be removed with care as one of them extracts the negative pressure developed in the venturi. With the bolts removed lift the float chamber from the throttle chamber.

6 Unscrew the accelerator pump plunger unit retaining screws and then invert the float chamber to extract the plunger assembly (Fig. 3.10).

7 Disconnect the fuel pipe nipple joint, strainer and float needle valve unit as in Fig. 3.11 and then very carefully remove the strainer to ensure that it does not get damaged or distorted.

8 Unscrew the level gauge cover retaining screws and disconnect the cover and float. Take care not to lose the float collar, and if

Fig. 3.3. Removing the Series V model air cleaner unit

Fig. 3.4. The thermosensor in the air cleaner

Fig. 3.5. Side elevation view of the DRJ-340 type carburetor

1 Float
2 Needle valve
3 Fuel nipple
4 Sec. slow air bleed
5 Sec. slow jet
7 Sec. main air bleed
8 Sec. small venturi
9 Sec. main nozzle
10 Sec. air vent
11 Choke valve
12 Pri. air vent
13 Pri. main nozzle
14 Vapor hole
15 Pri. main air bleed
16 Accelerator air bleed
17 Pri. slow air bleed: 1st
18 Plug
19 Pri. slow air bleed: 2nd
20 Vacuum piston
21 Diaphragm spring
22 Diaphragm
23 Sec. main jet
24 Sec. emulsion tube
25 Coasting hole
26 Sec. throttle valve
27 Sec. vacuum jet
28 Pri. vacuum jet
29 Pri. throttle valve
30 Pri. small venturi
31 Bypass hole
32 Idle hole
33 Inner emulsion tube
34 Outer emulsion tube
35 Pri. main nozzle
36 Pri. slow jet
37 Power valve

Fig. 3.6. Exploded view of the DRJ-340 type carburetor

1 Choke chamber assembly
2 Float chamber assembly
3 Throttle chamber assembly
4 Throttle adjusting screw
5 Idle adjusting screw
6 Adjusting spring screw
7 Adjusting screw spring
8 Diaphragm, chamber assembly
9 Diaphragm assembly
10 Diaphragm spring
12 (23) Screw
24 (26) Washer
28 Gasket
29 Washer
30 Pin
31 Gasket
32 Washer
33 Gasket
34 Screw
35 Nut
36 (37) Washer
38 Inlet valve
40 (48) Gasket
49 Choke wire bracket
50 Spring hanger
51 Choke connecting rod
52 Choke connecting rod
53 Accelerator switch holder
54 Plate
55 Throttle lever
56 Accelerator switch lever
57 Return spring
58 Accelerator switch bracket
59 Accelerator pump piston
60 Pump return spring
61 Injector weight
62 Pri. small venturi
63 Outer emulsion tube
64 Pump lever
65 Pump connecting lever
66 Return spring
67 Piston plate
68 Sec. Small venturi
69 Float
70 Dust cover
71 Choke connecting lever
72 Sleeve (B)
73 Spring
74 Rubber seal
75 Level gauge
76 Level gauge cover
77 Adjust lever
78 Return plate
79 Sleeve (A)
80 Set screw
81 Joint nipple
82 Spring
83 Float collar
84 Sec. emulsion tube
85 Injector weight plug
86 Main jet plug
87 Strainer
88 Pri. slow jet plug
89 Float needle valve assembly
90 Collar
91 Pri. main air bleed
92 Accelerator air bleed
93 Sec. slow air bleed
94 Sec. main air bleed
95 Pri. slow air bleed
96 Coasting jet
97 Vacuum jet
98 Coasting air bleed
99 Pri. main jet
100 Sec. main jet
101 Pri. slow jet
102 Sec. slow jet
103 Power valve
104 Anti dieseling solenoid
105 Coasting valve solenoid
106 Accelerator switch

5.8 Disconnect the fuel supply pipe from the float chamber needle valve connection

6.4 View showing 'A' the diaphragm, 'B' the diaphragm return spring, 'C' the throttle return spring and 'D' the throttle switch

6.19d The float chamber with cover removed, showing the needle valve

Fig. 3.7. Disconnect the accelerator pump lever

Fig. 3.8. Undo the retaining screws

Fig. 3.9. Lift the choke chamber and detach the connecting rod

Fig. 3.10. The pump plunger assembly

Fig. 3.11. The float needle valve assembly

Fig. 3.12. The upper float chamber and jet locations

possible avoid damaging the gaskets.

9   The coasting valve unit, throttle switch and solenoid units are now removed, taking care not to damage the coasting valve shaft and solenoid valve.

10 Remove the diaphragm chamber and unscrew the diaphragm cover retaining screws. Lift off the cover and separate the spring and diaphragm, but do not lose the ball and spring (Fig. 3.30).

11 From the upper part of the float chamber, the various jets can now be unscrewed and removed as required. If they are all to be removed, mark out their respective locations as in Fig. 3.12 on a piece of paper, and as they are extracted place them in position on the paper accordingly.

12 From the primary and secondary barrels, remove the small venturi then invert the float chamber to remove the outer emulsion tube (Fig. 3.13).

13 Unscrew the accelerator pump plug and invert the chamber to extract the balance weight as in Fig. 3.14.

14 Unscrew and remove the power jet taking care to correctly locate the screwdriver in the slot to avoid damaging the valve rod (Fig. 3.15).

15 Unscrew the two jet plugs (see Fig. 3.16) to remove the primary and secondary main jets.

16 Unscrew the primary vacuum jet and remove it (Fig. 3.17).

17 Apart from the primary and secondary throttle valve and the choke valve, the carburetor is now dismantled for cleaning and inspection. Do not remove the two throttle valves or choke valve as they are preset and sealed to prevent air leaks.

18 Clean the various components in petrol and blow dry. Do not probe the jets with wire. Inspect the parts carefully for signs of wear, damage and cracks in the carburetor body. Renew any parts that are suspect.

19 Reassembly is the reverse of dismantling but the following points should be observed.

General
a) Ensure that the jets are fitted into their correct locations.
b) If for any reason the throttle and choke valves (butterflies) have been removed refit them and on adjustment, to ensure that they close correctly, apply some adhesive solution to prevent air leaks.
c) When the accelerator pump has been reassembled, fill the cylinder with gasoline and check that the fuel is injecting smoothly.

Float level adjustment
d) The correct fuel level is when it is in line with the float chamber window glass line with the engine stationary. Should the fuel level be incorrect, adjustment can be made by bending the float seat accordingly. The effective needle valve stroke should be approximately 0.059 in. This can be adjusted by bending the float stopper.

e) Primary throttle valve opening adjustment
The primary throttle valve is opened by the choke connecting rod. When the choke valve is fully closed the throttle valve should be at an angle of 15° on Series 1 models or 18.5° on Series 2. To check this completely close the choke valve and measure the distance between the wall of the throttle valve chamber in the center of the valve and the throttle valve. The standard clearance is 0.05 to 0.06 inch on Series 1 and 3 or 0.06 to 0.07 in for Series 2 models. See GI in Fig. 3.18. Fully screw in the throttle stop screw before measuring.

To adjust, bend the connecting rod accordingly.

7   Carburetor (DRJ-340 - Series 1 and 2 models) - linkage adjustment

Refer to Fig. 3.19

1   With the primary throttle valve open at an angle of 50°, the adjust plate and interlocking primary throttle valve are in contact with point 'A' of the return plate. If the primary throttle valve is further opened, the return plate is pulled from the stopper 'B' which allows the secondary throttle valve to open.

2   Measurement of the opening point of the secondary throttle valve is made by measuring the distance between the primary throttle valve and the center of the valve at the throttle chamber wall (G2). The normal clearance is 0.26 to 0.32 in. Adjustment if necessary is made by bending the return plate at point 'A' as required.

Fig. 3.13. The primary and secondary venturi

Fig. 3.14. Extract the injector weight

Fig. 3.15. The power jet location

Fig. 3.16. Extract the main jets

Fig. 3.17. Unscrew the primary vacuum jet

Fig. 3.18. The primary throttle valve adjustment

Fig. 3.19. The linkage adjustment

8 Carburetor (DRJ-340 Series 1 and 2 models) - idle adjustment

1 With the engine running at its normal operating temperature, tighten fully the idle adjustment screw and then unscrew it 3½ turns.
2 Now adjust the throttle adjustment screw to give an idle speed of 700 rpm.
3 The idle adjustment screw is then further adjusted so that the engine runs smooth on a fast idle and the throttle screw is then readjusted to enable the engine to run at the correct idle speed.

9 Carburetor (DRJ-340 4C - Series 3 models) - dismantling and reassembly

1 Clean off the outside of the carburetor and remove to the workbench. When dismantling and assembling the various components always use the correct type of tools and lay the parts out on a clean area in sequence of removal.
2 Refer to Fig. 3.21 and detach the accelerator pump lever. Unclip the return spring and remove with bracket and connecting rods. Disconnect the wire arm and choke spring hanger.
3 Withdraw the cotter pin located between the diaphragm rod and secondary throttle lever. Detach the lever and diaphragm unit, disconnect the solenoid valve harness clips and loosen the three bolts retaining the float chamber. Take out the diaphragm (Fig. 3.20).
4 Lift the choke chamber from the float chamber unit, noting that the choke spring hanger is retained by one of the fixing bolts.
5 Remove the float chamber assembly from the throttle unit as in Fig. 3.22 after unscrewing the three lower retaining bolts and one upper bolt. Remove the bolts carefully - one of them relieves the negative pressure from the venturi.
6 Under no circumstances remove the slow cut solenoid and coasting richer solenoid from the float chamber.
7 Unscrew the accelerator pump retaining screws, invert the float chamber and remove the plunger unit.
8 Unscrew the fuel pipe nipple and remove with strainer and float needle valve unit. Do not distort the strainer.
9 Undo the three screws securing the level gauge cover, and remove with cover, baffle plate and float (Fig. 3.24).
10 To dismantle the diaphragm chamber follow the instructions in paragraph 10 in Section 6 and then follow paragraph ʜ ʜ to remove the jets.
11 From the primary and secondary carburetors remove the small venturi, invert the float chamber to remove the accelerator air bleed, main air bleeds and the secondary emulsion tube (Fig. 3.25), but do not remove the primary emulsion tube.
12 Unscrew the injector weight plug, invert the float chamber and extract the injector weight (Fig. 3.26).
13 Now follow paragraphs 14 to 18 in Section 6, In addition to those items mentioned in paragraph 18, check solenoid and valve wires are in good condition and their connections are firm. If the solenoid

Fig. 3.20. The diaphragm assembly

Fig. 3.22. Remove the float chamber

and valve are defective they must be renewed as a unit for they cannot be removed separately

14 Reassembly of the carburetor is a direct reversal of dismantling, but note instructions given in paragraph 19 of Section 6, and check the float level, primary throttle linkage and idle adjustments, as described in the following paragraphs.

Float level adjustment

15 Refer to paragraph 19 in Section 6, sub-paragraph 'd'.

Primary throttle valve adjustment

16 Refer to paragraph 19 in Section 6, sub-paragraph 'e'. The instructions are identical but the throttle valve should be at an angle of 17.5° when the choke valve is closed.

---

10 Carburetor (DRJ-340 4C - Series 3 models) - linkage adjustment

To set the linkage adjustment, refer to Section 7 - the instructions are identical.

---

11 Carburetor (DRJ-340 4C - Series 3 models) - idle adjustment

1   Run the engine at its normal operating temperature and adjust the idle to 700 rpm.

2   Detach the vacuum line from the air cleaner hot idle compensator and plug at the inlet manifold.

3   Tighten fully the idle adjustment screw and then unscrew it 3½ turns.

4   Adjust the throttle adjustment screw to give an idle speed of 700 rpm.

5   The idle adjustment screw is then further adjusted so that the engine runs smoothly on a fast idle and the throttle screw is then readjusted to enable the engine to run at the correct idle speed.

6   If air conditioning equipment is fitted turn AC on maximum cold and high blower, then open the throttle about a 1/3 rd and allow it to close. The speed up adjustment screw is now set so that the idle speed is 900 rpm. Re-open the throttle 1/3 rd and allow it to close and check that the engine idles at 900 rpm. If not readjust the speed up control adjustment screw.

7   Reconnect the hot air vacuum line from the air cleaner.

---

12 Carburetor (DCP-340 - Series 4 to 6 models) - dismantling and reassembly)

1   Clean off the outside of the carburetor and remove it to the workbench. When dismantling and assembling the various components always use the correct type of tools and lay the parts out on a clean work area in the sequence of removal.

Fig. 3.21. The DRJ-340 4C model carburetor. Illustration numbers 68 to 72 are only fitted to those models having air conditioning

1	Choke chamber assembly	37	Sleeve
2	Float chamber assembly	38	Filter set screw
3	Throttle chamber assembly	39	Spring
4	Throttle adjust screw	40	Collar
5	Idle adjust screw	41	Secondary emulsion tube
6	Throttle adjust screw apring	42	Plug
7	Idle adjust screw spring	43	Drain plug
8	Diaphragm chamber assembly	44	Filter
9	Diaphragm	45	Slow jet plug (primary)
10	Diaphragm spring	46	Needle valve
11	Screw and washer kit, A	47	Accelerator air bleed
12	Screw and washer kit, B	48	Main air bleed (primary)
13	Gasket	49	Slow air bleed (secondary)
14	Choke control arm	50	Main air bleed (secondary)
15	Choke connecting rod	51	Slow air bleed (primary)
16	Choke connecting rod	52	Coasting jet
17	Throttle lever (primary)	53	Vacuum jet
18	Accelerator pump piston	54	Coasting air bleed
19	Piston spring	55	Main jet (primary)
20	Injector weight	56	Main jet (secondary)
21	small venturi (primary)	57	Slow jet (primary)
22	Accelerator pump lever	58	Slow jet (secondary)
23	Connecting rod	59	Power valve
24	Throttle return spring	60	Thrust washer
25	Plate	61	Pump lever return spring
26	Small venturi (secondary)	62	Kick lever
27	Float	63	Crank
28	Dust cover	64	Choke control cable hanger
29	Starting lever	65	Coasting adjust screw
30	Sleeve	66	Locknut
31	Spring	67	EGR vacuum pipe clip
32	Rubber seal	68	Fast idle lever
33	Fuel level gauge	69	Spring
34	Cover	70	Collar
35	Adjust lever, B	71	Fast idle adjust spring
36	Return plate	72	Fast idle adjust screw

Fig. 3.23. The DCP 340 carburetor component parts

1	Choke chamber assembly	22	Fast idle lever	43	Accelerator pump rod
2	Choke connecting rod	23	Fast idle lever spring	44	Fast idle lever collar
3	Counter lever	24	Thermostat cover assembly	45	Accelerator pump piston
4	Nipple	25	Fast idle cam spring	46	Piston return spring
5	Hose	26	Gasket kit	47	Injector weight
6	Float chamber assembly	27	Fast idle cam	48	Vacuum jet plug
7	Anti-dieseling solenoid	28	Small venturi (primary)	49	Throttle return spring
8	Coasting richer solenoid	29	Fuel level gauge	50	Lock lever
9	Hose	30	Primary emulsion tube	51	Float
10	Diaphragm chamber assembly	31	Baffle plate	52	Rubber seal
11	Diaphragm	32	Throttle adjusting lever	53	Cover
12	Diaphragm spring	33	Throttle return plate	54	Plate
13	Nipple	34	Kick lever sleeve	55	Small venturi (secondary)
14	Nipple stop plate	35	Throttle lever sleeve	56	Dust cover
15	EGR vacuum hose clip	36	Kick lever	57	Fast idle adjusting screw
16	Throttle chamber assembly	37	Fast idle lever	58	Collar
17	Throttle adjusting screw	38	Auto choke piston spring	59	Secondary emulsion tube
18	Adjusting screw spring	39	Screw and washer kit, A	60	Thrust washer
19	Idle adjusting screw	40	Screw and washer kit, B	61	Filter set screw
20	Adjusting screw spring	41	Accelerator pump lever	62	Injector weight plug
21	Throttle lever (primary)	42	Pump lever return spring	63	Filter

64	Drain plug
65	Needle valve
66	Piston spring carrier
67	Piston spring stop pin
68	Main jet (primary)
69	Main jet (secondary)
70	Slow air bleed (primary)
71	Main air bleed (secondary)
72	Slow jet (primary)
73	Slow jet (secondary)
74	Slow air bleed (Secondary)
75	Main air bleed (primary)
76	Power valve
77	Coasting jet
78	Coasting air bleed
79	Vacuum jet
80	Connecting lever
81	Collar A
82	Down shift lever
83	Pump rod

FLOAT   COASTING VALVE SOLENOID

Fig. 3.24. The float chamber and coasting richer solenoid

PRIMARY SMALL VENTURI

SECONDARY SMALL VENTURI

ACCEL AIR BLEED

SECONDARY MAIN AIR BLEED

PRIMARY EMULSION TUBE

PRIMARY MAIN AIR BLEED

SECONDARY EMULSION TUBE

Fig. 3.25. The primary venturi and main air bleed, the secondary venturi and air bleed and the accelerator air bleed

INJECTOR WEIGHT

INJECTOR WEIGHT PLUG

Fig. 3.26. Extracting the injector weight

2   Detach the accelerator pump lever and throttle return spring (Fig. 3.27).

3   Remove the automatic choke lead and unscrew the three thermostat cover to housing screws. Unscrew the fuel pipe nipple and remove with strainer.

4   Unscrew the choke lever to choke shaft retaining screw and move the choke lever fully in towards the choke chamber. Detach the choke connection rod from the counter lever, then remove the choke chamber unit by unscrewing the four securing screws.

5   Withdraw the cotter pin from the diaphragm rod and secondary lever, and detach the lever and diaphragm unit. Unclip the solenoid valve harness clips, slacken the diaphragm chamber attachment bolts to remove the diaphragm unit.

6   Carefully remove the three lower and one upper float chamber to throttle chamber retaining bolts and separate the two assemblies. Note that one of the bolts removes the negative pressure developed in the venturi and must be handled carefully.

7   Unscrew the two screws attaching the accelerator pump plunger unit and invert the float chamber to extract the unit.

8   Unscrew and remove the float needle valve assembly and then unscrew the gauge level cover (Fig. 3.23) retaining screws. Detach the cover and remove the baffle plate and float and note the float collar.

9   To dismantle the diaphragm chamber follow the instructions given in paragraphs 10 to 13 in Section 9.

10 Reassembly of the carburetor is a direct reversal of dismantling but note paragraph 19 of Section 6, and check the float level, primary throttle valve linkage and idle adjustments as described below.

Float level adjustment

11 Refer to paragraph 19 in Section 6, sub-paragraph 'd'.

Primary throttle valve adjustment

12 Refer to paragraph 19 in Section 6, sub-paragraph 'e'. The instructions are identical but the throttle valve should be at an angle of 17° when the choke valve is closed and the standard clearance between the throttle valve chamber and valve is 0.04 to 0.05 in.

---

13 Carburetor (DCP-340 Series 4 and 5 models) - linkage adjustment

Refer to Section 7. The instructions are identical to those of the DRJ-340 carburetor but with the exception of the angle of the primary throttle valve, which should be open at 47° and the normal clearance between the primary throttle valve and the center of the valve at the chamber wall is 0.24 to 0.30.

---

14 Carburetor DCP-340 - Series 4 models - idle adjustment

1   Run the engine to its normal operating temperature, and plug the air pipe at the vacuum pipe connection of the idle compensator.

2   Tighten fully the idle adjustment screw and then unscrew it exactly 2½ turns.

3   Adjust the throttle adjustment screw to give an engine speed of 700 rpm, and then reset the idle adjustment screw to obtain the maximum inlet manifold vacuum.

4   Tighten the idle adjustment screw by 1/8 turn and reset the throttle adjustment to give 700 rpm.

5   If air conditioning is fitted, turn AC to maximum cold and high blower, open the throttle by about 1/3 and allow it to close. Now adjust the speed up controller setting screw to idle at 900 rpm. Open the throttle (1/3) and allow it to close and recheck the rpm. If it does not idle at 900 rpm, repeat the above procedure until correct.

6   Refit the air cleaner hot idle compensation line.

7   If a CO meter is available, follow the instructions in paragraphs 1 and 2 above and then set the throttle adjustment screw so that the engine idles at 700 rpm.

8   Adjust the idle adjustment screw to idle at CO 1%. Then reset the throttle screw to give the 700 rpm engine speed, and check that the idle CO is within 1 ± 0.5%.

9   The procedure for checking with a CO meter is otherwise identical including paragraph 5 concerning air conditioning if fitted.

Fig. 3.27. The accelerator pump lever and connecting rod

Fig. 3.28. The diaphragm unit showing the harness clip position

Fig. 3.29. Withdraw the accelerator pump plunger assembly

Fig. 3.30. The components of the diaphragm unit

Fig. 3.31. The principle components of the customatic choke

Fig. 3.32. The thick line mark for alignment of the thermostat housing and cover

Fig. 3.34. The fuel pump lid removed showing cap, seal and strainer

Fig. 3.33. The adjustment screw - check clearance at point 'L'

Fig. 3.35. The dismantled pump unit

15 Carburetor (DCP-340 - Series 5 and 6) - idling adjustment

1   Ensure that the parking brake is on and place chocks under the drive wheels, Check that the transmission is in neutral.
2   Run the engine to its normal operating temperature, and if fitted, turn off the air conditioner.
3   Disconnect the distributor vacuum line and also the idle compensator vacuum line which should be plugged on removal.
4   Tighten the mixture idle screw fully and then unscrew it 3 full turns.
5   Set the throttle adjusting screw so that the engine idles at 900 rpm, and then reset the idle adjusting screw to its fastest setting.
6   Re-adjust the throttle screw to 900 rpm, and then turn the idle mixture screw clockwise to reduce the engine speed to 850 rpm.
7   Re-adjust the idle screw turning it counterclockwise by a ½ turn and then reset the throttle screw to give 900 rpm engine speed.
8   If an air conditioning unit is fitted, set the idle as above and then turn the AC to maximum cold and high blower, open the throttle by about a 1/3 and allow the throttle to close. Now set the speed up controller adjustment screw so that the engine idles at 900 rpm.

16 Electric automatic choke - general

Refer to Fig. 3.31
1   An automatic choke assembly is fitted in place of the manually operated choke on some models. The automatic choke incorporates a thermostatic spring which operates the choke valve automatically according to the variation in ambient temperature.
2   The choke valve position is preset by the thermostatic spring when the accelerator pedal is fully depressed and released prior to starting. On starting the engine the negative pressure from the carburetor venturi actuator the choke diaphragm (A) and the choke valve is opened against bimetal spring tension, which in turn prevents the engine from being overchoked.
3   The choke diaphragm 'B' actuates to turn the spring slightly in the returning direction to shorten the choke valve opening. Additionally, on starting the engine, the current flow thru the heater relay unit and heater element flexes the bimetal and opens the choke valve.

4   Since the throttle valve does not automatically return to its position for idling, its opening angle is reduced by the fast idle cam during depressing and releasing of the accelerator pedal with the engine at fast idle and this causes the throttle valve to be repositioned for normal idling. This occurs when the fast idle screw is released from the fast idle cam.

17 Electric automatic choke - adjustment

1   Fit the choke cable lever end to the bimetal hook and align the thick line marking on the housing to that of the cover (Fig. 3.32) and fit the cover.
2   Ensure that the stopper on the bimetal lever side contacts the cover stopper and should a gap exist, adjust the bimetal rod accordingly.
3   Apply finger pressure to the diaphragm and measure the clearance between the cover side stopper and bimetal cover side stopper as in Fig. 3.33. The normal clearance should be 0.28 to 0.29 in.
4   If the measured clearance is incorrect, adjust the screw accordingly.

18 Fuel pump (mechanical) Series 1 to 3 models - removal and installation

1   Clean the outside surfaces of the fuel pump and connecting pipes.
2   Detach the hose from the side of the pump.
3   Unscrew the fuel pipe joint bolt and detach the pipe from the side of the pump.
4   Unscrew the pump unit retaining nuts and withdraw the pump unit.
5   Refitting is the reverse of removal but be sure to fit new joint bolt gaskets if the old ones are worn or broken.

19 Fuel pump (mechanical) - dismantling, inspection and reassembly

1   Unscrew the valve chamber cap retaining bolt and remove with washer. Detach the cap, strainer, seal and screen, Fig. 3.34.

2　To separate the fuel pump upper and lower body sections, unscrew and remove the five retaining screws and washers.

3　Unscrew the valve retainer screws and remove the valve retainers, the valves and seals.

4　With a suitable drift, drive out the rocker arm shaft and disconnect the rocker arm diaphragm, spring and return spring.

5　Clean the components in gasoline and blow dry. Check for cracks in the pump body and cap. If the pin hole in the body is worn the pump will have to be renewed. Similarly, if the diaphragm or valves are defective the pump unit must be renewed.

6　Reassemble the pump unit in the reverse order of dismantling and use new gaskets. Check on refitting for signs of leaks.

20 Fuel pump (electro-magnetic) - removal and installation

1　This type of pump is located on the inner-surface of the third crossmember on the left-hand side.

2　It is of the 'totally-enclosed' variety and cannot be dismantled for repair. If defective, the unit must therefore be renewed.

3　To remove the pump, disconnect the ground cable from the battery and then detach the lead and rubber hoses from the fuel pump.

4　Unscrew the retaining bolts and nut and remove the fuel pump unit.

5　Installation is the reverse of removal.

21 Fuel tank - removal and installation

1　Detach the battery ground cable.

2　Place a suitable clean metal container beneath the drain plug and unscrew the plug. When fully drained, withdraw the container and store in a safe area and place a lid over it.

3　Detach the fuel filler cap and unscrew the fuel filter pipe bracket bolts (Fig. 3.37).

4　From its fuel tank terminal, disconnect the sender unit.

5　Undo the retaining clips of the three rubber hoses on the left side of the fuel tank and detach the hoses.

6　Undo the clips retaining the two hoses from the check and relief valve to the fuel filter at the front of the tank and detach the hoses.

Fig. 3.36. The electro magnetic fuel pump location

Fig. 3.37. The fuel filler pipe bracket and retaining bolt location

Fig. 3.38. The emission control system - Series 1 to 4 models

Fig. 3.39. The fuel filter

Fig. 3.40. Exhaust emission control system - Series 1 to 4

Fig. 3.41. Air injector reactor system - Federal - Series 5

Fig. 3.42. Air injector reactor system - California models - Series 5

→ NORMAL PASSAGE

---→ AT DECELERATION

Fig. 3.43. End elevation showing component parts of the air pump

24.11 Withdraw the mounting bolts and remove the pump

24.16 The air manifold check valve

24.17 The mixture control valve

24.22 The coasting richer solenoid

7   Unscrew and remove the fuel tank mounting bolts from the front
and rear sides. Withdraw the fuel tank.
8   To install the fuel tank, reverse the above procedure but on
refilling, check that there are no signs of fuel leakage from the tank
and connection hoses.

22 Fuel filter element - removal and refitting

1   The fuel filter element must be renewed every 12000 miles or
sooner if contaminated or damaged.
2   To remove, simply unclip the connecting fuel hoses and withdraw
it.
3   Refit in the reverse sequence and ensure that the hose connections
are good.

23 Emission control system - description

1   The principle of the emission control system is to prevent the
discharge of harmful gases from the vehicle.
2   The emission control system is basically divided into three parts,
these being the exhaust emission control system to reduce the exhaust
gas; the crankcase emission control which recirculates the blow-by gases
from the crankcase, together with fuel vapours, into the combustion
chamber via the inlet manifold to be burned; and the evaporative emission
control system which stores fuel vapor from the fuel supply system and
leads it to the combustion chamber.
3   From Series 3 models, California versions were fitted with an exhaust
gas recirculation (EGR) valve and on Series 5 California models, a
catalytic converter is incorporated into the exhaust system and a over
temperature control system fitted which operate in conjunction with
each other.
4   A dual contact points distributor control system is fitted to all
models. This allows the ignition timing to be automatically selected
to suit the engine operating conditions. The retarded contact breaker
points operate when the engine is accelerating or decelerating which
momentarily causes the harmful content in exhaust gases to increase.
Details of the distributor setting and adjustments are given in Chapter
4.
5   The emission control system can only function correctly when the
engine and its associate components are in good condition and
correctly adjusted. All interconnecting hoses and electrical connections
within the system must be regularly checked and in good
condition in order that the system functions efficiently and complies
with the strict regulations.

24 Exhaust emission control system - component description and maintenance

Air pump - description
1   The air pump comprises mainly of the pump body, cover, vanes and
relief valve which is a press fit. The pump is driven by a connecting belt
to the water pump shaft pulley which in turn is driven by the crankshaft pulley.
2   Air enters the air cleaner and then into the pump suction chamber
where it is transferred by the vanes and rotor to the outlet chamber
which is interconnected to the air manifold. The relief valve
is normally closed, but when the outlet air pressure exceeds 2.84 to 4.98
psi the valve opens to release excess air. To operate efficiently the
pump drivebelt must be correctly adjusted at all times.

Air pump drive belt - adjustment
3   The tension of the air pump drivebelt should be periodically
checked at the same time as the fan belt.
4   If the belt is worn or cracked it must be renewed as soon as
possible.
5   To retension the air pump drivebelt, loosen the air pump mounting
bolts and hinge the pump unit away from the engine to tighten the
tension. Do not overtension the belt. The correct lateral play should
be 0.4 in when finger pressure is applied in the middle of the belt run
between the pulleys (Fig. 3.45).
6   When pivoting the pump, do not force it with a lever or the pump
may distort.

Fig. 3.44. Side elevation showing component parts of the air pump

Fig. 3.45. The Series 5 air pump

Fig. 3.46. The air pump and generator driving belts layout, showing the
adjustment deflection

SOLENOID VALVE

DISTRIBUTOR RELAY

IGNITION SWITCH

BATTERY

ACCELERATOR RELAY

TRANSMISSION RELAY

SPARK PLUG

ADVANCED BREAKER

CLUTCH RELAY

TRANSMISSION SWITCH

RETARDED BREAKER

CLUTCH SWITCH

ACCELERATOR SWITCH

Fig. 3.47. The coasting richer system - Series 1 to 3

VALVE SPRING

JOINT

VALVE SEAT

VALVE

EXHAUST MANIFOLD

FROM AIR PUMP

Fig. 3.48. The check valve

TO INTAKE MANIFOLD

VACUUM PIPE

DIAPHRAGM

PRESSURE AIR FROM AIR PUMP

AIR VALVE

ORIFICE

DIAPHRAGM CHAMBER

SPRING

AIR DISCHARGE TO INTAKE MANIFOLD

Fig. 3.49. The mixture control valve

IGNITION SWITCH

TRANSMISSION SWITCH

CLUTCH SWITCH

ACCELERATOR SWITCH

RESISTOR

BATTERY

IGNITION COIL

CONDENSOR

DISTRIBUTOR

COASTING RICHER SOLENOID VALVE

Fig. 3.50. The coasting richer system - Series 4 and 5

7   On adjustment, retighten the pump bolts and recheck the lateral belt play. If a new belt has been fitted check it again after usage as it may have stretched and need readjusting.

Air pump relief valves - checking

8   Start the engine and increase the speed to 2000 rpm, when at this point the relief valve will open and allow the airflow. If the air blows thru the valve prior to this, it will have to be removed and renewed.

Air pump, Series 1 to 4 - removal, inspection and reassembly

Note: *The air pump on Series 5 and 6 models is non-serviceable and therefore if defective is renewed as a unit.*

9   Slacken the adjustment bolt and the mounting bolts. Detach the hoses from their pump connections.
10 Pivot the pump towards the engine and remove the drivebelt from the pump drive pulley.
11 Withdraw the adjustment and pump mounting bolts (photo) and remove the pump.
12 Clean off the outside of the pulley if the pump is noisier than usual; the bearing may possibly be defective. To check this, turn the pulley ¾ of a turn clockwise and then ¼ of a turn counter-clockwise. If the pulley is binding and not very smooth then this is indicative that the bearing is at fault.
13 Dismantle the pump and lay the respective components on a clean work area. Clean the components and inner pump body.
14 Examine and check the vanes and rotor for wear also the inner pump body. Check the needle roller bearings and, if damaged or badly worn, then the pump unit should be renewed. The rear side seal must be renewed if it is worn or damaged. Renew the carbon shoes and/or vanes if they are badly worn or damaged.
15 Reassemble the pump in the reverse order and install in position in engine. Refit the drivebelt and tension as described in previous Section.

Check valve - description and inspection

16 This is located on the air manifold (photo) and ensures that the air flow under pressure from the air pump can only flow one way. Any counter flow of gases from the exhaust manifold shuts the valve and safeguards the air pump and hoses. To check the valve, disconnect it from the manifold, and blow air into the valve from the pump side and then from the manifold side. Air pressure should only be allowed thru the valve from the pump side. Should air be allowed thru the valve from the manifold side then the check valve is faulty and must be renewed, although a small leakage is allowable.

Mixture control valve

17 The mixture control valve (photo) supplies air to the inlet manifold to prevent the mixture from becoming rich when the throttle valve is closed suddenly. The valve is normally kept closed under pressure from the normal air supply in the intake manifold but when this pressure becomes negative, the valve opens and air is supplied via the air pump. To check the valve, detach the mixture control valve to inlet

manifold hose. Plug the inlet manifold side of the valve and start the engine. Depress the accelerator fully and then release it quickly. If the valve is normal, air will continue to blow from the mixture control valve for up to 5 seconds. If the air flow continues after this time, the valve is in need of renewal.

Air injection nozzle manifold - Series 1 to 4 - removal, inspection and installation

18 To remove the air injection nozzles it is first necessary to detach the camshaft carrier as described in Chapter 1. Disconnect the check valve hose and then unscrew each nozzle joint bolt and carefully detach the manifold. Slacken the air injection nozzle nipple and disconnect it by rotating it thru 180°.
19 Wash each nozzle and blow dry with an air line. Inspect them carefully for signs of burning, cracks or distortion. If defective in any way they must be renewed.
20 Installation is the reversal of removal but on restarting the engine, check for leaks.

Series 5 and 6

21 Disconnect the check valve hose and unscrew each of the nozzles from their position near the exhaust valves. Now follow the instructions in paragraphs (19) and (20) above.

Coasting richer system - description

22 This system incorporates a solenoid valve attached to the secondary side of the carburetor (photo). The solenoid is connected in relay to a series of switches which detect engine coasting conditions. These switches are as follows.
Federal manual transmission models:- accelerator switch, clutch switch, transmission 4th/3rd gear switch.
California manual transmission models:- accelerator switch, clutch switch, transmission neutral switch and engine speed sensor.
California automatic transmission models:- accelerator switch, inhibitor switch, engine speed sensor.
23 When these switches are activated, the solenoid valve and magnet are energised and open the secondary valve. On opening the valve, the fuel supply from the float chamber is metered into the wasting jet, mixed with air and metered thru the coasting air bleed.
24 This mixture then enters the lower secondary throttle valve via the wasting valve. This enrichens the mixture drawn into the engine to assist the exhaust gas reburning. An engine speed sensor fitted to California models only detects the engine revolutions via the ignition pulse from the coil. When the speed of the engine exceeds 1600 rpm the sensor turns on to operate the coasting richer circuit.
25 When the accelerator or clutch pedal are depressed or the transmission shifted to neutral, the series circuit automatically switches off and the wasting valve shuts.
26 To check the operation of the coasting richer system, listen carefully for the noise that accompanies the operating of the solenoid valve. If a malfunction of the system is suspected, check the respective adjustments of the clutch and accelerator switches and the transmission

Fig. 3.51. The air manifold and air injection nozzles (Series 1 to 4)

Fig. 3.52. The air manifold and air injection nozzles, Series 5

Fig. 3.53. The accelerator switch and adjustment to pedal

Fig. 3.54. The clutch switch and adjustment to pedal

Fig. 3.55. The transmission switch showing on and off positions

switch, (see below). If these are in order, and the system remains inoperative, have it checked by your local dealer.

Accelerator switch and clutch switch - checking

27 Check the respective pedal to switch clearances and if necessary adjust by loosening the locknut and turning the switch accordingly to the correct clearance as in Fig. 3.53 and Fig. 3.54. Test the switches by disconnecting the wires and connect a circuit tester. The switch must be on when the pedal is depressed and off when released. Renew the switch if faulty.

Transmission switch - checking

28 Disconnect the switch wiring and connect a circuit tester. The switch is operating correctly when, with the gearshift moved into 3rd or 4th gear, the switch is turned on. If not, the switch is defective and must be renewed.

Engine speed sensor (California only) - checking

29 Detach the wiring connector from the engine speed sensor and with suitable interconnecting cables connect 'B', 'BR' and 'BY' color coded wiring terminals together. Start the engine and check the continuity between 'LgB' color coded wiring terminals. If continuity exists when the engine speed is in excess of 1500 to 1700 rpm, then the sensor is in order. If not it should be renewed.

Accelerator relay - checking

30 Ensure that the supply voltage is being received at the relay terminals. If the voltage at terminal 3 (Fig. 3.56) equals that measured at terminal 1 with the switch in the off position, then the relay is in order. If the voltage measured at terminal 3 is lower or not being supplied then the contact breaker points are defective and in need of renewal or attention.

31 If the supply of voltage to terminal 3 is interrupted when the accelerator pedal is depressed, then the accelerator relay is in working order. If however, the voltage supply to terminal 3 is not discontinued on depressing the pedal, the relay coil is faulty and should be renewed.

Clutch relay - checking

32 Ensure that the accelerator pedal is released so that the switch is off. Engage 3rd or 4th gear to turn on the transmission switch. Check that the relay terminals 1 and 2 (Fig. 3.56) have a voltage supply and that the clutch switch is operating.

33 If relay terminal 3 has voltage and terminal 4 has not when the clutch pedal is released then the clutch relay is in order. If, however, terminal 3 has no voltage supply or a reduced supply to that of terminal 1, the breaker points are in need of attention or should be renewed.

34 If the supply of voltage to terminal 3 continues when the clutch pedal is depressed or there is no voltage reading at terminal 4 when the pedal is depressed, the relay coil is open or the points seized up, in which case they must be repaired or renewed.

Fig. 3.56. The coasting richer system relay circuit

CARBURETOR

EGR VALVE

INTAKE MANIFOLD

EXHAUST MANIFOLD

WATER GALLERY

SIGNAL PIPE

GAS PASSAGE TO INTAKE MANIFOLD

ORIFICE

THERMAL VACUUM VALVE

EGR PIPE (GAS PASSAGE TO VALVE)

Fig. 3.57. The exhaust gas recirculation system (California models)

ORIFICE

ORIFICE

SPRING

DIAPHRAGM

FULL STROKE

CARBURETOR

IDLE STOP

LOCK NUT

H.6192

DASH POT

THROTTLE SHAFT   THROTTLE LEVER   BRACKET

Fig. 3.58. The dash pot showing location in carburetor

Transmission relay - checking

35 Check the voltage supply at terminals 1 and 4 in Fig. 3.56, with the accelerator pedal released. If there is a supply at both terminals this indicates that the relay is operating normally. This is checked further if the voltage supply at terminal 5 is discontinued whilst terminal 6 receives voltage when in neutral (switch off). If there is no voltage supply at terminal 6 or a drop in voltage, the contact points are suspect and should be checked and renewed if necessary. As a further check, shift the transmission into 3rd or 4th gear and check that terminal 5 is receiving voltage but terminal 6 is not. If the voltage supply to these two terminals is not reversed when 3rd or 4th gear are selected then again the contact points are suspect.

Exhaust gas recirculation valve (EGR) - California only - description and checking

36 Mounted beneath the inlet manifold, the exhaust gas recirculation valve controls the recycled gas flow entering the inlet manifold from the exhaust manifold. When the vacuum caused by the throttle valve opening reaches 3.5 in Hg the diaphragm opens the exhaust gas metering valve allowing the exhaust gases into the engine intake. A thermal vacuum valve situated on the inlet manifold is connected between the vacuum port in the carburetor and the EGR valve. When the engine coolant temperature is below 118° to 126°F (46° to 51°C), the valve remains closed, as does the EGR valve. When the coolant temperature rises above these figures the valve opens and operates the EGR system.
37 To check the operation of the EGR valve, start the engine and open the throttle to give an engine speed of 2000 to 2500 rpm and ensure that the diaphragm operating shaft moves upwards, and when the engine speed drops to normal idle, returns downwards.
38 To check the diaphragm, a vacuum gauge is needed and also an alternative source of vacuum supply. If available, connect the vacuum supply to the top of the diaphragm chamber port tube to the carburetor. The diaphragm must not 'leak down' and should be fully raised at about 8 in of vacuum.

Dash pot (California models only) - inspection and adjustment

39 On California models, a throttle dash pot is incorporated into the emission control system and prevents the throttle valve from closing rapidly on deceleration. To check the dash pot, ensure that it operates smoothly when the shaft is moved endwise by hand. If defective or

Fig. 3.59. The exhaust gas recirculation valve

Fig. 3.60. The air bypass valve

* — MANUAL TRANSMISSION MODELS ONLY

** — NEUTRAL SWITCH FOR MANUAL TRANSMISSION MODELS

— INHIBITOR SWITCH FOR AUTOMATIC TRANSMISSION MODELS

Fig. 3.61A. The over temperature control system

Fig. 3.61B. The catalytic converter

Fig. 3.62. The vacuum switching valve

bending, the dash pot unit must be renewed.
40 To adjust, slacken the dash pot locknut (Fig. 3.59) and unscrew the dash pot fully counter clockwise. The carburetor fast idle cam is now set to the 2nd stop position which should give a throttle valve opening of 13°. Now tighten the dash pot (clockwise) so that the end of the dash pot shaft just contacts the dash pot lever. Tighten the locknut. With the engine running and the fast idle cam in the second stop position the engine speed should be within 2400 to 2800 rpm. Any deviation from this necessitates readjustment of the dash pot.

Air bypass valve (Federal) - Series 5 and 6

41 Located between the air pump outlet and air distribution manifold, the air bypass valve controls the secondary air flow, and prevents after burning in the exhaust system when decelerating. To check that it is operating satisfactorily, depress fully the accelerator pedal and then release it suddenly. The secondary air flow thru the bypass valve should not blow out for more than 5 seconds. If it does then the air bypass valve is faulty and will need renewing.

Oxidizing Catalytic converter system (Series 5 and 6 models - California only) - description

42 A catalytic converter is incorporated into the exhaust system and the thru blow of exhaust gases from the engine are chemically changed. The harmful hydro carbon and carbon monoxide gases are processed by oxidation withing the converter to water and carbon dioxide. The catalytic converter operates in conjunction with the over temperature control system, see Fig. 3.61A. To remove the catalytic converter, apply the parking brake, jack up the vehicle and disconnect the catalytic converter flange bolts. Remove the catalytic converter and gaskets. Installation is the reversal of removal but use new gaskets, and check for leaks.

Over temperature control system (California - Series 5 and 6 models)

43 This prevents the catalytic converter overheating and operates in the following manner. When the engine is coasting, the coasting richer system operates to prevent the catalytic converter overheating due to poor combustion. The secondary air injection operates simultaneously. On reaching 1350°F in the catalyst due to continued high speed, hills or high load driving, the secondary air is diverted into the atmosphere to reduce chemical reaction within the catalyst. If the catalyst temperature reaches 1830°F due to engine faults, the warning light and buzzer are actuated by a thermo sensor and thermo controller to indicate a failure.

Vacuum switching valve

44 The vacuum switch valve incorporates three ports. Two of these ports are opened or closed by the electrically controlled solenoid plunger. This operates when the catalyst temperature reaches 1350°F in driving (not coasting conditions). When actuated the switch valve connects the diaphragm chamber 'B' to the inlet manifold, allowing the manifold vacuum to draw off diaphragm chamber 'B'. When deactivating, the solenoid plunger shuts the port and connects chamber 'B' to chamber 'A'. The vacuum switching valve is also actuated by the transmission controlled spark advance system (TCS) as described in Section 1, Chapter 4.

Air switching valve - checking

45 This valve switches the air flow from the air pump, and is actuated by manifold vacuum and air pump pressure, being switched by a vacuum switching valve. Air pump pressure in diaphragm chamber 'B' activates the vacuum switching valve, which flows the air from the pump to check valve. Manifold vacuum switched by the vacuum switching valve acts in diaphragm chamber 'B'. The valve shuts

TO VACUUM SWITCHING VALVE
FROM AIR PUMP
TO CHECK VALVE
DIAPHRAGM
DIAPHRAGM CHAMBER (B)
DIAPHRAGM CHAMBER (A)
SHAFT
VALVE
TO ATMOSPHERE
TO MIXTURE CONTROL VALVE

Fig. 3.63. The air switching valve

AIR CLEANER
THERMO SENSOR
HOT IDLE COMPENSATOR
VACUUM MOTOR
HOT AIR CONTROL VALVE
HOT AIR HOSE
MANIFOLD COVER
EXHAUST MANIFOLD
VACUUM PIPE
INTAKE MANIFOLD
CARBURETOR
HOT AIR
VACUUM OR OUTSIDE AIR

Fig. 3.64. The automatic temperature controlled air cleaner system

SIDE COVER
FLAME ARRESTOR
AIR CLEANER
CAMSHAFT CHAMBER
BAFFLE PLATE
CARBURETOR
INTAKE MANIFOLD
ADAPTOR
REGULATING VALVE (PCV VALVE)
BLOWBY GAS
FRESH AIR
BLOWBY GAS + FRESH AIR

Fig. 3.65. The crankcase emission control system on Series 1 to 4 models

VALVE   WASHER
SPRING   SNAP RING

Fig. 3.66. The regulator valve

Fig. 3.67. The crankcase emission control system on Series 5 models

the air passage to the check valve and opens the atmosphere port to divert the air flow from the air pump.

46 To check the switching valve, with the engine off electrically operate the switching valve and start the engine. The secondary air should continue to blow out the air switching valve. If it does not, then it is faulty and in need of replacement.

Automatic temperature - controlled air cleaner system - checking

47 The air cleaner contains a viscous type filter element which must be renewed at the specified service intervals. Removal of the element for inspection and/or renewal is described in Section 2 and 3. Additionally check that the vacuum motor, idle compensator and thermo sensor retaining screws are tight. Check the hose connections and condition. Renew where necessary.

25 Crankcase emission control - description and maintenance

1 The crankcase emission control system forces the blowby gases from the engine crankcase into the intake manifold so that they are recirculated into the engine with the fuel air mixture.

2 This system has a baffle plate in the side cover to separate the oil particles from the gases, a regulating valve to control the suction of gases and interconnecting hoses, including a hose to supply fresh air from the air cleaner, (Fig. 3.65). Series 5 models differ in that the baffle plate is located in the head cover as in Fig. 3.67.

Fig. 3.68. The evaporative emission control system - Series 1 to 3

Fig. 3.69. The evaporative emission control system - Series 4 models

EVAPORATIVE GAS →
OUTSIDE AIR --->

Fig. 3.70. The evaporative emission control system - Series 5 models

Fig. 3.71. The check and relief valve

Fig. 3.72. The vapor tank access cover and retaining bolt positions

Fig. 3.73. The exhaust system layout (California models)

Baffle plate - removal inspection and refitting

3 Detach the hoses from the side cover on the camshaft carrier on Series 1 to 4 models or from the head cover in Series 5. Undo and remove the nuts and bolts and washers securing the side cover/head cover.
4 Remove the side cover/head cover. The baffle plate is located on the inner face of the right-hand side cover on Series 1 to 4 or on the underside of Series 5 models. Wash the inner parts of the baffle plate in detergent oil and blow clean with compressed air. If the cover, or baffle plate is damaged in any way, it must be renewed.
5 Refit the cover in the reverse order and fit a new sealing gasket. Ensure the hose connections are good.

Regulating valve - inspection and overhaul

6 Detach the regulating valve hose and carefully inspect the inner valve parts for signs of wear or damage. When applying finger pressure, the valve movement must be light and return easily, if not the valve must be overhauled or renewed. Similarly if the valve is lower in the manifold side and/or the inner valve is clogged or fouled up, it must be renewed or overhauled.
7 To remove the regulator valve from inlet manifold, unscrew it, and then with a pair of snap-ring pliers extract the snap-ring and withdraw the washer valve and spring (Fig. 3.66). Wash the parts in detergent, oil and inspect the parts for damage. Renew the unit if any parts are found to be defective. Reassemble in reverse ensuring that the narrow end of the spring is inserted upwards into the body.

26 Evaporative emission control system - description

1 This system enables fuel vapor from the fuel tank to be directed into the engine crankcase and together with the blow by gases is redirected into the inlet manifold.
2 The system consists of a vapor separator tank, a check and relief valve and interconnecting tubes (Figs. 3.68, 3.69, and 3.70).

Check and relief valve - inspections

3 To inspect the check and relief valve, disconnect the hoses and remove the attachment bolts. Remove the valve unit and check for

leakage by blowing air into parts. If found to be defective the unit will have to be renewed.
4 The check valve is normal if on applying air from the fuel tank side air passes thru the crankcase side but not the air cleaner side.
5 Apply air from the check side and if the passage of air is restricted then the valve is normal.
6 Apply air from the relief side (from the air cleaner) and air should pass into the fuel tank side but not the check side. Renew the rubber connecting tubes if they are found to be cracked or perished.

Vapor separator tank - removal and installation

7 Unscrew and remove the four access panel mounting bolts on the rear body and also the four vapor tank unit bolts (Fig. 3.72). Remove the panel.
8 Detach the three rubber hoses from the vapor tank. Remove the tank unit.
9 Reassemble in the reverse order and ensure that the hose connections are good.

27 Exhaust system - removal and installation

1 Position the vehicle over a pit or jack it up with the parking brake firmly applied. Secure with chassis stands or blocks.
2 Remove the respective mounting bracket bolts and exhaust pipe to manifold flange retaining bolts.
3 It may be necessary to wire brush the bolt threads clean and apply penetrating oil if they are corroded into position.
4 Remove the exhaust pipe and muffler and on California models, the catalytic converter.
5 Installation is the reversal of removal but semi-tighten the mounting bolts when the system is in position and ensure that the pipes and muffler are clear of surrounding body and fittings, then tighten the bolts to 11 lb f ft (15 Nm).
6 Check for leaks and if necessary apply a sealant to the pipe connections.

28 Fault diagnosis - Carburetion; fuel, exhaust and emission control systems

Symptom	Reason/s
Fuel consumption excessive	Air cleaner choked and dirty giving rich mixture. Fuel leaking from carburetor, fuel pump, or fuel lines. Float chamber flooding. Generally worn carburetor. Distributor condenser faulty. Balance weights or vacuum advance mechanism in distributor faulty. Carburetor incorrectly adjusted, mixture too rich. Idling speed too high. Contact breaker gap incorrect. Valve clearances incorrect. Choke valve incorrectly set. Incorrectly set spark plugs. Tires under-inflated. Wrong spark plugs fitted. Brakes dragging. Emission control system faulty (see later in this Section).
Insufficient fuel delivery or weak mixture due to air leaks	Partially clogged filter in pump, carburetor or fuel line. Incorrectly seating valves in fuel pump. Fuel pump diaphragm leaking or damaged. Gasket in fuel pump damaged. Fuel pump valves sticking due to fuel gumming. Too little fuel in fuel tank (prevalent when climbing steep hills). Union joints on pipe connections loose. Split in fuel pipe on suction side of the fuel pump. Inlet manifold to-block or inlet manifold-to-carburetor gaskets leaking. Fuel tank relief valve stuck closed.

Power reduced

Clogged main jets.
Accelerator linkage requires adjustment.
Fuel filter blocked.
Air cleaner blocked.

Erratic idling

Slow jet clogged.
Secondary throttle valve operating incorrectly.
Worn throttle valve shafts.
Broken carburetor flange gasket.
Incorrect adjusted carburetor.

Flat spot or hesitation

Clogged jets.
Emulsion tube clogged.
Secondary throttle valve operating incorrectly.

Engine will not start

Fuel level incorrect.
Lack of fuel.
Incorrect setting of mixture screw.
Incorrect fast idle adjustment.

Emission control system faults
Engine lacks power - difficult to start

Loose vacuum pipes/hose connections.
Manifold retaining nuts loose.
Faulty EGR valve.
Hot air control valve defective.
Fuel vapor control valve defective.
Coasting richer solenoid defective.
Mixture control valve defective.
Air pump drivebelt loose/worn.
Check valve defective.
Air pump/relief valve defective.

Chapter 4 Ignition system

Contents

Condenser - testing, removal and installation...	4	
Distributor contact points - removal, installation and adjustment ...	3	
Distributor - dismantling, servicing, and installation	6	
Distributor - removal and installation	5	
Dwell angle - checking	7	
General description	1	

Ignition coil	10
Ignition system (mechanical contact breaker) - fault diagnosis ...	11
Ignition timing	8
Routine maintenance	2
Sparking plugs and HT leads	9

Specifications

Spark plugs

Series 1 to 4 models

Type	NGK BP6ES
Thread diameter	0.55 in
Pitch	1.25 in
Reach	0.75 in
Spark gap:	
Series 1 models	0.028 - 0.032 in
Series 2 and 3	0.030 - 0.040 in
Series 4	0.030 in
Spark plug torque setting	18 - 25 ft lbs (2.4 to 3.4 kg fm)

Series 5 and 6 models

Type	NGK BPR6ES
Reach	0.75 in
Spark gap	0.030 in

Firing order ... ...   1 - 3 - 4 - 2

Ignition coil

Make	Nippon Denso
Model - Series 1 to 4	6CR - 200
- Series 5	C6R - 207 029700 - 3500
Voltage	12V
Secondary voltage (Series 1 to 4)	15,000V @ 1,500 rpm
Primary resistance (Series 1 to 4)	1.5 ohms
Secondary resistance (Series 1 to 4)	11.5 K ohms
Resistance (Series 5)	1.3 to 1.7 ohms

Distributor

Make	Nippon Denso
Model - Series 1	D414 - 62
- Series 2	D414 - 64
- Series 3	D417 - 62
- Series 4	D417 - 64 (Fed.) or D417 - 62 (California)
- Series 5	029100 - 3280
- Series 6	029100 - 3281
Rotational direction	Counter-clockwise (from top)
Ignition interval (Series 1 to 4)	$90° \pm 1°$
(Series 5 and 6)	$88.5° - 91.5°$

Contact breaker point pressure - Series 1 to 4		...	...	...	...				1.1 - 1.43 lbs
- Series 5 and 6			...	...	...	...			0.83 - 1.27 lbs

Contact breaker points gap

Series 1 and 2	...	...	...	...	...	...	...	...	...	0.018 - 0.022 in (advance)
										0.016 - 0.024 in (retard)
Series 3 and 4	...	...	...	...	...	...	...	...	...	0.018 - 0.022 in
Series 5 and 6	...	...	...	...	...	...	...	...	...	0.016 - 0.020 in

Dwell angle

Series 1 to 4	...	...	...	...	...	...	...	...	...	49° to 55° with 0.020 in point gap
Series 5 and 6	...	...	...	...	...	...	...	...	...	47° to 57°

Condenser capacity

Series 1 and 2 - advanced	...	...	...	...	...	...	...	...	...	0.20 - 0.24 Micro Farads
- retarded	...	...	...	...	...	...	...	...	...	0.05 Micro Farads $\pm$ 15%
Series 3 and 4 - advanced	...	...	...	...	...	...	...	...	...	0.20 - 0.24 Micro Farads
Series 5 and 6	...	...	...	...	...	...	...	...	...	0.25 Micro Farads
Maximum speed (Series 1 to 6)	...	...	...	...	...	...	...	...	...	3,000 rpm
Weight (approx) ...	...	...	...	...	...	...	...	...	...	2.2 lbs (2.4 Series 5)

1 General description

In order that the engine can run correctly, it is necessary for an electrical spark to ignite the fuel/air mixture in the combustion chamber at exactly the right moment in relation to engine speed and load. The ignition system is based on feeding low tension (LT) voltage from the battery to the coil where it is converted to high tension (HT) voltage. The high tension voltage is powerful enough to jump the spark plug gap in the cylinders many times a second under high compression pressures, providing that the system is in good condition and that all adjustments are correct.

The ignition system is divided into two circuits: the low tension circuit and the high tension circuit.

The low tension (sometimes known as the primary) circuit consists of the battery lead to the ignition switch lead, from the ignition switch to the low tension or primary coil windings (+ terminal) and the lead from the low tension coil windings (– terminal) to the contact breaker points and condenser in the distributor.

The high tension circuit consists of the high tension or secondary coil windings, the heavy ignition lead from the center of the coil to the center of the distributor cap, the rotor arm, and the spark plug leads and spark plugs.

The system functions in the following manner. Low tension voltage is changed in the coil into high tension voltage by the opening and closing of the contact breaker points in the low tension circuit. High tension voltage is then fed via the carbon brush in the center of the distributor cap to the rotor arm of the distributor cap, and each time it comes in line with one of the four metal segments in the cap, which are connected to the spark plug leads, the opening and closing of the contact breaker points causes the high tension voltage to build up, jump the gap from the rotor arm to the appropriate metal segment and so via the spark plug lead to the spark plug, where it finally jumps the spark plug gap before going to earth.

The ignition is advanced and retarded automatically, to ensure the spark occurs at just the right instant for the particular load at the prevailing engine speed.

The ignition advance is controlled both mechanically and by a vacuum operated system. The mechanical governor mechanism comprises two weights, which move out from the center under centrifugal force and are connected to the shaft by two light springs, and it is the tension of the springs which is largely responsible for correct spark advancement.

The vacuum control consists of a diaphragm, one side of which is connected via a small bore tube to the carburetor, and the other side to the contact breaker plate. Depression in the inlet manifold and carburetor, which varies with engine speed and throttle opening, causes the diaphragm to move, so moving the contact breaker plate and advancing or retarding the spark. A fine degree of control is achieved by a spring in the vacuum assembly. A resistor is incorporated in the ignition circuit for Series 5 and 6 models so that during starting, with the engine being cranked by the starter motor, full battery voltage is applied at the coil to maintain a good spark at the plug electrodes which would not be the case should a drop in voltage occur.

On vehicles equipped with a full emission control system a spark timing control system is employed. The system is designed to advance or retard the ignition timing in accordance with the prevailing engine operating conditions in order to reduce the emission of noxious exhaust fumes particularly during periods of deceleration. A dual point distributor was used for this purpose on Series 1 and 2 models.

The contact breaker point sets are connected in parallel and the retard contact breaker circuit incorporates a relay.

The accelerator and transmission relays and throttle and ignition switches are connected to the distributor relay in parallel (Fig. 4.3).

The advance contact breaker points are actuated when the relay is energized by the following:

a) *The transmission is not engaged in 3rd or 4th gear, and the throttle valve is not open in excess of 7°.*
b) *The clutch pedal is depressed.*
c) *The throttle valve is fully open.*
d) *When the ignition switch is turned on.*

On California Series 5 and 6 models, an engine speed sensor is incorporated into the ignition circuit, which detects the ignition pulse from the coil. At engine speeds in excess of approximately 1,600 rpm, the speed sensor is actuated and this then energizes the coasting richer circuit in the emission control system.

On some California models, a transmission controlled spark advance (TCS) system is fitted. This again works in conjunction with the emission control system, and consists of a transmission switch and a vacuum switching valve, which controls the ignition timing to reduce the nitrogen oxide and hydrocarbon emissions. When this system is fitted, the vacuum advance is eliminated in third gear, and is operated in the following manner.

The vacuum switching valve incorporates a three way port system. Two of the ports are opened or closed by the electrically controlled solenoid plunger. When the vehicle transmission is in 1st, 2nd, 4th or reverse gear, the solenoid leads have continuity and retain the plunger spring in the compressed position, and the carburetor and distributor port sides are in contact. The ignition timing can then be advanced in the normal manner according to the throttle movement.

When the transmission is in third gear the circuit opens and the plunger, actuated by the return spring, closes the carburetor to distributor vacuum port. The air cleaner side port then opens to allow negative pressure in the distributor advance unit to be released, thus preventing the ignition timing being advanced.

2 Routine maintenance

1   The ignition system is one of the most important and most neglected systems in any vehicle, and attention to routine maintenance cannot be over-emphasized. The maintenance intervals are given in the Routine Maintenance Section at the beginning of this Manual.

Spark plugs

2   Remove the plugs and thoroughly clean away all traces of carbon. Examine the porcelain insulation round the central electrode inside the

Fig. 4.1. The dual point ignition circuit - Series 1 and 2

Fig. 4.2. The single point ignition circuit - Series 3 and 4

Fig. 4.3. The dual point distributor ignition and associate emission control circuit

plug, and if damaged discard the plug. Reset the gap between the electrodes. Do not use a set of plugs for more than 12,000 miles; it is false economy. For further information on spark plugs, see Section 9.

Distributor contact points

3   Remove the distributor cap and rotor, and carefully pry open the contact points with a small screwdriver. Provided that the points are clean (and this is not very likely since there is normally a build-up on one contact and a cavity in the other), all that needs to be done is to check and reset the gap, as described in Section 3. If the points require attention, refer to Section 3, and remove them; then rub the faces smooth using an oilstone. It is important to remove all the build-up on the one contact, and as much as is practically possible of the cavity on the other contact. Also remember that the faces must be square to each other when re-installed or correct setting of the gap will not be possible; a slightly domed profile can assist for this purpose. After cleaning, install the contacts and set the gap, as described in Section 3. The ultimate life of contact breaker points cannot be predicted, but with correct attention at the appropriate maintenance intervals, they should be capable of lasting for at least 12,000 miles (20,000 km).

Distributor cap, rotor and HT leads

4   Remove the distributor cap and HT leads from the ignition coil and spark plugs. Wipe the end of the coil, the HT leads and spark plug caps and the internal and external surfaces of the distributor cap with a lint-free cloth moistened with gasoline (petrol) or a cleaning solvent. Ensure that all traces of dirt and oil are removed, then carefully inspect for cracked insulation on the leads, spark plug caps, distributor cap and ignition coil end. At the same time, check that the carbon brush in the center of the distributor cap is intact and returns under the action of its spring when pressed in. Carefully scrape any deposits from the distributor cap electrodes and from the rotor; if any serious erosion has occurred, replacement parts should be fitted.

Lubrication

5   Apply two drops of engine oil to the screw head in the center of the distributor cam, and through the aperture in the baseplate to lubricate the advance mechanism. Apply a trace of the same oil to the breaker point pivot(s), and a trace of petroleum jelly to the cam profile.

Ignition timing

6   After completing the aforementioned, check and adjust the dwell angle and ignition timing, as described in Sections 7 and 8.

---

3   Distributor contact points - removal, installation and adjustment

Series 1 to 4

1   Spring back the distributor cap retaining clips, remove the cap and pull off the rotor.
2   Remove the screws retaining the distributor point set(s) and, where applicable, loosen the nut so that the lead can be detached. Take care that no screws, nuts or washers are dropped inside the distributor.
3   Lift out the respective contact sets. If they are to be cleaned, refer to Section 2; alternatively obtain a new set of the correct type from your vehicle main dealer.
4   Installation is the reverse of the removal procedure, but before finally tightening down the points it is necessary to set the contact point gap as described in the following paragraph. For most practical purposes this is all that is required, although it is advantageous to obtain a final setting by the dwell angle method, as described in Section 7.

Series 5 and 6

4   Remove the distributor cap, rotor and dust proof cover.
5   Remove the points as in paragraphs 2 and 3 above and renew or service the existing set(s).
6   To refit and set the clearance refer to Section 6, paragraph 29, sub-paragraphs (d) and (e).

---

4   Condenser - testing, removal and installation

1   A faulty condenser will cause rapid burning of the contact breaker points at best and at worst total failure of the ignition system.
2   Without special test equipment, a faulty condenser cannot be readily diagnosed, but where there is an indication of malfunction it is the best policy, considering the moderate cost, to renew it/them.
3   If renewing one or both of the condensers be sure to note from where each was removed and refit in their original positions as the advance and retard condensers have different microfarad ratings (see Specifications).

Fig. 4.5. The crankshaft pulley and front cover timing mark positions - Series 5 models

Fig. 4.4. The dual point distributor showing advance and retard breaker respective positions

THIS MARK IS AT
20° B.T.D.C.

THIS MARK IS AT
10° B.T.D.C.

YELLOW MARK
IS AT T.D.C.

POINTER

CRANKSHAFT
PULLEY

Fig. 4.6. The crankshaft pulley and front cover timing mark positions - Series 1 to 4 models

5.6 Removing the distributor

CAP   CAM   CONDENSER

CENTER
CARBON

SIDE   ROTOR   BREAKER   GOVERNOR
PLUG   HEAD   PLATE   WEIGHT   CONDENSER

VACUUM CONTROLLER

POINT GAP
ADJUSTING SCREW

ADVANCED BREAKER
POINT ARM

ADVANCED
CONDENSER

POINT GAP
ADJUSTING SCREW

RETARDED
CONDENSER

PHASE ANGLE
ADJUSTING SCREW

RETARDED BREAKER
POINT ARM

Fig. 4.7a. The Series 1 and 2 distributor component parts

5   Distributor - removal and installation

1   On Series 5 models, disconnect the battery ground cable.
2   To remove the distributor complete with cap, detach the sparking plug leads from the plugs (note their respective positions). Detach the HT lead from the ignition coil.
3   Disconnect the low tension lead from the coil.
4   Detach the vacuum line from the distributor.
5   To simplify re-installation of the distributor, rotate the crankshaft by turning the crankshaft, using a wrench on the pulley retaining nut clockwise and align the crankshaft pulley and front cover timing pointer at the TDC position (see Fig. 4.5). Index mark the relative position of the distributor body with the fixing plate and cylinder block, and the rotor in relation to the distributor body.
6   Unscrew and remove the distributor fixing plate retaining bolt, and withdraw the distributor from the engine (photo).
7   Installation is a direct reversal of removal, but ensure that when the distributor is fully located, that the relative marks are in alignment with the crankshaft at the TDC position.

6   Distributor - dismantling, servicing and reassembly

Series 1 to 4
1   With the distributor cap removed, lift out the rotor.
2   Remove the vacuum control unit retaining screw and lift the connecting rod from the pivot pin. Withdraw the vacuum controller unit.
3   Unscrew the low tension lead retaining screw and disconnect the lead.

Series 1 and 2
4   Lift out the two sets of contact breaker points, but do not disturb the adjustment plate setting retaining the retarded side breaker points.

Series 3 and 4
5   Undo the retaining screws and withdraw the contact breaker points.
6   Detach the primary side terminal and withdraw the breaker plate.
7   Support the distributor shaft and coupling in a 'V' block and using a suitable drift, remove the roller pin.
8   Undo and remove the screw from the cam head and detach the timing lever.

CAP CAM

CENTER CARBON
SIDE PLUG
ROTOR HEAD
BREAKER PLATE
GOVERNOR WEIGHT

VACUUM
CONTROLLER

DISTRIBUTOR
CAP

ROTOR

Fig. 4.8. The distributor with vacuum controller, cap rotor and retaining plate removed

VACUUM CONTROLLER

POINT GAP ADJUSTING SCREW

BREAKER POINT ARM

CONDENSER

Fig. 4.7b. The Series 3 and 4 distributor component parts

BREAKER
POINT ASSY.

Fig. 4.9. Remove the contact breaker points - Series 1 and 2

BREAKER POINT ASSY.

Fig. 4.10. Remove the contact breaker points - Series 3 and 4

COUPLING

Fig. 4.11. Removing the roll pin

CAM

GOVERNOR
SPRING

GOVERNOR
WEIGHT

Fig. 4.12. The distributor, shaft, governor weights and springs

Measuring plug gap. A feeler gauge of the correct size (see ignition system specifications) should have a slight 'drag' when slid between the electrodes. Adjust gap if necessary

Adjusting plug gap. The plug gap is adjusted by bending the earth electrode inwards, or outwards, as necessary until the correct clearance is obtained. Note the use of the correct tool

Normal. Grey-brown deposits lightly coated core nose. Gap increasing by around 0.001 in (0.025 mm) per 1000 miles (1600 km). Plugs ideally suited to engine and engine in good condition

Carbon fouling. Dry, black, sooty deposits. Will cause weak spark and eventually misfire. Fault: over-rich fuel mixture. Check: carburettor mixture settings, float level and jet sizes; choke operation and cleanliness of air filter. Plugs can be re-used after cleaning

Oil fouling. Wet, oily deposits. Will cause weak spark and eventually misfire. Fault: worn bores/piston rings or valve guides; sometimes occurs (temporarily) during running-in period. Plugs can be re-used after thorough cleaning

Overheating. Electrodes have glazed appearance, core nose very white - few deposits. Fault: plug overheating. Check: plug value, ignition timing, fuel octane rating (too low) and fuel mixture (too weak). Discard plugs and cure fault immediately

Electrode damage. Electrodes burned away; core nose has burned, glazed appearance. Fault: initial pre-ignition. Check: as for 'Overheating' but may be more severe. Discard plugs and remedy fault before piston or valve damage occurs

Split core nose (may appear initially as a crack). Damage is self-evident, but cracks will only show after cleaning. Fault: pre-ignition or wrong gap-setting technique. Check: ignition timing, cooling system, fuel octane rating (too low) and fuel mixture (too weak). Discard plugs, rectify fault immediately

GOVERNOR SPRINGS

Fig. 4.13. The primary and secondary springs and their respective positions

9   Note their respective positions and unhook the two governor springs and remove with governor weights (Fig. 4.12).
10 Clean thoroughly the respective parts and inspect for wear and damage.
11 Refer to Section 2, paragraph 5, for checks and cleaning details of the cap and rotor. Unless the points are known to be in good condition it is advisable to install new ones. Check the weights for excessive looseness on their pivots; it is advisable to fit new springs in view of their modest cost. Suck (by mouth) on the vacuum diaphragm unit and check that the link is drawn in. When the vacuum is held by placing the tongue or a finger over the tube, the link should remain in; if it fails to do so, the vacuum unit must be renewed. Ensure that the driven gear is securely pinned to the cam spindle, and that the gear is undamaged. Also check the shaft for wear, and the governor weights and springs. Renew any suspect parts.
12 Apply a trace of grease to the bearings and sliding surfaces.
13 Refit the cam and pinion taking care to refit the respective components to their original positions. Two types of governor springs are used in the centrifugal advance.
    The primary stage spring has a round hook on its end.
    The secondary stage spring has a sharp hook on one end as in Fig. 4.13. Do not overstretch these springs when refitting.
14 The primary stage spring is hooked to the governor weight. The governor weight pin locates into the longest hole in the cam plate.
15 The secondary stage spring is hooked to the governor weight and the weight pin fits into the shorter hole.
16 Refer to Fig. 4.14 and note that the coupling is installed with the rotor head tip end facing to the coupling side on which the slot is offset.
17 Apart from the above items, reassembly is basically a reversal of removal procedures but be sure to fit a new roller pin when refitting the distributor coupling.

Series 5 and 6
18 Lift off the distributor cap and remove the rotor and dust proof cover.
19 Unscrew the terminal bolt locknut and remove the terminal complete with insulator (Fig. 4.15).
20 Remove the condenser from the vacuum housing.
21 Extract the circlip securing the vacuum advance rod and withdraw the vacuum advance unit.
22 Remove the dust proof gasket (Fig. 4.17). Unscrew the breaker

Fig. 4.14. Rotor head to coupling installation position

Fig. 4.15. Remove the cap, rotor and dust proof cover for access to the points

arm retaining screws and withdraw the breaker arm, points and damper spring (Fig. 4.18).

23 Detach the distributor cap clamps and the lead wire. Now extract the breaker plate.

24 Undo the screw in the end of the cam assembly and unhook the governor springs and cam. Note the respective spring positions before removing them.

25 Unclip the governor weights retaining circlips and withdraw the governor weights.

26 Remove the caulking from the distributor shaft set pin and then remove the pin from the shaft. Finally remove the collar and distributor shaft (Fig. 4.20)..

27 With the distributor dismantled, wash and clean off the various components but do not wash the inner face of the vacuum advancer.

28 Inspect and service as required the distributor components as described in paragraphs 10 and 11.

29 Reassembly of the distributor is a direct reversal of the removal procedure, but note the following:

a) Ensure that the governor springs and weights are fully located as in Fig. 4.19 and that they are suitably lubricated.

b) Fit the cam drive plate with its rear face (marked), turned to the governor plate stop pin.

c) The cap clip is installed with its projected portion facing the terminal side.

d) When installing the damper spring, ensure that the clearance between the flat face of the cam and heel is 0.0020 - 0.0040 in (0.05 - 0.10 mm) - see Fig. 4.21.

e) To fit and adjust the breaker point gap, rotate the cam so that the heel of the breaker arm is against the tip of the cam lobe. The breaker point assembly can now be fitted to the breaker plate and the gap adjusted to the specified clearance (0.015 - 0.019 in) (0.38 to 0.48 mm).

7 Dwell angle - checking

1 For most practical purposes, the breaker points can be set by adjusting the gap, as described in Section 3. However, a more accurate method of setting the points is obtained by the dwell angle method which requires the use of a proprietary dwell angle meter. This type of meter is supplied complete with operating and connecting instructions.

2 To check the dwell angle, first disconnect the distributor vacuum line.

3 Connect the dwell angle meter and set it up in accordance with the manufacturer's instructions for 4-cylinder engines.

4 Start the engine and run it at idle speed.

5 Check the dwell angle and compare it with that specified. If it is satisfactory, all that needs to be done is to disconnect the meter and its connections.

6 If adjustment is required, you will need to increase the breaker point gap, if the angle was too large, or decrease the gap, if the angle

Fig. 4.16. The component parts of the Series 5 model distributor

1	Cap	13	Governor spring (high-speed side)
2	Rotor	14	Governor weight
3	Dust-proof cover	15	Cap washer
4	Breaker plate	16	Thrust washer
5	Lead wire	17	Dust-proof gasket
6	Breaker point	18	Cap clamp
7	Circlip	19	Terminal
8	Vacuum control	20	Housing
9	Condenser	21	Shaft
10	Governor	22	'O' ring
11	Cam assembly	23	Collar
	Governor spring (high-speed side)	24	Pin

Fig. 4.17. The distributor with dust cover removed

Fig. 4.18. Remove the contact breaker arm

Fig. 4.19. The governor weights and springs

Fig. 4.20. The distributor shaft and collar

Fig. 4.21. The damper spring to cam position

10.1 The ignition coil and connections - Series 1-4

was too small. This can be done by readjustment, as described in Section 3. However, it is possible to do it whilst the engine is being cranked by an assistant while you carry out the adjustment. First remove the coil HT lead from the distributor and ground it, then remove the distributor cap and rotor. Loosen the breaker point attaching screws then, whilst the engine is being cranked, alter the contact position until the correct dwell angle is obtained. Stop the engine cranking, tighten the attaching screw(s) then recheck the angle. On completion, remove the meter, remake the HT connection, then install the rotor and distributor cap.

8   Ignition timing

1   Check that the distributor points gap are set correctly as in Section 3, and that the advance contact breaker side is operational.
2   Run the engine until it reaches its normal operating temperature (180ºF - 82ºC).
3   Stop the engine and connect a timing light lead to number 1 or 4 cylinder. A 12 volt bulb of fairly low wattage together with two leads is ideal.
4   Slacken the distributor location clamp plate bolt, so that the distributor can be rotated for adjustment.

5   Using a suitable wrench, turn the crankshaft pulley to align the pulley mark with the timing cover pointer as in Figs. 4.5 or 4.6 accordingly.
6   For accurate setting of the timing refer to the Specifications for your model.
7   The instant of time at which the distributor contact breaker points open is the time at which the spark is delivered. Therefore, if the appropriate timing mark is aligned with the timing pointer, the breaker points should just be opening. To be able to judge this more accurately, connect the test bulb leads across the breaker points and switch on the ignition. Rotate the crankshaft at the pulley about 20º counter-clockwise from top-dead-center (TDC) at which time the bulb should be extinguished. Now rotate the crankshaft clockwise until the bulb illuminates (ie. the breaker points are just opening) and check the position of the pulley with respect to the pointer. If the marks are correctly aligned, all is well and good. If the marks are not aligned, it will mean slackening the distributor clamp bolt, turning the distributor slightly, tightening the clamp bolt and rechecking. If the timing is too far advanced (ie. the timing mark is too far from the pointer when the points open) you will need to rotate the distributor clockwise; if it is too far retarded (ie. the timing mark is too near the pointer or has gone past it), you will need to rotate the distributor counter-clockwise (photo).
8   With the ignition timing set, tighten the distributor clamp plate and refit the distributor cap and leads.

9 Spark plugs and HT leads

See page 91 for illustrations

1 The correct functioning of the spark plugs is vital for the proper running and efficient operation of the engine.

2 At the intervals specified, the plugs should be removed, examined, cleaned, and if worn excessively, renewed. The condition of the spark plug can also tell much about the general condition of the engine.

3 If the insulator nose of the spark plug is clean and white, with no deposits, this is indicative of a weak mixture; or too hot a plug (a hot plug transfers heat away from the electrode slowly - a cold plug transfers heat away quickly).

4 If the insulator nose is covered with hard black looking deposits, then this is indicative that the mixture is too rich. Should the plug be black and oily then it is likely that the engine is fairly worn, as well as the mixture being too rich.

5 If the insulator nose is covered with light tan to greyish brown deposits, then the mixture is correct, and it is likely that the engine is in good condition.

6 If there are any traces of long brown tapering stains on the outside of the white portion of the plug, then the plug will have to be renewed, as this shows that there is a faulty joint between the plug body and the insulator, and compression is being allowed to leak away.

7 Plugs should be cleaned by a sand blasting machine, which will free them from carbon more than cleaning by hand. The machine will also test the condition of the plugs under compression. Any plug that fails to spark at the recommended pressure should be renewed.

8 The spark plug gap is of considerable importance, as, if it is too large or too small the size of the spark and its efficiency will be seriously impaired. The spark plug gap is given in the Specifications Section.

9 To set it, measure the gap with a feeler gauge, and then bend open, or close, the outer plug electrode until the correct gap is achieved. The centre electrode should never be bent as this may crack the insulation and cause plug failure, if nothing worse.

10 When installing the plugs, remember to connect the leads from the distributor cap in the correct firing order which is 1, 3, 4, 2, No. 1 cylinder being the one nearest the radiator.

11 The plug leads require no maintenance other than being kept clean and wiped over regularly. The leads used are of the carbon cored type which are used to suppress high frequency radio interference from the ignition system. Although these leads can give trouble-free performance for many years, they can sometimes cause starting problems after a considerable period of usage. A procedure is given for checking them in Section 11, paragraph 6, but if they are found to be faulty, consideration should be given to replacing them with the copper cored conductor type and using suppressor-type plug caps. Your automobile electrical specialist will be able to help with the supply of approved types.

10 Ignition coil - removal, checking and installation

1 On Series 1 to 4 models remove the primary and secondary leads, noting their positions.

2 On Series 5 and 6 models, disconnect the battery ground cable, then detach the positive and negative wires from the coil. In addition, remove the resistor lead.

3 Unscrew the coil retaining screws/bolts and nuts/washers and remove the coil.

4 To test the coil requires specialised equipment and this should, therefore, be entrusted to your GM dealer or local auto electrician.

5 Installation is a direct reversal of removal.

11 Ignition system (mechanical contact breaker) - fault diagnosis

Engine fails to start

1 If the engine fails to start and the car was running normally when it was last used, first check there is fuel in the fuel tank. If the engine turns over normally on the starter motor and the battery is evidently well charged, then the fault may be in either the high or low tension circuits. First check the HT circuit. **Note:** If the battery is known to be fully charged; the ignition light comes on, and the starter motor fails to turn the engine check the tightness of the leads on the battery terminals and also the secureness of the earth lead to its connection on the body. It is quite common for the leads to have worked loose, even if they look and feel secure. If one of the battery terminal posts gets very hot when trying to work the starter motor this is a sure indication of a faulty connection to that terminal.

2 One of the commonest reasons for bad starting is wet or damp spark plug leads and distributor. Remove the distributor cap. If condensation is visible internally, dry the cap with a rag and also wipe over the leads. Refit the cap.

3 If the engine still fails to start, check that current is reaching the plugs by disconnecting each plug lead in turn at the spark plug end, and hold the end of the cable about 3/16th (5 mm) away from the cylinder block. Spin the engine on the starter motor.

4 Sparking between the end of the cable and the block should be fairly strong with a regular blue spark. (Hold the lead with rubber to avoid electric shock). If current is reaching the plugs, then remove them and clean and regap them. The engine should now start.

5 If there is no spark at the plug leads take off the HT lead from the centre of the distributor cap and hold it to the block as before. Spin the engine on the starter once more. A rapid succession of blue sparks between the end of the lead and the block indicate that the coil is in order and that the distributor cap is cracked, the rotor arm faulty, or the carbon brush in the top of the distributor cap is not making good contact with the spring on the rotor arm. Possibly the points are in bad condition. Clean and reset them as described in this Chapter.

6 If there are no sparks from the end of the lead from the coil check the connections at the coil end of the lead. If it is in order start checking the low tension circuit.

7 Use a 12v voltmeter or a 12v bulb and two lengths of wire. With the ignition switch on and the points open test between the low tension wire to the coil (it is marked SW or +) and earth. No reading indicates a break in the supply from the ignition switch. Check the connections at the switch and resistor to see if any are loose. Reinstall them and the engine should run. A reading shows a faulty coil or condenser, or broken lead between the coil and the distributor.

8 Take the condenser wire off the points assembly and with the points open, test between the moving points and earth. If there is now a reading, then the fault is in the condenser. Install a new one and the fault is cleared.

9 With no reading from the moving point to earth take a reading between earth and the negative terminal of the coil. A reading here shows a broken wire which needs to be renewed between the coil and distributor. No reading confirms that the coil has failed and must be renewed, after which the engine will run once more. Remember to reinstall the condenser wire to the points assembly. For these tests it is sufficient to separate the points with a piece of dry paper while testing with the points open.

Engine misfires

10 If the engine misfires regularly, run it at a fast idling speed. Pull off each of the plug caps in turn and listen to the note of the engine. Hold the plug cap in a dry cloth or with a rubber glove as additional protection against a shock from the HT supply.

11 No difference in engine running will be noticed when the lead from the defective circuit is removed. Removing the lead from one of the good cylinders will accentuate the misfire.

12 Remove the plug lead from the end of the defective plug and hold it about 3/16th inch (5 mm) away from the block. Restart the engine. If the sparking is fairly strong and regular the fault must lie in the spark plug.

13 The plug may be loose, the insulation may be cracked, or the points may have burnt away giving too wide a gap for the spark to jump. Worse still, one of the points may have broken off. Either renew the plug, or clean it, reset the gap, and then test it.

14 If there is no spark at the end of the plug lead, or if it is weak and intermittent, check the ignition lead from the distributor to the plug. If the insulation is cracked or perished, renew the lead. Check the connections at the distributor cap.

15 If there is still no spark, examine the distributor cap carefully for tracking. This can be recognised by a very thin black line running between two or more electrodes, or between an electrode and some other part of the distributor. These lines are paths which now conduct electricity across the cap thus letting it run to earth. The only answer is a new distributor cap.

16 Apart from the ignition timing being incorrect, other causes of misfiring have already been dealt with under the Section dealing with the failure of the engine to start. To recap - these are that:

   a) *The coil may be faulty giving an intermittent misfire;*

   b) *There may be a damaged wire or loose connection in the low tension circuit;*
   c) *The condenser may be short circuiting;*
   d) *There may be a mechanical fault in the distributor (broken driving spindle or contact breaker spring).*

17 If the ignition timing is too far retarded, it should be noted that the engine will tend to overheat, and there will be a quite noticeable drop in power. If the engine is overheating and the power is down, and the ignition timing is correct, then the carburetor should be checked, as it is likely that this is where the fault lies.

Chapter 5 Clutch

Contents

Clutch adjustments 2
Clutch hydraulic system - bleeding 3
Clutch - inspection and renovation 9
Clutch installation 11
Clutch master cylinder - removal and installation 4
Clutch master cylinder - servicing 5

Clutch - removal 8
Clutch slave cylinder - dismantling and reassembly 7
Clutch slave cylinder - removal and installation 6
Fault diagnosis 12
General description 1
Release bearing - removal, inspection and reassembly 10

Specifications

Series 1 models

Type	Single dry plate, diaphragm spring, hydraulically operated

Clutch driven plate

Clutch face material	Woven SF 105 M
Clutch face diameter (outside diameter x inside diameter x thickness) ...	8 in x 5¾ in x 9/64 in (203 x 127 mm 0.75 x 0.140 mm)
Total friction area	24 sq in x 2 (154.8 cm^2)
Driven plate thickness	
Free	11/32 in (8.73 mm)
Compressed	5/16 in (7.93 mm)
Number of damper springs	6
Clutch surface to rivet head minimum thickness	0.008 in (0.203 mm)
Driven plate run out (maximum)	0.039 in (1.016 mm)

Diaphragm spring to flywheel distance	1.496 in (37.9 mm)
Maximum spline play in direction of rotation	0.079 in (2.032 mm)
Clutch pedal height	6.3 to 6.7 in (160 to 170 mm)
Clutch pedal play	Approximately 25/32 in (19.84 mm)
Clutch shift fork play	0.118 (3.0 mm)
Clutch master cylinder bore	5/8 in (15.87 mm)
Slave cylinder bore	3/4 in (19.05 mm)
Minimum diaphragm spring load	655 lbs (297 kgs)

Series 2 to 6 models
As per Series 1 but with the following differences

Diaphragm spring to flywheel distance	1.299 in (33 mm)
Clutch face diameter (outside diameter x inside diameter x thickness) ...	7.87 x 5.12 x 9.64 in (197.6 x 130 x 3.5 mm)
Total friction area	28 sq in x 2 (180.6 cm^2)
Driven plate thickness - free	21/64 in (8.33 mm)
Number of damper springs	4
Maximum spline play in direction of rotation	0.113 in (2.9 mm)
Clutch pedal height (Series 2/4/5 and 6 models)	5.9 to 6.3 in (150 to 160 mm)
Series 3	6.3 to 6.7 in (160 to 170 mm)

Torque wrench settings

							lb f ft	kg f m
Shift fork ball stud								
Series 1 to 4 models	...	...	...	...	...	...	70	9.6
Series 5 and 6 models	...	...	...	...	...	...	30	4.1
Clutch cover/flywheel bolts								
Series 1 models	...	...	...	...	...	...	50	6.9
Series 2 to 6 models	...	...	...	...	...	...	13	1.7
Clutch push rod to pedal arm nut								
Series 1 models	...	...	...	...	...	...	25	3.4

1 General description

1   The clutch unit fitted is of the single dry plate (disc) type. The unit comprises the disc assembly, the pressure plate assembly, the clutch cover, and the shift fork assembly.

2   The clutch housing is integral with the transmission casing and contains the clutch shaft (input shaft) bearing retainer and seals.

3   The clutch is hydraulically operated by means of a master cylinder and a clutch slave cylinder. The master cylinder is located in the engine compartment and is attached to the rear panel. The slave cylinder is mounted to the clutch housing.

4   The respective clutch components are riveted together to prevent dismantling for repair and it therefore follows that if the clutch disc or clutch cover unit is worn or damaged, then they must be replaced as a unit. The master cylinder and slave cylinder repairs are confined to the renewal of the rubber seals. The shift fork (operating lever) is adjustable with the pushrod. Periodic checking of this clearance and also topping up the master cylinder is all the maintenance normally required on the clutch system.

2 Clutch - adjustment

Clutch pedal
1   The clutch pedal height is adjusted in the same manner as the brake pedal adjustment. The clutch pedal pushrod and switch correspond to the brake pedal pushrod and stoplight switch. Refer therefore to Chapter 9, Section 3.

Clutch shift fork
2   Disconnect the shift fork return spring and ease the shift fork rearwards slightly. Slacken the adjustment nut (Fig. 5.2) and adjust the pushrod so that it is in contact with the shift fork.

3   Unscrew the pushrod approximately 1¾ turns and lock in position by tightening the locknut. The correct clearance should be 5/64 in (1.98 mm).

4   Any excess clearance between the diaphragm spring fingers and the release bearing will cause the clutch to drag. Too little clearance will cause it to slip.

3 Clutch hydraulic system - bleeding

1   Bleeding the cylinders and fluid lines is necessary when air gets into the system. This is caused by a joint or seal leakage usually, but the system must also be bled when a component in the system is removed and/or replaced. Bleeding entails the process of removing air from the hydraulic circuit.

2   Hydraulic fluid is harmful to paintwork so be very careful not to spill any on the surrounding areas when bleeding or topping up the reservoir.

Fig. 5.1. Section view of the clutch unit

3   Always commence bleeding by ensuring that the reservoir is topped up to the level required with the specified type of hydraulic fluid. This level must be kept topped up during the bleeding operation and must not be allowed to drop below ½ of the specified level.

4   Bleeder screws are fitted to both the master cylinder and slave cylinder. Both are bled in the same manner. To bleed the master cylinder, have an assistant pump the clutch pedal several times and then whilst holding it down, slacken the bleeder screw slowly. Now tighten the bleeder screw whilst the assistant gradually releases the clutch pedal. Repeat this operation until the air bubbles disappear from the fluid being pump out.

5   Detach the clutch slave cylinder bleed screw dust cap and connect a length of suitable rubber or vinyl tube to the nipple. Insert the other end of the tube into a clean jar and put about 1 inch (2.5 cm) of fluid into the jar.

6   Slacken the bleed nipple and get the assistant in the cab to depress the clutch pedal slowly and fully down. Tighten the bleed valve.

7   The pedal is now released and the bleed valve loosened again and the procedure repeated until the air bubbles in the circuit are fully expelled. Check that the reservoir is topped up during the operations and that the end of the tube is kept submerged in the fluid within the jar.

8   Remove the tube on completion and refit the bleed valve caps. Always discard the old fluid as it is a false economy to use it again, since it will undoubtedly be contaminated with dirt and moisture.

9   Check the clutch operation on a test drive and readjust the pedal or linkage as described in Section 2.

Fig. 5.2. Adjustment of the clutch push-rod - Series 5

4   Clutch master cylinder - removal and installation

1   Detach the clutch pedal arm from the pushrod.

2   Disconnect the fluid line from the master cylinder and drain the fluid into a suitable container, taking care not to spill any fluid on the paintwork.

3   Remove the master cylinder flange retaining bolts and withdraw the unit from the engine compartment.

4   Installation is the reverse of removal but check the pedal height and linkage adjustment as previously described and bleed the system (Sec. 3)

5   Clutch master cylinder - servicing

1   Drain off the hydraulic fluid from the master cylinder into a container and commence dismantling by removing the rubber boot and circlip to remove the pushrod.

Fig. 5.3. Slacken the bleed nipple on the slave cylinder

Fig. 5.4. The master cylinder
      component parts

1   Piston assembly
2   Piston cup
3   Retainer
4   Clip
5   Boot
6   Push rod
7   Clevis
8   Lock nut
9   Cap
10 Reservoir
11 Seal
12 Retaining strap
13 Fitting
14 Body
15 Mounting parts

Fig. 5.5. Take care when fitting the cup seal and position as shown

8.4 Remove the clutch pressure plate and disc (driven plate)

Fig. 5.6. The slave cylinder component parts fitted to Series 1 to 4. Series 5 models have a different mounting flange,
otherwise they are identical

1	Piston	4	Boot	7	Push rod	10	Bolt
2	Piston cup	5	Bleeder screw	8	Nut	11	Spring
3	'O' ring	6	Cap	9	Nut		

2   Withdraw from the body of the master cylinder the stopper, piston, cup and return spring, noting the order of sequence and fitting.

3   Lay the respective parts out in order on a sheet of clean paper. Wash all the components in clean hydraulic fluid, isopropyl alcohol or methylated spirit. Examine carefully the surface of the piston and the bore of the cylinder for scoring or bright wear areas. Where these are evident, renew the master cylinder complete.

4   Where components are in good condition, discard the rubber seals and obtain a repair kit.

5   Reassembly of the master cylinder is the reversal of removal procedure but lubricate all parts with clean hydraulic fluid before fitting. When fitting the cup seal take care not to damage the lipped portions.

6   Clutch slave cylinder - removal and installation

1   Undo the slave cylinder securing bolts and remove the pushrod from the shift fork.

2   Disconnect the flexible hydraulic hose from the slave cylinder and plug the hose to prevent further loss of fluid and also the ingress of dirt. Remove the cylinder.

3   To reinstall the slave cylinder, reverse the removal instructions and top up the master cylinder fluid level. Bleed the system as described in Section 3 and if necessary, readjust the pedal and pushrod to shift fork clearance to 5/64 inch (1.98 mm) as described in Section 2.

7   Slave cylinder - dismantling and reassembly

1   Although not normally requiring attention, if the slave cylinder is to be dismantled be sure to obtain a repair kit containing the necessary parts before dismantling. It is recommended that all rubber parts are renewed.

2   Having removed the slave cylinder from the vehicle, clean the outside using a lint-free cloth. Do not attempt to clean the slave cylinder or its components with gasoline (petrol), kerosene or cleaning solvents. It is normally adequate to use new hydraulic fluid for cleaning but isopropyl alcohol or methylated spirits is also suitable.

3   Remove the dust boot from the cylinder and withdraw the pushrod.

4   Remove the piston by tapping the pushrod end of the cylinder sharply on a wooden block. Alternatively, compressed air applied at the inlet connection can be used.

5   Clean all the components as described in paragraph 2, but discard the rubber cups. Examine the bore for wear, scoring or roughness; check the clearance of the piston in the bore and replace any parts which are unsatisfactory. Check the bleed valve and inlet valves are clean and that the bleed valve is in good working condition.

6   When reassembling, dip the respective components in clean hydraulic fluid before fitting, Ensure that the piston cup is carefully fitted and positioned as shown in Fig. 5.6.

7   On refitting the slave cylinder, recheck the pushrod to shift fork clearance and adjust if required. Bleed the system and top up the reservoir.

8   Clutch - removal

1   Remove the transmission unit as described in Chapter 6 or alternatively the engine and/or transmission unit as described in Chapter 1.

2   As applicable, separate the engine and transmission by removing the clutch housing to engine securing bolts.

3   Prior to removing the clutch unit from the flywheel, mark their respective positions in relation to each other, so that they may be refitted in the correct position.

4   Unscrew the clutch assembly securing bolts a turn at a time in diametrically opposed sequences until the tension of the diaphragm

Fig. 5.7. The clutch unit component parts

1	Plate assembly	6	Clutch shift block
2	Disc assembly	7	Bearing
3	Pin	8	Spring
4	Bolt	9	Fork assembly
5	Washer		

spring is released. Withdraw the bolts and lift the pressure plate assembly clear.

5   The driven plate (clutch disc) will fall from the location between the flywheel and pressure plate.

9   Clutch - inspection and renovation

1   Clean off the clutch components and wipe dry with a clean cloth.

2   Commence inspection by examining the pressure plate and flywheel surfaces for signs of scoring. Slight score marks may be left but if deep marks are apparent, then the pressure plate will have to be renewed. If the flywheel is badly scored then it must be dismantled (as described in Chapter 1) and taken to your GM dealer or auto engineering specialist for further inspection. It may prove possible to machine across the face to resurface it, without upsetting the balance of the engine and flywheel. If a new flywheel is the only answer, then it must be balanced to match the original.

3   Check the driven plate (friction disc) linings for wear, loose rivets or damaged torsion springs. Also check the driven plate hub to input shaft splines, which must be an easy sliding fit. The driven plate must be renewed if the lining surface is worn to within 0.008 in (0.203 mm) of the rivet head. If the lining surfaces show signs of breaking up or black areas where oil contamination has occurred, it should also be renewed. If facilities are readily available for obtaining and fitting new friction linings to the existing disc this may be done but the saving is relatively small compared with obtaining a complete new disc assembly which ensures that the shock absorbing springs and the splined hub are renewed also. The same applies to the pressure plate assembly which cannot be readily dismantled and put back together without specialised riveting tools and balancing equipment. An allowance is usually given for exchange units.

4   If on inspection oil is present on the driven plate, then check the pilot bush, the transmission input shaft seal and the engine rear main bearing oil seal. Also inspect the front bearing support gaskets and renew defective items as necessary before reassembling the clutch unit.

10.3 The shift fork showing spring clip in position over the ball stud

Fig. 5.8. The clutch release bearing and shift fork

10.9 Refit the shift fork

11.5 Centralizing the driven plate using an old input shaft

10.6 Check the clutch release (throwout) bearing for excessive wear or damage

10 Clutch release bearing - removal, inspection and reassembly

1   To inspect or renew the clutch release bearing it is necessary to
remove the engine and/or transmission unit from the vehicle as
described in Chapters 1 and 6.
2   Detach the shift fork cover from the transmission casing.
3   The shift fork spring clip is now disconnected from the ball stud
(photo) and the shift fork and release bearing removed. If required the
shift fork ball stud can be unscrewed and removed from its location
in the front cover.
4   Clean the respective parts with a clean rag - do not wash the release
bearing in gasoline, oil or any other cleaning solvent.
5   Check the clutch fork ball socket and fingers for signs of wear and
inspect the retaining spring for any damage. The spring must be able
to retain the fork to the ball stud firmly.
6   To check the clutch release bearing, splin it and listen for noisy
operation or if it vibrates, renew it. Renew any other suspect clutch
release fork components and reassemble as follows.
7   Screw the shift fork ball stud into position in the front cover and
tighten to a torque figure of 30 lb f ft (4.147 kg f m).
8   Lubricate the inner collar groove of the shift block and the shift
fork ball seat and fingers with graphite grease and refit the shift fork
and clutch release bearing unit together with the shift fork spring clip.
Ensure that the fork is fully engaged with the ball stud and that the

release bearing can operate smoothly.
9   Finally refit the shift fork (photo) cover to the transmission casing.

11 Clutch - installation

1   Clean the flywheel and pressure plate surfaces.
2   Apply a little Lubriplate or a similar lubricant to the splines of the
driven plate, and also smear the pilot bearing in the center of the flywheel with a high melting point grease.
3   Locate the driven plate against the flywheel.
4   Postion the pressure plate assembly on the flywheel and
ensure that the relative marks are in alignment.
5   Insert the retaining bolts, but do not tighten. The disc must now be
centralized on the flywheel and this can be best achieved using the
transmission input shaft (if the transmission has also been dismantled)
as alignment tool. An old input shaft, if available, would also align
the disc (photo). Alternatively a suitable round shaft of wood or steel
may be utilized.
6   When the disc is centralized, tighten the respective bolts evenly in
a diametrically opposed manner to a specified torque of 13 lb f ft
(1.79 kg f m).
7   Remove the alignment shaft, and check that the clutch release
lever operates freely before installation of the transmission/engine.

12 Fault diagnosis - Clutch

Symptom	Reason/s
Judder when taking up drive	Loose engine transmission mountings. Badly worn friction surfaces or contaminated with oil. Worn splines on transmission input shaft or driven plate hub. Worn input shaft spigot bush (pilot bearing) in flywheel.
Clutch spin (failure to disengage) so that gears cannot be meshed	Incorrect release bearing to diaphragm spring finger clearance. Driven plate sticking on input shaft splines due to rust. May occur after vehicle standing idle for long period. Damaged or misaligned pressure plate assembly.
Clutch slip (increase in engine speed does not result in increase in vehicle road speed - particularly on gradients)	Incorrect release bearing to diaphragm spring finger clearance. Friction surfaces worn out or oil contaminated.
Noise evident on depressing clutch pedal	Dry, worn or damaged release bearing. Insufficient pedal free travel. Weak or broken pedal return spring. Weak or broken clutch release lever return spring. Excessive play between driven plate hub splines and input shaft splines.
Noise evident as clutch pedal released	Distorted driven plate. Broken or weak driven plate cushion coil springs. Insufficient pedal free travel. Weak or broken clutch pedal return spring. Weak or broken release lever return spring. Distorted or worn input shaft. Release bearing loose on retainer hub.

Chapter 6 Part A: Manual transmission

Contents

Clutch gear shaft unit - dismantling 5	Transmission - Series 5 and 6 - dismantling 4
General description 1	Transmission - Series 1 to 4 - reassembly 8
Mainshaft dismantling 6	Transmission - Series 5 and 6 - reassembly 9
Transmission - cleaning and inspection 7	Transmission - Series 1 to 6 - removal and installation 2
Transmission - Series 1 to 4 models - dismantling 3	

Specifications

Series 1 to 4

Type	4 forward and 1 reverse gear with synchromesh on all forward gears
Model	MSE

Control ratios

1st	3.51 : 1
2nd	2.18 : 1
3rd	1.42 : 1
4th	1.00 : 1
Reverse	3.93 : 1

Speedometer gear ratios

Series 1 and 2	17.5
Series 3 and 4	5.18

Lubricant capacity	1.3 qt
Lubricant type	SAE 30

Synchromesh blocker ring to gear face maximum clearance

allowance	0.040 to 0.080 in (1.01 to 2.03 mm)

Series 5 and 6

Type	4 forward and 1 reverse gear with synchromesh on all forward gears
Control system	Direct with floor mounted shift lever

Gear ratios

1st	3.51 : 1
2nd	2.81 : 1
3rd	1.42 : 1
4th	1.00 : 1
Reverse	3.83 : 1

Speedometer gear ratio	6.20

Lubricant type

Below 50°F (10.0°C)	SAE 10W - 30
Above 50°F (10.0°C)	SAE 40
Between 0°F and 90°F (17.8°C and 32.2°C)	SAE 30

| Lubricant capacity ... ... | 1.35 qt |

Dimensions and backlash specifications

Reverse idle shaft gear to bush clearance - maximum allowance	0.006 in (0.152 mm)
Reverse idler shaft standard outside diameter	
Series 5	0.709 in (18 mm)
Series 6	0.866 in (22 mm)
Maximum allowance for 1st gear width to collar width	0.019 in (0.5 mm)
Mainshaft run out limit	0.002 in (0.05 mm)
Synchromesh blocker ring to gear clearance allowance	0.032 in (0.8 mm)
Synchromesh hub spline to mainshaft spline clearance allowance	0.008 in (0.20 mm)

Minimum shift arm thickness

3rd/4th	0.256 in (6.5 mm)
1st/2nd and reverse	0.276 in (7.1 mm)
Shift rod detent spring length - minimum allowance	1.084 in (27.5 mm)

Standard gear backlash

1st	0.0039 to 0.0071 in (0.07 to 0.17 mm)
2nd	0.0039 to 0.0067 in (0.07 to 0.15 mm)
3rd	0.0039 to 0.0067 in (0.07 to 0.15 mm)
4th	0.0039 to 0.0067 in (0.07 to 0.15 mm)
Reverse gear - main	0.0039 to 0.0071 in (0.07 to 0.17 mm)
Reverse idle gear	0.0039 to 0.0071 in (0.07 to 0.17 mm)
Maximum limit allowance	0.016 in (0.40 mm)

Inside diameter for gears

1st	1.773 in (45.03 mm)
2nd	1.615 in (41.02 mm)
3rd	1.615 in (41.02 mm)
Limit allowance	0.004 in (0.101 mm)

Torque wrench settings

Series 1 to 4

	lb f ft	kg f m
Mainshaft rear bearing nut	80	11.0
Rear extension retaining bolts	10	1.3
Top cover bolts	36 - 48	4.9 - 6.6
Front cover bolts	10	1.3
Clutch shift fork ball stud	65 - 70	8.9 - 9.6

Series 5 and 6

	lb f ft	kg f m
Idler gear shaft lock plate bolt	14	1.9
Countershaft reverse gear nut	100	13.8
Mainshaft locknut	94	12.9
Rear extension bolts	27	3.7
Shifter cover bolts -		
Series 5	10	1.3
Series 6	14	1.9
Front bearing retainer bolts	14	1.9
Clutch fork ball stud	30	4.1

1 General description

The transmission fitted to all Series 1 to 4 models is a four forward speed and one reverse type with synchromesh on all forward gears. Gear selection is via a floor mounted shift lever.

The aluminium transmission casing incorporates the clutch housing at the front and there is a detachable rear cover, the top part of which is a quadrant box containing the transmission control mechanism.

All forward gears are helically cut to ensure quiet operation. The reverse gear and reverse idler gear are straight cut spur gears.

The Series 5 and 6 models gearbox is similar in construction except that the mainshaft and counter gear shafts are located in a detachable centre support.

The overhaul procedures differ on the Series 5 and 6 models to that of the earlier types and reference should therefore be made to the relevant Section when major work is undertaken.

Automatic transmission is also available on the Series 5 and 6 models and for information on this refer to Part B of this Chapter.

Fig. 6.1. Undo the gearlever retaining bolts

2 Transmission - Series 1 to 6 - removal and installation

To remove the engine and transmission units complete refer to Chapter 1, Section 6.

1 Detach the ground cable from the battery.

2 Remove the air cleaner unit from the carburetor and detach the accelerator linkage from the carburetor throttle lever.

3 Remove the starter motor attachment bolts and connecting cable. Withdraw the starter motor.

4 From inside the cab, lift the gearshift lever boot up the lever and with a suitable wrench, unscrew and remove the gearshift lever attachment bolts. Lift the lever clear.

5 Unless vehicle is located over a work pit, jack up and block up sufficiently to enable work to be carried out underneath the vehicle.

6 Unscrew and remove the exhaust pipe to transmission hanger.

7 Detach the speedometer cable from the transmission unit (photo).

8 Refer to Chapter 7 and remove the propeller shaft.

9 Drain the oil from the transmission, and plug the rear extension to prevent spillage of oil during removal.

10 Unscrew the clutch slave cylinder securing bolts and detach the slave cylinder. Tie it to the side frame with a piece of wire or cord to keep it out of the way.

11 Disconnect the flywheel stone shield and undo the three frame bracket to transmission rear mounting bolts.

12 Place jacks under the engine and transmission and raise the units sufficiently to undo and remove the crossmember to frame bracket bolts.

13 Lower the engine and gearbox and support the rear of the engine with blocks or jack.

14 From the top of the gearbox, detach the TCS switch (photo), and reverse lamp switch where fitted. On California models disconnect the neutral switch wires on Series 5 and 6 models.

15 Support the transmission and remove the engine bellhousing bolts. Withdraw the gearbox from the engine by pulling to the rear and when clear of the clutch, tilt the gearbox downwards and remove.

16 Installation of the transmission unit is direct reversal of removal but note the following.

a) When the slave cylinder and pushrod are reconnected adjust the shift fork as given in Chapter 5.

b) Adjust the clutch pedal height - see Chapter 5

c) Refit the propeller shaft and align the rear flange marks as described in Chapter 7.

d) Tighten all retaining bolts/nuts to the specified torque where given.

e) Refit the drain plug and refill the transmission with new oil of the correct grade and quantity.

3 Transmission - Series 1 to 4 - dismantling

1 Having removed the transmission unit from the vehicle, clean the exterior housing and fitting and drain any remaining oil. Remove to clean work area.

2 From the clutchhousing remove the clutch fork cover and disconnect the clutch fork and release bearing (Fig. 6.2) .

3 Unscrew and remove the front bearing retainer bolts and withdraw the retainer (photo).

4 Unscrew and remove the eight bolts securing the gearbox top cover. Prise the top cover from the gearbox and note the gasket and baffler plate (photo).

5 Extract the three detent springs and balls.

6 Remove the four retaining bolts from the gear shift quadrant and remove the quadrant (photo) and gasket.

7 Remove the TCS and reversing light switches if still fitted, taking care not to lose the reverse light switch detent ball and actuating pin.

8 Refer to photo and drive out the retaining pin from the shift control fulcrum and remove the fulcrum bracket, reverse idler gear control lever and shift block (Fig. 6.5). .

9 Remove the selector rod shift fork roll pins (photo).

10 Withdraw the reverse shifter shaft from the front and lift out the shift fork. Do not lose the detent balls at the front of the casing when removing the shifter shafts.

11 From the rear extension disconnect the speedometer adaptor

2.7 Unscrew to speedo cable connection

2.14 Remove the TCS switch from the top of the gearbox

3.3 Withdraw the bearing retainer

3.4 Remove the top cover

Fig. 6.2. Remove the clutch fork, cover and release bearing

3.6 Remove the gearshift quadrant

3.8 Remove the shift control fulcrum roll pin

3.9 The selector rod shift forks and locating roll pins

3.11 Remove the speedo motor adaptor from the rear extension

3.13 Remove the lockplate

3.14 Use a dummy shaft to remove the counter gearshaft

Fig. 6.3. Cross section view of the four speed manual transmission - Series 1 to 4 models

1 Clutch drive gear	7 3-4 shift fork	13 Extension housing bushing	19 Reverse idler gear shaft
2 Front bearing retainer	8 1-2 shift fork	14 Extension seal	20 Countergear
3 Front bearing	9 Rear bearing	15 Speedometer drive gear	21 Caged roller bearings
4 TCS switch	10 Shift quadrant	16 Mainshaft	22 Clutch gear pilot bearing
5 Shift rails	11 Shift lever assembly	17 Countergear shaft	23 Transmission case
6 Top cover	12 Rear extension housing	18 Reverse idler gear	

Fig. 6.4. The gearbox component parts - Series 1 to 4 models

1	Transmission case
2	Stud; starter to case
3	Plug; oil filler
4	Plug; magnetic
5	O-ring; drain plug to case
6	Packing; filler plug
7	Cover; clutch shift fork
8	Shaft; clutch gear
9	Bearing; front
10	Snap ring; bearing top gear
11	Cover assembly; front
12	Oil seal; front cover
13	Support; clutch fork
14	Gasket; front cover
15	Bearing; main shaft
16	Extension housing assembly
17	Bushing; prop shaft yoke
18	Oil seal; rear cover
19	Cover; dust rear cover
20	Gasket, rear cover
21	Cover assembly
22	Gasket, top cover
23	Plate
24	Main shaft
25	Snap ring; main shaft
26	Hub; 3-4
27	Sleeve; 3-4
28	Insert; clutch hub
29	Spring; insert
30	Blocker ring; 3-4
31	3rd gear assembly
32	2nd gear assembly
33	Hub; 1-2
34	Reverse gear
35	Insert; clutch hub
36	Spring; insert
37	Blocker ring; 1-2
38	Thrust washer
39	Low gear
40	Bearing; low, 2nd, 3rd
41	Collar, low
42	Adapter assembly; mainshaft
43	Pin; adapter
44	Spacer
45	Nut; main shaft
46	Bearing; main shaft
47	Speedometer drive gear
48	Snap ring; speedometer gear
49	Key; speedometer gear
50	Counter gear
51	Needle roller
52	Spacer; counter gear
53	Thrust washer
54	Thrust washer
55	Counter gear shaft
56	Lock plate
57	Shaft; reverse idle
58	Gear; reverse idle
59	Bushing; reverse idle gear
60	Speedometer driven gear
61	W/O-ring bushing
62	O-ring; speedometer gear bush
63	O-ring; speedometer gear
64	Cover; front transmission case
65	71 ball, detent, gear shift
66	Spring, detent ball, gear
67	Ball, inner lock, gear shift
68	Pin, lock, inner lock
69	Switch assembly, reverse lamp
70	Plunger, reverse lamp switch
71	Switch assembly, top-3rd
72	Gasket, switch
73	Arm, shift, top-3rd
74	Arm, shift low-2nd
75	Arm, shift, reverse
76	Block, shift w/pin, reverse
77	Rod, gear shift, top-3rd
78	Rod, gear shift, low-2nd
79	Rod, gear shift, reverse
80	Pin, spring, shift arm
81	Lever, reverse, idle gear control
82	Bracket, fulcrum, lever control
83	O-ring, fulcrum bracket
84	Box, quadrant
85	Pin, quadrant box
86	Plunger, reverse stop
87	Spring, reverse stop, inner
88	Spring, reverse stop, outer
89	Cap, reverse stop, spring
90	Gasket, quadrant box
91	Lever assembly, gear shift control
92	Spring, control lever
93	Cage, control lever
94	Cover, control lever
95	Grommet, lever, gear shift
96	Knob, lever, gear shift control
97	Cover, dust, control lever

Fig. 6.5. Remove the shift blocks and control fulcrum

(photo) then undo the retaining bolts and remove the rear housing.
12 The 3rd/4th and 1st/2nd shifter shafts can now be withdrawn thru the rear of the gearcase, and the shift forks extracted.
13 Detach the backplate from its location between the reverse idler shaft and the countershaft on the rear of the gearcase (photo).
14 Drive the countershaft thru the rear of the gearcase using a dummy shaft (photo).
15 The mainshaft assembly can now be removed from the rear (photo).
16 Withdraw the clutch shaft (primary shaft) assembly from the front of the gearcase (photo) taking care not to lose any of the needle roller bearings from the mainshaft aperture.
17 Lift the countergear and reverse collar out of the gearcase.

4 Transmission - Series 5 and 6 - dismantling

1   Drain any remaining oil from the casing.
2   Detach the clutch fork, rubber boot and throwout bearing.
3   Undo and remove the bearing retainer bolts and withdraw the retainer gasket and spring washer (Fig. 6.9).
4   Unscrew the speedometer gear bush retaining bolt and withdraw the speedometer driven gear assembly.
5   Undo the retaining bolts and remove the gear shift cover and gasket.
6   Remove the reverse light switch and CRS switches.
7   Remove the rear extension retaining bolts and detach the rear extension and gasket.
8   Remove the reverse idler gear and thrust washers from the gear shaft (Fig. 6.10).

Fig. 6.6. Cross section of the gearbox - Series 5 and 6 models

1 Clutch gear shaft	15 Oil seal
2 Bearing retainer	16 Speedometer drive gear
3 Clutch gear shaft bearing	17 Reverse gear
4 3rd-4th switch (for Federal)	18 Mainshaft
5 Shift rods	19 Self-locking nut
6 3-4 shift fork	20 Counter reverse gear
7 1-2 shift fork	21 Reverse idle gear shaft
8 Mainshaft rear bearing	22 Reverse idle gear
9 Center support	23 Collar
10 Shifter cover	24 Counter gear rear bearing
11 Shift lever assembly	25 Caged roller bearing
12 Reverse shift fork	26 Counter gear
13 Neutral switch (for California)	27 Counter gear front bearing
14 Rear extension	28 Clutch gear roller bearing

Fig. 6.7. The gearbox casing and selector control components - Series 5 and 6 models

1 Fork, 3rd-4th shifter
2 Fork, 1st-2nd shifter
3 Fork, reverse shifter
4 Rod, gear shift, 3rd-4th
5 Rod, gear shift, 1st-2nd
6 Rod, gear shift, reverse
7 Pin, spring, shift fork
8 Pin, spring, reverse rod
9 Ball, detent, gear shift
10 Spring, detent ball
11 Plate, detent spring
12 Gasket
13 Pin, interlock
14 Plug, interlock
15 Switch assembly, reverse lamp
16 Gasket
17 Switch assembly, 3rd-4th (Federal spec.)
18 Gasket (Federal spec.)
19 Shifter cover (Federal spec.)
20 Shifter cover (California spec.)
21 Plunger, reverse, stop

22 Spring, inner
23 Spring, outer
24 Cap, reverse, stop
25 Rod, neutral switch
26 Damper pad
27 Spring
28 Switch assembly, neutral
29 Gasket
30 Gasket, shifter cover
31 Bracket
32 Gear, speed, driven
33 Bush, W/O-ring
34 O-ring, bush outer
35 O-ring bush inner
36 Cover, front, transmission case
37 Lever assembly, gear shift control
38 Spring, control lever
39 Seat, spring
40 Cover, control lever
41 Cover, dust, control lever
42 Grommet, lever, gear shift
43 Knob, control lever

3.15 Remove the mainshaft assembly

Fig. 6.8. The gearcase and components parts - Series 5 and 6 models

1 Case, w/center support
2 Pin, guide
3 Bearing, needle
4 Plug, shift rod
5 Stud
6 Plug, oil filler
7 O-ring, oil filler
8 Dust cover, shift fork
9 Ring, snap, mainshaft
10 Ring, snap, counter gear
11 Gasket, case and rear cover
12 Ball stud
13 Washer, lock
14 Washer, plain
15 Plug, screw
16 Gasket, plug (Calif. spec.)
17 Plug, screw (Calif. spec.)
18 Gasket, plug (Calif. spec.)
19 Shaft, clutch gear
20 Bearing, ball
21 Ring, snap
22 Ring, snap
23 Spring, belleville
24 Bearing, needle
25 Bearing retainer
26 Seal, oil, bearing retainer
27 Gasket, bearing retainer
28 Bolt
29 Extension assembly, rear, w/bushing and seal
30 Bushing
31 Seal, oil, rear extension
32 Breather assembly
33 Plug, oil drain
34 O-ring, oil drain
35 Bolt
37 Shaft main
38 Ring, snap
39 Hub, synchronizer, 3rd-4th
40 Sleeve, synchronizer
41 Key, synchronizer
42 Spring, synchronizer
43 Ring, blocker
44 Gear assembly, 3rd
45 Gear assembly, 2nd
46 Hub, synchronizer, 1st-2nd
47 Sleeve, synchronizer
48 Key, synchronizer
49 Spring, synchronizer
50 Ring, blocker
51 Gear assembly, 1st
52 Bearing, needle, 1st
53 Bearing, needle, 2nd
54 Collar, needle bearing
55 Washer, thrust, 1st
56 Bearing, mainshaft
57 Washer, lock, mainshaft
58 Nut, mainshaft
59 Gear, reverse
60 Gear, speed drive
61 Ring, snap, drive gear
62 Key
63 Gear, counter
64 Bearing, angular ball
65 Gear, counter reverse
66 Spacer
67 Washer, plain
68 Nut, self lock
69 Shaft, reverse idle
70 Plate, lock
71 Bolt, lock
72 Washer, spring
73 Gear, reverse idle
74 Washer, thrust
75 Synchronizer assembly, 3rd-4th
76 Synchronizer assembly, 1st-2nd

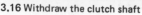
3.16 Withdraw the clutch shaft

Fig. 6.9. Withdraw the bearing container

9 From the mainshaft, unclip the snap-rings, and remove the speed-ometer drive gear and key.

10 Drive the spring pin from the reverse shifter fork using a suitable drift and, remove the shift fork and reverse gear (Fig. 6.11).

11 Using a pair of snap-ring pliers (Fig. 6.12) remove the snap-ring retaining the clutch gear shaft ball bearing in place.

12 Withdraw the center support unit from the gearcase as shown in Fig. 6.13.

13 Support the center support unit and drive the spring pins from the 1st/2nd, and 3rd/4th shifter forks. Support the shift rods during removal to prevent the rods bending and to ease removal of the pins.

14 Undo the detent spring retaining plate bolts and remove the plate and gasket. Extract the detent springs and balls.

15 Now remove the respective shifter rods, taking care not to lose detent interlock plugs in the rods in the center support. The reverse shifter rod is fitted with a stop pin and must therefore be removed forwards.

16 To prevent the mainshaft rotating, move the synchronizers to the rear. If they are reluctant to move, tap them with a hammer handle as shown in Fig. 6.15.

17 Flatten the mainshaft nut lockwasher tab, and undo the locknut. Remove nut and washer.

18 Undo the locknut from the countershaft and remove the washer, reverse gear and collar (Fig. 6.16).

19 Disengage the snap-ring from the center support using a pair of snap-ring pliers as shown in Fig. 6.17. Tap the front of the center support while expanding the snap-ring.

20 Expand the mainshaft retaining snap-ring and remove the center support.

5 Clutch gear shaft unit - dismantling

1 To remove the front bearing from the clutch gear shaft, extract the snap-rings from the shaft, retaining groove and the bearing outer race groove.

2 Remove the bearing from the shaft using a suitable puller.

6 Mainshaft dismantling

Series 1 to 4

1 Using snap-ring pliers, extract the speedometer drive gear snap-rings and withdraw the speedometer gear and drive key from the shaft.

2 Undo the rear bearing retaining nut and remove with lockwasher. Remove the rear bearing retainer.

3 Withdraw 1st gear thrust washer, caged roller bearing sleeve and blocker ring.

4 Withdraw the 1st/2nd synchronizer hub and gear unit.

5 Withdraw 2nd speed gear, roller bearing and blocker ring.

6 Disengage the 3rd/4th synchronizer hub snap-ring and withdraw the synchronizer unit, blocker ring and roller bearing.

7 Clean and lay the respective parts out ready for inspection.

Fig. 6.10. Remove the reverse idler gear

Fig. 6.11. Drift out the spring pin

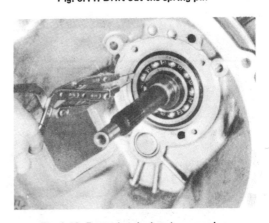

Fig. 6.12. Removing the bearing snap ring

Fig. 6.13. Withdraw the center support

Fig. 6.14. Remove the shifter rods

Fig. 6.15. Move the synchronizers to the rear

Fig. 6.16. Remove the counter gear self-locking nut

Fig. 6.17. Using snap ring pliers to expand the snap ring for removal of the center support from mainshaft and counter gear

Fig. 6.18. Remove the rear bearing retainer

Fig. 6.19. The mainshaft components

1 Blocker ring	6 1st gear	11 1st gear thrust washer	16 Clutch gear pilot roller
2 Blocker ring	7 1st and 2nd synchronizer hub	12 Reverse idler gear	17 Sleeve
3 Blocker ring	8 2nd gear	13 Caged roller bearings	18 Mainshaft
4 Blocker ring	9 3rd gear	14 Caged roller bearings	19 Clutch gear
5 Rear bearing and retainer	10 3rd and 4th synchronizer hub	15 Caged roller bearings	20 Front bearing

J-22912

Fig. 6.20. Removing the mainshaft rear bearing using special tool
J-22912

Fig. 6.21. Remove 1st speed gear unit

Fig. 6.22. Measure the blocker ring to gear clearance

Series 5 and 6

8   Remove the mainshaft rear ball bearing using a suitable puller or press. If special tool J - 22912 is available, this should be used together with an arbor press to remove the bearing as shown in Fig. 6.20. NB. This tool can also be used to remove the countershaft bearing.
9   Withdraw the 1st speed gear assembly complete with thrust washer, needler roller bearings, collar and blocker ring as in Fig. 6.21.
10 Withdraw the 1st/2nd synchronizer assembly.
11 Withdraw 2nd gear with blocker ring and needle roller bearing.
12 Disengage and remove the snap-ring, then withdraw 3rd/4th synchronizer assembly and blocker ring.
13 Withdraw 3rd speed gear from the shaft with needle roller bearings.

7   Transmission - cleaning and inspection

Cleaning

1   All parts, except seals and ball bearing assemblies, should be soaked in gasoline (petrol) or kerosene (paraffin), brushed or scraped as necessary, and dried with compressed air.
2   Ball bearing assemblies may be carefully dipped into clean gasoline or kerosene, and spun with the fingers. Whilst being prevented from turning, they should be dried with compressed air. After inspection (paragraphs 12 thru 14) they should be lubricated with SAE 90EP transmission oil and stored carefully in clean conditions until ready for use.

Inspection - general

3   Inspect the transmission case and extension housing for cracks, worn or damaged bearings and bores, and damaged threads and machined surfaces. Small nicks and burrs can be locally dressed out using a fine file.
4   Examine the shift levers, forks, shift rods and associated parts for wear and damage.
5   Renew roller bearings which are chipped, corroded or rough running.
6   Examine the countershaft (layshaft) for damage and wear; renew it if this is evident.
7   Examine the reverse idler and sliding gears for damage and wear. Renew them if this is evident.
8   Renew the input shaft and gear if damaged or worn. If the roller bearing surface in the counterbore is damaged or worn, or the cone surface is damaged, renew the gear and gear rollers.
9   Examine all the gears for wear and damage, renewing as necessary.
10 Renew the mainshaft if bent, or if the splines are damaged.
11 Renew the seal in the transmission front bearing cover.

Ball bearing assemblies - inspection

12 Examine the inner and outer raceways for pitting and corrosion, renewing any bearings where this is found.
13 Examine the ball cage and races for signs of cracking, renewing any bearings where this is found.
14 Lubricate the raceways with a small quantity of SAE 90EP transmission oil then rotate the outer race slowly until the balls are lubricated. Spin the bearing by hand in various attitudes, checking for roughness. If any is found after the bearings have been cleaned (paragraph 2) they should be renewed. If they are satisfactory they should be stored carefully whilst awaiting assembly into the transmission.

Synchronizer mechanism

15 Inspect the clutch hub, sliding sleeve, blocker rings and inserts for signs of excessive wear or damage - renew as required.
16 Check the hub taper, the gear teeth and inspect fitting grooves of the blocker rings for excessive wear or damage and renew as required. To inspect the tapered portions locate the blocker ring against the conical section of the gear and, using a feeler gauge, measure the clearance as shown in Fig. 6.22 and renew the blocker ring if the clearance exceeds that specified.
17 Measure the clearance of the clutch hub splines and mainshaft splines and renew if the clearance exceeds that specified.

Mainshaft run-out

18 Place the mainshaft on two 'V' blocks and check for run-out using a dial test indicator. If the run-out exceeds that specified, renew the mainshaft.

8.2 Fit the 3rd gear and roller bearing to the mainshaft ...

8.3 ... followed by the synchronizer hub unit ...

8.4 ... and retain with snap ring

8.5 Locate the needle roller bearing and 2nd gear

8.6 Fit the 1st/2nd synchronizer hub and reverse sliding gear

8.7 Fit the needle roller bearing over the 1st gear sleeve

Reverse idler gear

19 Check the reverse idler gear for wear, damage and the amount of clearance between the gear and bushings. Renew the bushing if clearance is beyond that specified.

8 Transmission - Series 1 to 4 - reassembly

Mainshaft assembly

1 Before reassembling the various components of the transmission ensure that all items are clean and old gaskets and sealant solution are removed from mating surfaces. Lubricate where specified with the recommended transmission oil.
2 Commence reassembly by lubricating the 3rd gear bearing journal on the mainshaft, then fit the caged roller bearing and 3rd gear (photo).
3 Refit the blocker ring and the 3rd/4th synchronizer hub assembly (photo) - the synchronizer hub chamfer faces forwards. Ensure that the blocker rings are assembled with their notches aligned with the synchronizer keys.
4 Retain the gear and synchronizer hub with the snap-ring (photo).
5 Lubricate the 2nd speed journal on the mainshaft and slide the needle roller bearings into position followed by 2nd gear (photo).
6 Fit the blocker ring and 1st/2nd synchronizer hub (see Fig. 6.24) and reverse sliding gear (photo).
7 Lubricate the 1st speed journal and install the needle roller bearing, over the sleeve as shown in the photo.
8 Fit the blocker ring and 1st gear into position (photo).
9 Fit the thrust washer against the 1st gear with its oil groove towards 1st gear.
10 If the rear bearing has been removed from the retainer, this should now be reinstalled with the sealed side towards the front of the retainer (photo).
11 Assemble the bearing and retainer unit to the rear end of the main shaft. Fit the lockwasher and nut (photo) and torque the nut to 80 lb f ft (11 kg f m). Bend over the lock tab on the washer over a flat of the nut to retain it in position.
12 Refit the speedometer drive gear and locate with snap-rings (photo).

13 Install the reverse idler into the casing with the shift fork groove to the rear (photo), and the shaft slot facing the countershaft hole.

Countergear shaft assembly

14 Insert the inner bearing thrust washers into the front and rear of the countergear shaft assembly.
15 Lubricate the needle roller bearings with grease and locate them into the respective housings followed by the outer thrust washers (photo). There are 46 roller bearings in all, 23 to fit in each end.
16 Position the countershaft thrust washers into position in the gearcase (photo) and install the countergear into position in the gearcase with the large diameter gear to the front of the case (photo). Locate temporarily with dummy shaft.

Clutch gear shaft assembly

17 If it has been removed, press the bearing onto the clutch gear and retain with snap-ring (photo), and fit the locating ring to the outer bearing race.
18 Fit the clutch gear shaft unit into position in the front of the gearcase. When locating the bearing into the housing ensure that the gear does not foul the housing wall when pressing or drifting into position.
19 Smear the clutch gear pilot roller bearing with grease and insert into position (photo).
20 Fit the blocker ring to the clutch gear cone.

Transmission final assembly

21 Install the mainshaft assembly into position in the gearcase (photo). Locate the lug on the rear bearing retainer into the recess in the rear face of the gearcase (photo).
22 Rotate the mainshaft assembly to position the countergear for the insertion of the countershaft.
23 Lightly lubricate the countershaft and check that the thrust washers are correctly located. Install the countershaft thru the rear of the casing and tap carefully into position; extract the dummy shaft. The slot in the end of the countershaft is to face the reverse idler shaft (photo).
24 Position the reverse idler gear shaft and countergear shaft and

8.8 Fit the blocker ring and 1st gear

8.10 Install the bearing with the sealed side to the front of the retainer

8.11a Fit the lockwasher and nut

8.11b The assembled mainshaft unit

8.12 Locate the speedometer drivegear with snap rings

8.13 The reverse idler positioned in the gearcase

8.15 The countershaft gear needle bearings and washers in position

8.16a The countershaft thrust washer in position

8.16b Insert the countershaft into the gearcase

8.17 Retain the clutch shaft bearing with snap ring

8.19 Insert the clutch shaft gear pilot roller bearing and fit the blocker ring to the cone

8.21a Install the mainshaft assembly

8.21b The locating lug in the rear face recess

8.23 Fit the countershaft with the slot towards the reverse idler shaft

8.25 The shifter forks located

8.27 The front detent balls, pin and plunger positions:
A = Inner lock pin   B = Plunger

8.31 Installing the detent balls

8.32 Fit the shifter fork to shaft roll pins

8.34 Fit the reverse lampswitch

8.35 Drift the roll pin into position thru the reverse shift block and shaft

8.37a Fit the rear detent balls ...

8.37b ... and springs into position

8.38 Fit the top cover with gaskets and baffle plate

Fig. 6.23. 3rd/4th synchronizer hub directional location

locate the lock plate into position in the key slots of the respective shafts. Carefully tap the lock plate flush to the rear of the case.
25 Position the shift forks into their respective 1/2nd, 3/4th synchronizer sleeve grooves, and the reverse gear shift fork into its groove on the reverse idler gear (photo).
26 Drive the interlocking pin into the 1st/2nd shifter shaft and insert the shaft into the gearcase thru the rear and locate with the 1st/2nd shifter fork.
27 Install two detent balls into the front shifter shaft bosses. See photo for respective ball, pin and reverse plunger positions.
28 Insert the 3/4th shifter shaft from the rear and locate thru the shifter fork and into the front of the casing to retain the detent balls.
29 Fit the rear extension and gasket into position and retain with bolts tightened to the specified torque.
30 If the rear extension oil seal has been removed, carefully lift the new one into position.
31 Install the two detent balls into position (photo) and then insert the reverse shifter shaft thru the front of the casing and reverse shifter fork.
32 Fit the respective roll pins into position thru the shifter forks and shafts (photo).
33 Fit the speedometer driven gear unit into position.
34 Install the detent ball and plunger followed by the reverse lamp switch (photo). Fit the TCS switch.
35 Fit the reverse shift block, fulcrum bracket and reverse idler gear control lever and locate with the roll pin (photo).
36 Refit the top shift quadrant and gasket tighten the retaining bolts to the specified torque.
37 Select neutral position and insert the three detent balls, (photo) and springs (photo) into their location in the top of the rear face of the casing.
38 Fit the gaskets and baffle plate and then the top cover into position (photo). Locate the retaining bolts and tighten to the specified torque.
39 Locate the front cover gasket and fit the front cover. Tighten the retaining bolts to the specified torque.
40 Refit the clutch shift fork and release bearing.

9 Transmission - Series 5 and 6 - reassembly

Mainshaft

1 Smear the needle roller bearing with grease and fit to the mainshaft together with the third speed gear. The gear is fitted with its tapered side to the front.
2 Fit a blocker ring with clutching teeth upwards over the third speed gear synchronising surface.
3 To reassemble the 3rd/4th synchronizer unit, locate the synchronizer hub face with its heavy boss to the sleeve face as in Fig. 6.23. Locate the keys into the groove and insert the springs into the hole in the side face of the synchronizer hub. Check that the hub and sleeve slide smoothly.
4 Fit the 3rd/4th synchronizer into position on the mainshaft with the small chamfer on the sleeve face to the rear of the shaft. Retain with the snap-ring.
5 Invert the mainshaft and fit the 2nd speed gear and needle bearing onto the shaft-grease the bearing before assembly and ensure that the 2nd gear taper face is to the rear of the shaft.
6 Fit the blocker ring with its clutching teeth downwards over the

Fig. 6.24. Fit the reverse sliding gear and sleeve

Fig. 6.25. 1st/2nd synchronizer directional location

Fig. 6.26. Install the rear bearing with snap ring groove forward

Fig. 6.27. Fit the clutch gear bearing retaining snap ring

Fig. 6.28. Tighten the lockplate to the specified torque

Fig. 6.29. Tighten the detent retainer bolts to specified torques

Fig. 6.30. The detent plug positions in center support

Fig. 6.31. Assemble the counter shaft and main shaft to the center support using special tool no. J-26545-5 if available to keep the shaft assemblies in mesh and parallel

Fig. 6.32. Fit the reverse shifter fork and reverse gear

Fig. 6.33. Fit the reverse idler shaft

Fig. 6.34. Thrust washer location in extension

2nd gear synchronizer surface.

7 To reassemble the 1st/2nd synchronizer, position the hub with the chamfer on the inner edge facing to the heavy chamfer on the outer edge of the sleeve as in Fig. 6.25. Locate the keys into their grooves and synchronizer spring in the hole in the synchronizer hub side face. Check that the hub and sleeve slide smoothly.

8 Fit the 1st/2nd synchronizer unit into position with its sleeve chamfer facing forwards.

9 Fit the blocker ring with its clutching teeth rearwards.

10 Smear the 1st speed gear roller bearing with grease and fit it together with its collar and gear onto the mainshaft. The gear is fitted with the tapered side facing forwards.

11 Fit the 1st speed gear thrust washer with its grooved side against the gear.

12 Press the rear bearing into position on the shaft with the snap-ring groove off set to the front of the mainshaft (Fig. 6.26).

13 Fit the bearing to the clutch gear shaft if it has been removed. The snap-ring groove is positioned offset to the front of the shaft. Retain the bearing with the snap-ring as in Fig. 6.27.

14 Smear the clutch gear pilot needle roller bearing with grease and fit it together with the blocker ring and clutch gear to the mainshaft.

15 Press the countergear ball bearing into position with the snap-ring groove offset to the rear.

16 Refit the snap-rings to their grooves in the mainshaft and counter-gear shaft locations in the center support.

17 Install the idler gear shaft into position in the center support with the lock plate grooved side positioned correctly. Fit the lock plate and tighten the retaining bolt to the specified torque of 14 lb f ft (1.9 kg f m).

18 The mainshaft assembly and countergear shaft unit are meshed together in parallel and fitted to the center support. If special tool No. J-26545-5 is available this should be used to retain the two gear shaft assemblies in parallel mesh when fitting the center support.

19 Expand the countergear bearing and mainshaft bearing snap-rings in the center support and get an assistant to press the center support over the bearings so that the snap-rings are fitted in their respective grooves.

20 Push the synchronizers to the rear to prevent the mainshaft rotating. If the synchronizers are reluctant to move, tap them with a wooden hammer handle.

21 Now locate on the rear of the countergear the collar, countershaft reverse gear, washer and self-locking nut. Always use a new self-locking nut, and tighten to a torque of 100 lb f ft (13.8 kg f m).

22 Fit the mainshaft locknut and washer. Tighten the nut, fitted with its chamfered side facing the washer, to 94 lb f ft (12.9 kg f m).

23 Grease the detent plugs and install them into their location holes from the middle hole of the center support as in Fig. 6.30.

24 Position the 1st/2nd and 3rd/4th shifter forks into their location grooves in the synchronizers.

25 Insert the 3rd/4th shifter rod thru the rear of the center support, the middle hole, and into the respective shifter forks. The 3rd/4th

9.45 Refit the ball stud and tighten to specified torque

shifter rod has two detent grooves on the side of the rod.

26 Insert the 1st/2nd shifter rod thru the rear of the center support and into the 1st/2nd shifter fork.

27 Align the shifter forks and shaft spring pin holes.

28 Install the stopper pin in the reverse shifter rod so that the pin is protruding equally from each side of the shaft. Fit the reverse shifter rod from the front of the center support.

29 Support the shifter rods and drift the spring pins into position to locate the shifter forks and shafts.

30 The detent balls, springs and retainer are now installed and the retainer securing bolts tightened to 14 lb f ft (1.9 kg f m).

31 Position the transmission casing upright on wooden blocks and fit the center support assembly and gasket into the casing. Align the dowel pin holes with the dowel pins.

32 Fit the reverse shifter fork to reverse gear and then fit them into position from rear of the mainshaft, and connect to the reverse shifter rod.

33 Drive the spring pin into the reverse shifter fork.

34 Fit the thrust washer and then the reverse idler gear to the idler shaft. The flange on the thrust washer locates in the center support stopper. The undercut teeth on the reverse idler gear face forwards (Fig. 6.33).

35 Locate the speedometer drive gear snap-ring and key onto the mainshaft.

36 Fit the speedometer drive gear in alignment with the key groove and retain with snap-ring.

37 Carefully fit a new oil seal to the rear extension, then smear the outer thrust washer of the reverse idler shaft with grease and fit to the rear extension (Fig. 6.34).

38 Fit the rear extension and gasket into position aligning the dowel pin and hole. Tighten the retaining bolts to 27 lb f ft (3.6 kg f m).

39 Refit the reverse lamp switch and CRS switch.

40 Fit the shifter cover and gasket and tighten the retaining bolts to 10 lb f ft (1.3 kg f m).

41 Apply some oil to the 'O' ring on the speedometer driven gear unit and fit it into position in the rear extension. Tighten the retaining bolt.

42 Fit the new front bearing retainer seal into position.

43 Fit the snap-ring to the outer clutch gear bearing race. Grease the retainer spring washer and position it in the bearing retainer. The dished face of the washer must face the bearing outer race.

44 Fit the bearing and retainer into position in the front of the gear-case and retain with bolts. The shorter bolts are fitted to the counter-gear front bearing side of the retainer. Tighten the bolts to 14 lb f ft (1.9 kg f m).

45 If it has been removed, refit the ball stud, (photo) and tighten to a torque of 30 lb f ft (4.1 kg f m).

46 Refit the clutch fork, dust boot and throwout bearing, and install the retaining spring. Grease the shift fork support with molybdenum disulphide grease, and ensure that the clutch fork hook is correctly located to the support.

Chapter 6 Part B: Automatic transmission

Contents

Fault diagnosis - Automatic transmission 20	Shift lever - dismantling, inspection and reassembly 16
Fluid level - checking 11	Shift linkage - adjustment 13
General description 10	Throttle valve control cable - removal, installation and
Inhibitor switch - adjustment 17	adjustment 14
Rear oil seal - renewal 19	Transmission - draining and refilling ... ' 12
Shift control lever - removal and installation 15	Transmission - removal and installation 18

Specifications

Type	3 speed, fully automatic
Torque ratio	2.6

Gear ratios

1st	2.74 : 1
2nd	1.57 : 1
3rd	1.00 : 1
Reverse	2.07 : 1

Lubricant capacity	6.5 US quarts (5.4 Imp qts)
Lubricant type	Dexron 11

Torque wrench settings

	lb f ft	kg f m
Screen to valve body bolts	6 to 10	0.8 to 1.3
Oil pan baths	10 to 13	1.3 to 1.7
Shift lever to control shaft nut		
Series 5	16	2.2
Series 6	22	3.0
Flexplate to converter bolts	30	4.1

10 General description

1   The fully automatic Turbo-Hydromatic 200 Transmission unit basically consists of a three element hydraulic torque converter and a compound planetary gear set.

2   To obtain the required actuation of the compound planetary gear set there are three multiple - disc clutches, a band and a roller clutch. The hydraulic torque is applied via the torque converter which connects the engine to the planetary gears thru oil, and the planetary gears consist of three forward and one reverse gear.

3   The torque converter comprises a pump (driving member), a turbine (driven member) and stator unit. The stator works in conjunction with a one-way roller clutch, which allows the stator to rotate in a clockwise direction only.

4   The engine crankshaft is coupled to the torque converter by a flex plate which only rotates at engine speed. The torque converter housing is filled with oil and the converter pump directs the oil to the turbine. Oil passing thru the turbine causes it to rotate. The stator redirects the oil flow from the turbine so that it does not adversely affect the converter blade action, at higher engine speeds. At lower speeds, the stator roller clutch is actuated and this activates the stator causing it to direct the oil at the converter pump. This has the effect of assisting the converter pump to deliver power or increase engine torque at the lower speeds.

5   The friction components and automatic controls are operated by a hydraulic system, pressurized by a gear pump, which supplies the working pressure required to operate the controls and components.

6   The transmission has six selector positions:

P   *Parking position which locks the out shaft to transmission case and incorporates a locking pawl. This is a safety device to prevent the vehicle moving when on an incline. The engine may be started with 'P' selected and this position must always be selected when adjusting the engine while it is running. 'P' must only be engaged when the vehicle is completely stationary.*

R   *Reverse gear*

N   *Neutral. Select this position to start the engine or when idling for long periods such as in heavy traffic.*

D   *Drive, for all normal motoring conditions. The drive range has three gear speeds from starting ratio to direct drive. This range gives maximum economy. Detent down shifts can be made by depressing the accelerator pedal to the floor.*

L2 *This range gives the same starting ratio as 'D' range but stops the transmission from engaging a higher gear, and can be used for acceleration or engine braking as required. Once engaged, the transmission will remain in 2nd until the vehicle speed or throttle are changed to obtain 1st gear as in 'D' range.*

L1 *The selection of this gear above a road speed of approximately 30 mph (48 kph) will engage 2nd gear and as the speed decreases below this figure the transmission will shift into 1st gear.*

7   Due to the complexity of the automatic transmission unit, any internal adjustment or servicing should be left to a GM dealer or automatic transmission specialist. The information given in this Chapter is therefore confined to those operations which are considered within the scope of the home mechanic. An automatic transmission should give many tens of thousands of miles service provided normal maintenance and adjustment is carried out. When the unit finally requires major overhaul consideration should be given to exchange the old transmission for a factory reconditioned one, the removal and installation being well within the capabilities of the home mechanic as described later in this Chapter.

8   The hydraulic fluid must be periodically drained and refilled as specified in Section 12, and the fluid level regularly checked (see next Section).

9   Periodically the outside of the transmission housing should be cleaned as an accumulation of dirt and oil is liable to cause overheating of the unit under adverse conditions.

10 The engine idle speed must be set as specified.

11 If a new or reconditioned transmission unit has been installed, the maximum speed must not exceed 70 mph for the break-in period of the first 600 miles.

11 Fluid level - checking

1   The transmission fluid level must be checked at every engine oil change period.

2   The oil must be checked at its normal operating temperature (93°C - 200°F) and this is achieved after a minimum of 15 miles highway driving or equivalent city driving.

Fig. 6.35. The principle components of the automatic transmission

3 To check the level, park the vehicle on a level surface with the
shift lever in 'P' position, and the parking brake applied.
4 Run the engine at its normal idle speed.
5 Withdraw the fluid level indicator and wipe clean. Fully re-insert it
until the cap seats and then remove the indicator for a level reading,
which should be at the 'F' (full) mark.
6 Top up if necessary, but do not over-fill, with the correct grade of
transmission oil as specified.
7 If for any reason the vehicle cannot be driven to warm up the
transmission for oil level checking as above, it can be checked at an
ambient temperature of 21°C (70°F), as follows.
8 Follow the instruction in paragraphs 3 and 4 above, but do not race
the engine under any circumstances!
9 Move the selector shift lever thru each range.
10 Now check immediately the fluid level with the selector engaged
in the 'P' position with the engine running. The fluid level on
the indicator should be between the two dimples below the 'ADD'
mark.
11 If it is necessary to top up the transmission only add sufficient
fluid to bring the level up to the point between the two dimples on the
dipstick.
12 The need for frequent topping-up indicates a leakage and should
be rectified as soon as possible.

Fig. 6.36. The control rod showing adjustment nuts position

12 Transmission - draining and refilling

1 The transmission oil pan must be drained and the screen cleaned
every 60,000 miles, and new fluid added. Under extreme working
conditions this should be undertaken every 15,000 miles.
2 Drain the fluid immediately after the vehicle has been used so that
the oil is at its normal working temperature, but take care - transmission
fluid can exceed 177°C (350°F).
3 Raise the vehicle and support the transmission vibration damper
with a jack.
4 Place a suitable container under the oil pan and unscrew the oil
pan attachment bolts, from the front and side.
5 Slacken the oil pan rear securing bolts approximately four turns and,
using a suitable screwdriver, prise the oil pan loose and allow the fluid
to drain.
6 When the oil has drained, remove the rear oil pan bolts and lower
the pan and gasket.
7 Drain the remaining fluid from the oil pan, and clean the pan using
a solvent and blow dry using compressed air.
8 Unscrew and remove the screen to valve body bolts, screen and
gasket.
9 Clean thoroughly the screen in solvent and blow dry with compressed
air.
10 Fit a new gasket to the screen and refit it, tightening the retaining
bolts to 6 - 10 lb f ft (8 - 14 Nm).
11 Fit a new gasket to the oil pan and refit it to the transmission,
tightening the retaining bolts to 10 - 13 lb f ft (14 to 18 Nm).
12 Lower the vehicle and top up the transmission with approximately
6 pints (1.4 liters) of the recommended fluid.
13 Now check the transmission oil level as described in paragraphs
7 to 11 in the previous Section.

Fig. 6.37. Throttle valve cable location

13 Shift linkage - adjustment

1 Detach the control rod from the shift lever side by withdrawing
the cotter pin and removing the washers.
2 Turn the transmission manual shaft to stop in the counter clockwise direction viewed from the transmission left side (position '1'),
then back the shaft off three stops to the Neutral position.
3 Retain the parts in this position and move the shift lever in the
cab to Neutral, and push rearward to remove play.
4 Slacken the control rod locknuts and adjust the rod length by
turning it so that its end is in alignment with the shift lever hole.
5 Reconnect the control rod and shift lever and retain with washers
and cotter pin. Tighten the lock nuts.
6 Finally check the shift lever movement and that the vehicle moves
when the shift lever is in 'D' range and reverses when in 'R' range.

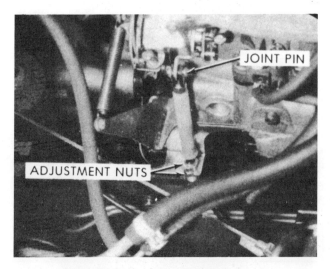

Fig. 6.38. Throttle valve cable adjustment nuts

Fig. 6.39. Check the cable stroke between wide open and fully closed

Fig. 6.40. Inhibitor switch showing adjustment positions

14 Throttle valve control cable - removal, installation and adjustment

1   Slacken the throttle valve control cable adjusting nuts and detach the cable from the carburetor lever by removing the cotter pin from the connector pin.
2   Detach the throttle valve cable clip from its location on the right rear side of the cylinder body. Undo the throttle valve control cable flange to transmission retaining bolt, and pull the cable upwards to detach the inner cable end from the throttle lever linkage on the transmission side.
3   Remove the cable assembly.
4   Installation is a direct reversal of removal and when in position must be adjusted as follows.
5   Ensure that the carburetor lever and throttle valve control cable bracket are free from distortion and normal.
6   Slacken the cable adjustment nuts (Fig. 6.38) and fully open the carburetor lever. The inner cable adjustment is set by turning the lower adjustment nut on the outer cable by hand to give the inner cable approximately 0.04 in (0.01 mm) play. Tighten the upper lock nut to secure.
7   Check that the inner cable stroke from wide open to closed position is within 1.37 to 1.41 in (34 to 35.8 mm).

15 Shift control lever - removal and installation

1   Locate the shift lever in Neutral position.
2   Withdraw the cotter pin and remove the washers and disconnect the control rod from the shift lever side.
3   Remove the console cover retaining screws and remove the console cover.
4   Disconnect the inhibitor switch and indicator light wiring from the connector.
5   Unscrew the four bolts retaining the shift lever unit and remove it.
6   Installation is a direct reversal of removal but readjust the shift lever setting if required as in Section 13.

16 Shift lever - dismantling, inspection and assembly

1   Unscrew the lever knob setscrew, remove the knob assembly from the lever.

2   Unscrew the four indicator upper cover retaining screws and remove the cover, slider and lower the cover, with indicator light, from the shift lever bracket.
3   Remove the inhibitor switch from the bracket by unscrewing the two securing screws and then prise the rubber boot from the bracket.
4   Undo the nut and remove with the spring washer from the control shaft to shift lever and remove them from the bracket.
5   Remove the shift lever bracket bushings.
6   To disconnect the shaft lever rod, turn it counterclockwise and withdraw it from the upper opening in the shift lever.
7   Now compress the shift lever rod return spring and withdraw the selector pin via the lower shift lever slot by turning it 90° and then remove the spring.
8   Clean and inspect the various components for signs of excessive wear or damage. Test the inhibitor switch for continuity using a circuit tester. The moving piece of the switch must be tested in its various positions of P - R - N - D.
9   Commence reassembly by fitting the shift rod return spring into its location thru the opening in the upper part of the lever.
10 Fit the select pin into its slot in the lower part of the lever by compressing the spring and turning the pin 90°. Smear the pin with a small amount of grease prior to fitting and when fitted its long side end must be positioned to the shift lever bracket.
11 Insert the shift lever rod into the lever with its end projecting from the upper face of the lever by approximately 1.686 in (42.8 mm) on Series 5 models or 1.8 in (46 mm) for Series 6. Screw the select pin into the lever and set the shift lever rod with its taper face to the push button.
12 Fit the two bushings to the control shaft fitting face of the lever bracket. Lightly grease the control shaft, select pin and control shaft fitting face of the bracket and install the control shaft and shift lever. Fit the washer and nut and tighten to a torque of 16 lb f ft (2.2 kg f m) on Series 5 models or 22 lb f ft (3 kg f m) on Series 6 models.
13 Fit the rubber boot to the bracket, and then insert the projected portion of the inhibitor switch in the slot in the shift lever. Fit parts to the bracket and locate the screws but do not fully tighten them. A small amount of grease should be applied to the projected portion of the inhibitor switch but be careful not to grease the points within the switch.
14 Fit the indicator light to the lower cover and assemble to the bracket complete with slider and upper cover. Do not fully tighten the setscrews.
15 Adjust the position of the upper cover by moving the shift lever

to each of its positions and the red color mark on the slider is in
alignment with the indicator plate window.
16 Fit the knob assembly to the shift lever and retain using a new
setscrew. The free play of the push button should be 0.008 to 0.048 in
(0.2 to 1.2 mm) for Series 5 or 0.028 to 0.048 in (0.7 to 1.2 mm) with
the lever in the N or P position. If adjustment is required refer to
paragraph 11. Check that the shift lever operates freely thruout the
range, adjust the inhibitor switch as follows.

17 Inhibitor switch - adjustment

1   If the engine can be started in any position other than Neutral or
Park adjust the switch as follows.
2   With the two inhibitor switch retaining screws slackened, adjust
the position of the switch so that the switch moving piece center
is in alignment with the neutral position on the indicator line on the
steel case, with the lever set in Neutral position. Tighten screws.

18 Transmission - removal and installation

1   Detach the ground cable from the battery terminal.
2   Slacken the throttle valve cable adjustment nuts, withdraw the
cotter pin and joint pin from the carburetor lever and then detach the
control lever.
3   Disconnect the oil level gauge from the transmission.
4   Jack up the vehicle and make secure with blocks.
5   Remove the dust cover from the lower part of the converter housing. Drain the transmission oil - see Section 12.
6   Unscrew and remove the starter mounting bolts and withdraw
the stator unit.
7   Refer to Chapter 7 and remove the propeller shaft.
8   Detach the control rod from the shift lever.
9   Disconnect the exhaust pipe retaining bracket from the transmission
and then detach the speedometer cable from the transmission.
10 Slacken the oil cooler pipe retaining nuts from the right-hand side,
remove the pipe securing clips and relocate the pipe towards the body.
11 Refer to Fig. 6.41 and remove the dust cover to gain access to the
three nuts and bolts coupling the converter to the drive plate. Turn the
drive plate accordingly to undo the negative bolts/nuts.
12 Undo and remove the three transmission to frame bracket mounting
bolts.
13 Place a jack under the engine and raise the engine and transmission
sufficiently to remove the frame bracket to crossmember bolts, and
remove the rear mount.
14 Support the transmission with a jack or blocks.
15 Undo and remove the bellhousing bolts.
16 Withdraw the transmission to the rear complete with the oil filler

VIEW A

BOLT;
CONVERTER TO
DRIVE PLATE

DUST COVER

A

Fig. 6.41. The converter to drive plate bolt position

tube and the throttle valve cable. When manoeuvring the transmission
clear of the vehicle take care not to let the torque converter become
detached from the transmission.
17 Installation of the transmission unit is a direct reversal of removal
sequence but note the following.
   *a) Prior to fitting the flexplate to converter bolts ensure that the
   welded converter brackets are flush with the flexplate, and the
   converter can be freely rotated by hand. Tighten all of the bolts
   finger tight before tightening to the specified torque to ensure
   correct converter alignment.*
   *b) The throttle valve cable and control rod must be re-adjusted as
   described in Sections 14 and 13.*
   *c) Refill the transmission with fluid of the correct type
   specified and check the fluid level as in Section 11.*

19 Rear oil seal - renewal

1   After a considerable mileage, leakage may occur from the seal which
surrounds the shaft at the rear end of the automatic transmission
extension housing. This leakage will be evident from the state of the
underbody and from the reduction in the level of the hydraulic fluid.
2   Remove the propeller shaft as described in Chapter 7.
3   Taking care not to damage the spline output shaft and the alloy
housing, pry the old oil seal from its location. Drive in the new one
using a tubular drift. Refit the propeller shaft.
4   Check the fluid level and replenish to the correct level as required.

20 Fault diagnosis - Automatic transmission

Symptom	Reason/s
Engine will not start in 'N' or 'P'	Faulty starter or ignition circuit. Incorrect linkage adjustment. Incorrectly installed inhibitor switch.
Engine starts in selector positions other than 'N' or 'P'	Incorrect linkage adjustment. Incorrectly installed inhibitor switch.
Severe bump when selecting 'D' or 'R' and excessive creep when idling	Idling speed too high.
Poor acceleration and low maximum speed	Incorrect oil level. Incorrect linkage adjustment.

**The most likely causes of faulty operation are incorrect oil level and linkage adjustment. Any other faults or mal-operation of the automatic
transmission unit must be due to internal faults and should be rectified by your GM dealer. An indication of a major internal fault may be gained
from the color of the oil which under normal conditions should be transparent red. If it becomes discolored or black then burned clutch bands
must be suspected.**

Chapter 7 Driveshaft

Contents

Driveshaft - balance and run-out check 5
Driveshaft - dismantling and reassembly 4
Driveshaft - removal and installation 2

General description 1
Universal joints - inspection 3

Specifications

Spider pin endplay	0.004 in
Snap-ring thickness	0.057 in ⎫ 0.059 in ⎬ as required 0.061 in ⎭

Torque wrench setting

Propeller shaft to companion flange	18 lb f ft (2.4 kg f m)

1 General description

Drive from the transmission to the rear axle is via a driveshaft (propeller shaft) comprising the coupling shaft, universal joints and rear connecting flange yoke.

The front end of the shaft is connected to the transmission unit by means of a splined sliding yoke which permits fore and aft movement of the driveshaft in accordance with axle movement. The rear end of the shaft is connected to the rear axle companion flange by the flanged yoke of the rear end universal joint.

The front and rear universal joints are retained in the yokes by snap-rings (circlips) which are available in varying thicknesses so that the joint spider can be correctly centered.

2 Driveshaft - removal and installation

1 Mark the relative position of the driveshaft rear yoke and rear axle companion flanges to ensure that they are refitted in the same relative position.

2 Unscrew the four bolts connecting the flange yoke with the companion flange. Support the shaft and remove the bolts.

3 Lower the rear of the shaft to clear the axle housing and carefully withdraw the driveshaft assembly from the transmission housing, taking care not to damage the rear oil seal in the transmission.

4 Plug the end of the transmission to prevent loss of lubricant (Fig. 7.2).

5 Installation is the reversal of removal but ensure that the transmission end of the driveshaft is well lubricated with transmission oil and take care not to damage the oil seal as the shaft is inserted.

Also check that the rear yoke and companion flange marks are aligned before fitting the bolts, which must be tightened to the specified torque. Top up the transmission if any lubricant has been lost.

3 Universal joints - inspection

1 Wear in the needle roller bearings is characterised by vibration in the transmission, 'clonks' on taking up the drive, and in extreme cases of lack of lubrication, metallic squeaking and ultimately grating and shrieking sounds as the bearings break up. If a bearing breaks up at high speed it could be lethal, so they should be changed in good time.

2 It is easy to check whether the needle roller bearings are worn with the driveshaft in position, by trying to turn the shaft with one hand, the other hand holding the companion flange when the rear universal is being checked, and the front half coupling when the front universal is being checked. Any movement between the shaft and the front and the rear half couplings is indicative of considerable wear. If, worn, the old bearings and spiders will have to be discarded and a repair kit, comprising new universal joint spiders, bearings, seals and snap-rings purchased. Check also by trying to lift the shaft and noticing any movement in the joints.

3 Examine the driveshaft spline for wear. If worn it will be necessary to purchase a new front half coupling, or if the yokes are badly worn, an exchange shaft. It is not possible to fit oversize bearings and journals to the trunnion bearing holes.

4 Driveshaft - dismantling and reassembly

1 Clean all traces of dirt from the universal joints. If the snap-rings

Fig. 7.1. The propeller shaft component parts

1 Propeller shaft	3 Cover	5 Flange yoke	7 Snap rings
2 Spline yoke	4 Plate plug	6 Bearing caps	

Fig. 7.2. Plug the end of the transmission

Fig. 7.3. Tap the yoke to withdraw the bearing cup

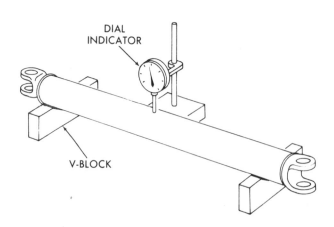

Fig. 7.4. Checking the propeller shaft run-out

have rusted into the yokes, use a wire brush to remove the surface rust and soak the snap-rings in penetrating oil.

2 Remove the snap-rings using suitable pliers or a small screwdriver. New snap-rings must be used on reassembly so it does not matter if they are distorted on removal. If they are difficult to remove, a hammer blow on the end of the joint spider may relieve the pressure on them.

3 To remove the bearing cups, hold the joint in one hand and with a mallet or copper hammer tap the yoke lightly as shown in Fig. 7.3. Alternatively, select two sockets, one being large enough to fit completely over the bearing cup and the other to fit on the end of the cup. By compressing in the jaws of a vice or by hammering on the smaller socket (providing that a degree of caution is exercised), the spiders and cups can be driven out of one side of the yoke. Having removed one cup, the opposite one can then be removed by reversing the direction of applied pressure. The remaining ones are then treated similarly.

4 Wash the respective parts in a solvent and wipe dry. Inspect the various components for wear and other damage. If a joint spider is worn below the limit. it must be renewed regardless of the condition of the bearings.

5 When reassembling the universal joints, ensure that all the parts are free from dirt, then lightly grease the holes in the yokes. Ensure that the bearing cups are approximately 1/3 full of molybdenum-disulphide grease.

6 Insert the spider into the yoke and carefully press in two opposing

cups and seals. The vise and sockets can be used for this job as they were when dismantling. Snap-rings are available in selective sizes of (0.057, 0.059 and 0.061 in) so that the universal joint can be positioned centrally and then all endplay can be taken up. Ensure that the opposing snap-rings are of equal size to obtain optimum balance. With the bearing cups in position the endplay of the spider pin must be within 0.078 in (2 mm).

5 Driveshaft - balance and run-out check

1 The driveshaft is balanced during manufacture and will not normally require any further balancing provided that the correct snap-rings have been used on the universal joints, and that accident damage has not occurred.

2 If vibration of the driveshaft is experienced, and the universal joints and coupling flange bolts and bolt holes are known to be in good order, then it may be possible that the driveshaft is misaligned and/or out of balance.

3 To check the alignment, remove the driveshaft from the vehicle and lay it with its ends supported in two 'V' blocks as shown in Fig. 7.4. Locate the probe of a dial indicator to locate centrally on the shaft. Turning the shaft slowly, note the dial indicator reading. Any excessive variation indicates that the shaft is misaligned and a replacement must be acquired.

Chapter 8 Rear axle

Contents

Axle housing - removal and installation	5	Fault diagnosis - rear axle 6
Axleshaft unit - removal and installation	2	General description 1
Differential carrier assembly - removal and installation	4	Rear wheel bearing and seal - removal and installation 3

Specifications

Type	Semi-floating, hypoid
Ratio	4.56 : 1 (manual)
	4.10 : 1 (speed automatic)
Ring gear to pinion backlash	0.005 to 0.008 in (0.127 to 0.203 mm)
Pinion to differential gears	0.001 to 0.003 in (0.02 to 0.07 mm)
Rated capacity	3.500 lbs (1533 kg)
Lubricant type	GL-5
Below 50°F (10°C)	SAE 80 W
0° to 90°F (17° to 32°C)	SAE 90
Consistently above 50°F (10°C)	SAE 140
Lubricant capacity	2.7 pints

Torque wrench settings

	lb f ft	kg f m
Axle to spring 'U' bolt	40	5.5
Shackle pins (Series 1 to 4)	130	17.9
Propshaft to companion flange	18	2.4
Axleshaft locknut	190	26.2
Bearing holder thru bolts	55	7.6
Bearing cap nuts	75	10.3
Pinion nut	190	26.2
Pinion nut initial torque	85	11.7
Ring gear to case bolts (with Loctite)		
Series 1	55	7.6
Series 2	65	8.9
Series 3, 4, 5 and 6	80 to 87	11.0 to 12.0
Carrier to housing bolts		
Series 1	35	4.8
Series 2	18	2.4

1 General description

1   The conventional rear axle is of the semi-floating type, located by semi-elliptic rear springs and telescopic double acting shockabsorbers. The differential carrier is detachable from the axle casing, permitting the crownwheel and pinion adjustments to be made on the workbench during any major servicing.

2   The final drive crownwheel and pinion are of the hypoid type with the pinion center line below the crownwheel center line. The pinion, which runs in two opposed taper roller bearings, is adjusted for depth of mesh to the crownwheel by means of shims. A collapsible spacer on the pinion shaft allows for the pinion bearing pre-load.

3   The crownwheel ring gear is bolted to the differential case and is located by two opposed taper roller bearings. Crownwheel side play adjustment is made by the use of shims.

4   The semi-floating axleshafts are retained at the outer ends by taper roller bearings located in housings bolted to the axle housing.

5   It is considered beyond the scope of a manual of this type to delve into the complexities of repair to and setting up of the differential since a number of special tools are required. Also, the procedure is rather complicated, and for those people without a good knowledge of this type of gear train there is a possibility of incorrect meshing and preload which will give rise to noise and backlash which will lead to early failure. In this Section you will find details of the removal procedures for the axleshafts and differential carrier. In the event of any failure of the differential assembly, it is recommended that a complete exchange assembly is purchased or the existing faulty assembly is repaired by a vehicle main dealer.

2 Axleshaft unit - removal and installation

1   Chock the front wheels and raise the rear of the vehicle.

2   Remove the rear roadwheel, brake drum, brake shoes and detach the parking brake inner cable. For further information on these procedures refer to Chapter 9.

3   Undo and release the brake pipe from the wheel cylinder, and plug the end of the pipe to prevent the ingress of dirt.

4   Undo and remove the four retaining nuts from the bearing holder.

5   Withdraw the axleshaft unit, and if available use special tool number J-5748.

6   If both axleshaft units have been removed and serviced, commence installation by inserting a 0.079 in (2 mm) shim between the axle tube end flange and the bearing holder. Refit the axleshaft unit into the axle tube and locate with the four flange retaining bolts. Tighten the flange bolts to a torque of 55 lb f ft (6.97 kg f m).

7   If only one axleshaft unit has been removed for servicing or when fitting the second proceed as follows. Refit the opposing axleshaft lens shims and when it is fully located against the thrust block in the differential, calculate the bearing holder to flange clearance, add 0.004 in (0.101 mm) to the measured clearance to determine the shim requirement.

8   Withdraw the shaft, and fit the necessary selected shims. Refit the shaft and tighten the flange bolts to 55 lb f ft (6.97 kg f m).

9   Reconnect the brake pipe/s, refit the brake shoes, the parking brake cable, brake drum and road wheels. The hydraulic brake system must now be bled and the parking brake readjusted before lowering the vehicle.

Fig. 8.1. The component parts of the axle, axle housing and differential carrier

1 Differential carrier and case assembly	5 Filler plug	10 Lock nut	15 Axle shaft
2 Mounting bolt	6 Vent	11 Lock washer	16 Wheel stud
3 Gasket	7 Thru bolt	12 Axle shaft bearing	17 Brake drum
4 Drain plug	8 Oil seal	13 Bearing holder	18 Wheel nut
	9 Shims	14 Grease seal	19 Drum to flange screw

Fig. 8.2. Sectional view of the rear axle and wheel hub assembly

shim
2mm (0.079 in)

Fig. 8.3. Fit shims to the value of 0.079 in (2 mm)

3 Rear wheel bearing and seal - removal and installation

1   Remove the axleshaft as described in the previous Section.
2   Bend over the locking tab on the convex lock washer, then support
the axleshaft in a soft jawed vise and undo the locknut using a suitable
wrench. If special tool number J-24246 is available, locate the
axleshaft in the vise so that the jaws clamp around the locknut - but
do not overtighten the vise. Locate the special tool over the flange
studs, and lock in position with two wheel nuts. Rotate the axleshaft
to loosen from the locknuts, using a box wrench, and 'L' bar as in
Fig. 8.4.
3   With the locknut and washer removed, press off the bearing and
holder and brake back plate.
4   The oil seal is now removed from the bearing holder and the bearing
outer race removed by drifting with a soft drift and hammer.
5   Commence reassembly by inserting a new bearing outer race into
the housing. This can be pressed in or carefully driven in using a hammer
and suitable diameter tube. Ensure that the bearing outer race is fully
located and not cocked at an angle.
6   Insert the new grease seal into position in the bearing holder
taking care not to damage the seal lip or distort it - always replace
the old seal with a new one of the correct type.
7   Smear the wheel bearing holder and inner race, also axle tube, with
a recommended grade of wheel bearing grease.
8   Locate the four bolts into the backing plate and then fit the
bearing holder into position with the oil seal side against the locking
plate. Fit the assembly over the axleshaft.
9   Fit the bearing over the axle and press it into position in the bearing
holder.
10 Fit a new lockwasher with the dished side away from the bearing
and thread the locknut onto the shaft. Tighten the locknut to a torque
setting of 190 lb f ft (26.25 kg f m). The shaft will have to be firmly
supported to achieve this figure and if special tool J-24246 is available
fit the axleshaft to the vise and the tool to the axleshaft as described
in paragraph 2, and then tighten the shaft to the nut. Remove the
tool.
11 Bend the lockwasher over the nut flat opposite the locating tab as in
Fig. 8.5.
12 Refit the axleshaft, brake and wheel assemblies as directed in
Section 2.

4 Differential carrier assembly - removal and installation

1   Remove the axleshaft as described in Section 2. It is not
necessary to fully remove the shafts unless required, as they only need
to be withdrawn sufficiently to allow the differential carrier to be
extracted.
2   Remove the axle drain plug and drain the oil into a suitable
container.
3   Mark the relative positions of the driveshaft flange to differential
companion flange (if not already marked), and disconnect the shaft
as described in Chapter 7.
4   Unscrew the ten retaining nuts from the differential carrier and
case unit and withdraw it from the axle housing.
5   Commence installation by cleaning down the faces of the
rear axle casing and the differential carrier. Also clean inside the axle
housing around the differential area to ensure that no particles
of metal are present.
6   Smear the gasket of the differential carrier with a coating of non-
setting gasket sealant and locate it round the carrier flange. Reposition the carrier to the axle housing and refit the retaining nuts.
Tighten them to a torque of 18 lb f ft (2.48 kg f m).
7   Relocate the driveshaft, referring to Chapter 7.
8   Relocate the axleshafts, referring to Section 2 if necessary.
9   Refit the drain plug into the axle housing and top up the axle with
lubricant of the specified grade.

Fig. 8.4. Method of undoing the locknut using special tool number
J - 24246

5 Axle housing - removal and installation

1   Jack up the rear of the car by placing a jack under the rear axle.
Chock the front wheels and place chassis stands or blocks under the
body to support.
2   Remove both rear wheels and brake drums. With a 12 mm box
wrench compress the retaining fingers and remove the brake springs
and shoes.
3   Detach the cables from the leaf spring clip (Fig. 8.6), and then
disconnect the brake hoses from the frame bracket (Fig. 8.7). To
prevent the ingress of dirt, plug the ends of the brake pipes.
4   Detach the driveshaft from the companion flange of the differential
as described in Chapter 7. If removing the driveshaft from the transmission unit, plug the end to prevent oil spillage.
5   Disconnect the shockabsorber lower retaining bolts, and also the
'U' bolts locating the axle to the leaf springs.
6   Get an assistant to steady the axle unit and undo and remove the
shackle bolt from each leaf spring at the rear and lower the springs.
Lower the trolley jack under the axle and withdraw it to the rear of the
vehicle, complete with axle. Take care not to damage the brake pipes.
7   Installation of the axle is a direct reversal of removal but be sure
to bleed the brakes and readjust the parking brake if necessary. Also
tighten all nuts and bolts to the specified torques, and top up the axle
oil level if drained.

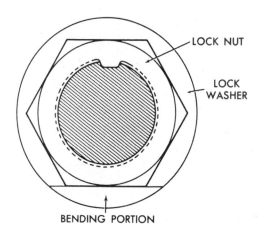

LOCK NUT

LOCK
WASHER

BENDING PORTION

Fig. 8.5. Bend the lock washer opposite the tab

Fig. 8.6. The leaf spring clip and cable

Fig. 8.7. The brake hose and retaining bracket

6   Fault diagnosis - rear axle

Symptom	Reason
Vibration	Worn axle shaft bearing. Loose bolts (driveshaft to companion flange). Wheels require balancing. Driveshaft out of balance.
Noise on turns	Worn differential gear.
Noise on drive or coasting*	Worn or incorrectly adjusted ring and pinion gear.
'Clunk' on accleration or deceleration	Worn differential gear cross shaft. Worn driveshaft universal joints. Loose bolts (driveshaft to companion flange).

*It must be appreciated that tire noise, wear in the rear suspension bushes and worn or loose shock absorber mountings can all mislead the mechanic into thinking that components of the rear axle are the source of trouble.

Chapter 9 Braking system

Contents

Bleeding the hydraulic system 5	Fault diagnosis 21
Brake adjustments 2	Front brake shoes (Series 1 to 4) - inspection, removal and
Brake/clutch pedal - removal and installation 18	installation 10
Brake disc/hub - removal, inspection and installation ... 13	Front disc brake shoe and lining (Series 5 and 6) - removal,
Brake hoses - inspection, removal and installation 9	inspection and installation 11
Brake master cylinder (single) - dismantling and reassembly ... 8	General description 1
Brake master cylinder (single and tandem) - removal and	Parking brake - adjustment 4
installation 6	Parking brake - removal and installation 19
Brake master cylinder (tandem) - dismantling and reassembly ... 7	Parking brake cables - removal and installation 20
Brake pedal - adjustment 3	Power cylinder - dismantling, inspection and reassembly 17
Brake wheel cylinders - removal, servicing and installation ... 15	Power cylinder - removal and installation 16
Disc brake caliper - overhaul 12	Rear brake shoes - inspection, removal and installation 14

Specifications

Type	Hydraulic, duo servo assisted
Front	
Series 1 to 4	Two leading shoe drum brake
Series 5 and 6	Disc type
Rear	Duo servo type
Parking brake	Rear wheels only - cable operated by hand
Brake drum inside dia.	
Front	10.000 in
Rear	10.000 in
Maximum refinish diameter	10.059 in
Replacement diameter	10.079 in
Brake lining replacement thickness	0.059 in
Wheel cylinder	
Bore diameter front	1.06 in
Bore diameter rear	0.75 in
Maximum piston to bore - clearance	0.006 in
Master cylinder	
Bore diameter	0.875 in
Maximum piston/bore clearance	0.006 in

Series 5 and 6 models specifications are as per above information but for the following items

Front brakes	
Maximum disc run out	0.005 in
Disc rotor thickness (standard)	0.709 in
Minimum refinish thickness	0.653 in
Front disc lining replacement thickness	0.067 in (Series 5) 0.236 in (Series 6)
Rear brakes	
Wheel cylinder bore diameter	1.25 in
Maximum piston to bore clearance	0.006 in

Torque wrench settings

	Series 1 to 4 lb/ft (kg fm)	Series 5 and 6 lb/ft (kg fm)
Flange plate to steering knuckle		
large bolt	55 (7.6)	
small bolt	35 (4.8)	
Flange plate to axle housing	55 (7.6)	55 (7.6)
Wheel cylinder - front		
large bolt	16 (2.2)	10 (1.3)
small bolt	10 (1.3)	10 (1.3)
Brake pipe nuts	12 (1.6)	12 (1.6)
Flexible hose nuts	12 (1.6)	12 (1.6)
Flexible hose bracket nuts	35 (4.8)	35 (4.8)
Master cylinder		
end plug	90 (12.4)	90 (12.4)
two way connector bolt	35 (4.8)	35 (4.8)
fluid reservoir clamp	30 (4.1)	30 (4.1)
mounting nuts	10 (1.3)	10(1.3)
brake lines to connector	12 (1.6)	12 (1.6)
stopper bolt	14 (1.9)	14 (1.9)
master cylinder bracket bolts	10 (1.3)	10 (1.3)
Power cylinder		
master cylinder flange to power cylinder	10 (1.3)	10 (1.3)
dash panel stud nuts	10 (1.3)	10 (1.3)
Connector to caliper		64 (8.8)
Bleeder to caliper		7 (0.9)
Rotor to hub		36 (4.9)
Support to adaptor		64 (8.8)

1 General description

Series 1 to 4

The braking system employed on all Series 1 to 4 vehicles consist of vacuum-hydraulic self-adjusting type drum brakes. The front drum brakes are of the twin leading shoe type where the front cylinder operates the lower shoe and the rear cylinder the upper shoe.

The rear drum brakes have a single cylinder operating the primary and secondary shoes. All shoe linings are the molded type bonded to the shoes and on the rear brakes the primary shoe lining is smaller than the secondary.

Self-adjusting brakes are fitted all round, the front brakes being adjusted on forward braking movements whilst the rears are taken up on reverse braking.

The master cylinder fitted to Series 1 models is a single acting type and is power assisted by vacuum.

On Series 2 onwards, the master cylinder is of the double-acting type having two separate master cylinder reservoirs and incorporates a primary and secondary piston. These operate the front and rear brakes simultaneously, but through separate circuits so that in the event of a failure in one circuit the other will still operate but with reduced braking efficiency.

The parking brake (handbrake) is operated by a hand controlled lever mounted to the dash on the right of the steering column and is locked on by means of a ratchet. The L-handled lever operates the interconnecting cables between the rear brakes and equalized unit by means of a front cable. The equalized unit is adjustable if required.

Series 5 and 6 models

Although the braking system on the Series 5 and 6 models is basically the same as the earlier series, the front brakes are now disc type, incorporating a single operating piston which actuates both inner and outer shoes. These are also self-adjusting.

With self-adjusting brakes all round, the maintenance requirements for the brake system is reduced considerably, but should never be neglected. The periodic maintenance and inspection tasks, as described in the maintenance section at the front of the book, must therefore be strictly followed.

2 Brake adjustments

1 Normally, adjustment of the brakes is not necessary as they are self-adjusting. However, after the brake linings have been renewed or the adjuster position altered, an initial adjustment can be made as follows.

2 With the car raised on a hoist and the road wheel removed, use the brake drum as an adjusting gauge, and adjust the upper and lower shoes by an equal number of notches so that the brake drum is slightly dragging against the brake linings.

3 On the front brakes, the upper and lower shoes are then retracted by two notches. On the rear brakes, turn the stave wheel 1¼ turns to retract the shoes.

4 Refit the drum to flange retaining screws.

5 Refit the roadwheels and lower the vehicle and remove the hoist. Refit the flange plate access plugs on the front.

6 The final adjustment is made by driving the vehicle in forward and reverse directions and applying the brakes firmly until the correct brake height is attained.

3 Brake pedal - adjustment

1 Disconnect the ground cable from the battery.

Series 1

2 Withdraw the cotter pin from the pushrod clevis pin and remove the clevis pin. Ensure that the brake pedal and return spring are connected.

3 Measure the distance from the floor pan to the surface of the foot pedal pad as shown in Fig. 9.2. The pedal must be fully released.

4 The correct distance requirement is 6.3 to 6.7 inches. If adjustment is required proceed as follows.

5 Detach the wiring harness from the stop light switch, and slacken the stop lamp switch locking nut. Rotate the switch to obtain the correct pedal height, and then retighten the switch locknut (photo).

6 Slacken the locknut on the pushrod clevis and turn the clevis on the rod until the clevis pin can be refitted. Check that the pedal does not bind and then insert the clevis pin and cotter pin. Note that the pin must not be forced in while depressing the pedal.

7 Securely tighten the clevis locknut, and reconnect the ground cable to the battery.

Series 2 to 6 models

Detach the battery ground cable and then proceed as follows.

8 The correct distance requirement is 5.9 to 6.3 inches. If adjustment is required, detach the stop light switch wiring harness and then remove the switch locknut. Rotate the switch counterclockwise to detach the switch from the bracket.

9 Slacken the pushrod locking nut and adjust the pedal to the

Fig. 9.1. General layout of the hydraulic circuit

VIEW B

VIEW C

VIEW A

STOP LAMP
SWITCH

LOCK NUTS

0.02—0.04 IN

PUSH ROD

90°

TOE PAN

5.9—6.3 IN

Fig. 9.2. Sectional view of the brake pedal adjustment and check points

3.5 The clutch and brake pedal (Series 1) layout, showing the pushrod clevises, return springs and switches

Fig. 9.3. The parking brake equalizer unit

Fig. 9.4. The hydraulic fluid full and minimum level in the dual master cylinder reservoirs

Fig. 9.5. Bleeding a rear wheel circuit

necessary height by rotating the pushrod accordingly. Retighten the pushrod locking nut when the height has been reached.

10 Refit the stop lamp switch and adjust the switch housing (not the pin) to brake pedal tab clearance which should be 0.02 to 0.04 in. Tighten the switch locknut to secure.

11 Reconnect the wiring and the ground cable.

4   Parking brake - adjustment

1   Raise the rear of the vehicle on a hoist and place chocks under the front wheels.

2   Fully release the parking brake and then re-apply it by two notches.

3   Refer to Fig. 9.3. Slacken the equalizer check nut and adjust the front jam nut by loosening or tightening to obtain a moderate drag when the rear wheels are turned frontwards.

4   Securely retighten the nuts, holding the front nut whilst tightening the jam nut.

5   Release the parking brake fully and rotate the rear wheels to check that they do not drag. Re-apply the parking brake and lower the vehicle and remove the hoist.

5   Bleeding the hydraulic system

1   In order that the hydraulic braking circuit is fully operational, it is essential that all air is removed from the system. This is necessary whenever any part of the circuit has been disconnected or when air may have entered the system.

2   Commence by checking the fluid level in the reservoir and top up to the level mark if necessary. Refit the cap. Ensure that the vent hole in the reservoir cap is clear, and clean any dirt from the master cylinder.

3   Check all brake line unions and connections for seepage, and check the flexible hoses for signs of cracking or perishing.

4   If any of the wheel cylinders condition is suspect, check for signs of leakage.

5   It is most important that the engine is running during the bleeding operation in order to prevent any damage to the pushrod seal. The exhaust system must be suitably ventilated if performing the operation inside.

6   Ensure that a supply of clean non-aerated brake fluid of the correct specification is to hand in order to replenish the reservoir during the bleeding process. It is essential to have someone available to help, as one person has to pump the brake pedal while the other attends to each wheel. The reservoir level has also to be continuously watched and replenished. Fluid bled out should not be re-used. A clean glass jar and a suitable length of rubber or plastic tube that will fit tightly over the bleed nipple are also required.

7   Make sure the bleed nipple is clean and put a small quantity of fluid in the bottom of the jar. Fit the tube onto the nipple and place the other end in the jar under the surface of the liquid. Keep it under the surface throughout the bleeding operation.

8   Loosen the bleed nipple, push the pedal down slowly thru its full travel then close the nipple and release the pedal. Repeat this operation until air ceases to flow from the bleed tube then finally tighten the nipple whilst the pedal is held depressed.

9   Remember to check the reservoir level then repeat this procedure for the next appropriate wheel cylinder. On completion, ensure that the fluid is between the 'Max' and 'Min' levels on the reservoir wall.

6   Brake master cylinder (single and tandem) - removal and installation

1   Detach the ground cable from the battery.

2   Clean the exterior of the master cylinder (photo) and connecting lines and as a precaution to protect the surrounding body paint, place a sheet of paper or piece of cloth beneath the master cylinder to soak up any spillage of fluid.

3   Remove the reservoir caps and filters and extract the hydraulic fluid.

4   Carefully detach the hydraulic lines from the master cylinder connectors and plug the lines to prevent spillage of fluid and the ingress of dirt.

5   Remove the master cylinder retaining bolts and also the power

Fig. 9.6. The hydraulic lines to the dual master cylinder connections

6.2 Clean the master cylinder and pipe connections prior to removal

cylinder attachment nuts and lockwashers. Remove the master cylinder unit from the car taking care not to spill fluid onto the paintwork.

6   Installation is the reverse of the removal procedure. After topping up the reservoirs, bleed the master cylinder and brake system as described in Section 5.

---

7   Brake master cylinder (tandem) - dismantling and reassembly

1   Dismantle the components of the master cylinder on a clean work surface and lay the parts out in the order of dismantling.
2   Remove the reservoir caps and filters. Drain any remaining fluid from the reservoirs.
3   Locate the master cylinder in a vise which has soft jaws fitted but do not overtighten the jaws. Slacken the reservoir clamp screws and remove the reservoirs from the cylinder body.
4   Unscrew the connector bolt and remove the connector and gaskets from the rear outlet of the cylinder (front system).
5   Unscrew the end plug and remove with the gasket, check valve, return spring and spring seat.
6   Unscrew the connector and remove with the gasket, check valve, return spring and spring seat from the front outlet of the master cylinder (rear system).
7   Press the primary piston fully into the cylinder bore and then unscrew the stopper bolt and remove with the gasket from the right-hand side of the cylinder.
8   With a pair of snap-ring pliers extract the primary piston snap-ring from the cylinder and then withdraw the primary and secondary piston units from the cylinder. Make a special note of which way round they are installed.
9   Remove the seals and again note which way they are located.
10 Clean all parts thoroughly in clean brake fluid. Do not use gasoline, kerosene or any other type of solvent. After drying the items with a lint free cloth, inspect the seals for signs of distortion, swelling, splitting, or hardening although it is normal practice and also recommended that new seals are always fitted after dismantling.
11 Inspect the bore and piston for signs of deep scoring which, if evident, means a new cylinder should be fitted. Ensure that the cylinder bore parts are clean.
12 As the respective parts are fitted to the cylinder bore ensure that they are thoroughly lubricated with clean hydraulic fluid of the specified type.
13 Install the new seals to the pistons making sure that they are fitted the correct way round as noted during dismantling.
14 Take care not to scratch the piston cups when fitting the secondary and primary piston units. If damaged they must be renewed.
15 Tighten the piston stopper bolt and the connector bolt to the specified torque.

Fig. 9.7. The dual master cylinder component parts

1	Master cylinder	15	Stopper bolt
2	Primary piston	16	Gasket
3	Secondary	17	Reservoir
4	Check valve	18	Filter
5	End plug	19	Clamp
6	Connector bolt	20	Filler cap
7	Connector	21	Plate
8	Gasket	22	Gasket
9	Check valve	23	Nut
10	Connector	24	Spring washer
11	Return spring	25	Bracket
12	Spring seat	26	Bolt
13	Gasket	27	Spring washer
14	Snap ring	28	Washer

8   Brake master cylinder (single) - dismantling and reassembly

1   The basic procedures given in the previous Section are applicable to single master cylinders. Ensure that the new secondary and primary seals are located in their piston grooves with the flared faces inwards. Install the connecting bolt and fluid reservoir to the cylinder and tighten to the specified torque.

9   Brake hoses - inspection, removal and installation

1   Inspect the condition of the flexible hydraulic hoses. If they are swollen, damaged or chafed they must be renewed.
2   Wipe the top of the brake master cylinder reservoir and unscrew the cap. Place a piece of polythene sheet over the top of the reservoir and install the cap. This is to stop hydraulic fluid syphoning out during subsequent operations. Note that tandem master cylinders have two reservoirs but it is not necessary to cover both cylinders unless both front and rear hoses are being removed.

Front brake hose
3   First jack-up the vehicle to take the weight off the suspension. To remove the hose, wipe the unions and bracket free of dust, and undo the union nut from the metal pipe end.
4   Withdraw the metal clip securing the hose to the bracket and detach the hose from the bracket. Unscrew the hose from the wheel cylinder.
5   Installation is the reverse of the removal procedure but ensure that the hose is connected at the wheel cylinder end first, with the wheels in the 'straight-ahead' position. On completion, the front brakes must be bled of air, as described in the previous Section.

Rear brake hose
6   To remove a rear flexible hose, wipe the unions, bracket and three way adaptor free of dust, and undo the union nut from the metal pipe end.
7   Withdraw the metal clip securing the hose to the bracket and detach the hose from the bracket. Unscrew the hose from the three-way adaptor.
8   Installation is the reverse of the removal procedure. Ensure that the hose is connected at the three-way adaptor end first, and on completion bleed the rear brakes.

10   Front brake shoes (Series 1 to 4) - inspection, removal and installation

1   Apply the parking brake and raise the front end of the vehicle. Remove the roadwheel.

2   Unscrew the brake drum retaining screws (photo) and withdraw the brake drum. If it proves difficult to remove the drum, disconnect the rubber hole plugs from the flange plate and insert a screwdriver thru the flange hole and locate in the hole in the brake shoe, refer to Fig. 9.8. Lift the end of the brake shoe return spring, freeing it from the serration and move the brake shoe towards the wheel cylinder.
3   Before removing the drum, mark the relative position to the hub to ensure correct reinstallation. With the drum removed do not depress the brake pedal.
4   Inspect the linings for excessive wear or shoe damage, and contamination from brake fluid or hub grease. Brake linings which are worn down to within 0.059 in of the shoes should be renewed. Shoes which are impregnated with oil or grease should be renewed as it is not very satisfactory to use proprietary solvents which tend to clean the surface but then allow the deposits which have soaked into the linings to come to the surface and form a glazed film.
5   At this stage, also inspect the condition of the drum. If the drum diameter exceeds that specified, or is heavily scored, a replacement item must be installed. If it is necessary to remove the brake shoes proceed as follows.
6   With a pair of pliers, detach the wheel cylinder piston springs (photo) from the shoes and pistons.
7   The hold down spring retainers are now pressed down and turned thru 90°, again using a pair of pliers, so that the springs and retainers can be removed (Fig. 9.9).
8   The upper and lower brake shoes can now be removed and if they are to be refitted, they should be marked so that they are reinstalled in their correct locations.
9   If the self-adjusting retainer, spring, washer pin and adjuster lever are to be removed from the brake shoe, an arbor press will be needed to depress the spring retainers. Hold the retainer and rotate the shoe thru 90° to separate.
10   To prevent the pistons coming out of the wheel cylinders during cleaning and inspection, rubber bands can be used to hold them in place.
11   Any grease or dirt retaining on the backing plate can now be removed using gasoline or other proprietary solvents. Dry off afterwards with a lint free cloth.
12   Inspect the flange plate and securing bolts to ensure that they are tight. Check the return springs for distortion, and weakness. Renew any suspect or damaged parts.
13   Reassemble the self-adjusting retainer and adjusting lever to the brake shoe in the reverse manner of removal. Ensure that the pin end of the spring is located in the retainer groove. Fit the washer with its lining side towards the lever The right- and left-hand adjuster levers are not interchangeable so be sure to fit them to their respective sides.
14   The brake shoe contact surfaces to flange plate must be lubricated with Delco Brake Lube 5450032 or an equivalent and also the wheel cylinder contact faces, see Fig. 9.10 before assembly.

10.2 The brake drum retaining screw

Fig. 9.8. The brake shoe and wheel cylinder assembly

Fig. 9.9. Press and turn the spring retainers to remove

Fig. 9.10. Arrows point to the lubrication points

Piston spring

Return spring

10.6 Remove the piston spring and brake shoe return spring

UPPER SHOE

ADJUSTER SPRING AND RETAINERS

PISTON SPRING

ADJUSTER PLATE

WHEEL CYLINDER

SHOE PULL-BACK SPRING

LOWER SHOE

SHOE HOLD-DOWN SPRING

Fig. 9.11. General view of the brake assembly on refitting

Fig. 9.12. Withdraw the caliper stops

Fig. 9.13. Remove the caliper

15 Hook the right- and left-hand return springs to their respective
brake shoes - they are not interchangeable. The left-hand side springs
are colored light blue, the right-hand side black.
16 Engage the grooved section of the adjuster lever to the guide pin
and then relocate the brake shoes into position. The shoes must be
correctly fitted to the guide pin. If the brake shoe end is not located
in the groove the shoes have lifted off of the ridged section. Check that
the return spring is correctly located to the adjuster lever.
17 Using a pair of pliers, refit the piston springs.
18 Relocate the shoe hold down springs and retainers. Compress the
spring with a pair of pliers and twist the retainer thru 90°, ensuring
that the pin end is correctly seated in the retainer groove.
19 Refit the brake drum and readjust the brakes as described in
Section 2.

Fig. 9.14. Remove the shoe and lining

11 Front disc brake, shoes and lining (Series 5 and 6) - removal, inspection and installation

1   Raise the vehicle on a hoist at the front and chock the rear wheels.
2   Remove the roadwheels.
3   With a pair of pliers extract the clip pins from the caliper stops and
then withdraw the stops (Fig. 9.12).
4   Withdraw the caliper from the support as in Fig. 9.13 and then
remove the stop plates from the caliper. Taking care not to distort or
damage the flexible brake hose, suspend the caliper unit from the
main frame or upper link using a piece of nylon cord or similar.
5   The respective shoe and lining assemblies with shims can now be
detached (Fig. 9.14). If they are to be refitted, they must be marked
so that they are refitted in their original location.
6   Clean off the respective components with a soft dry brush and
inspect for wear and distortion.
7   The anti rattle springs, stop pins, caliper, support and adaptors
must all be in good condition, if not, they must be renewed as
necessary. Check the disc for run-out and if badly scored or cracked
this must also be renewed.
8   The brake shoes and linings must be renewed when the lining is
worn to 0.039 in (approx) thickness over the shoe table. The shoes and
linings are renewed as sets.
9   Check the inner caliper for signs of leakage. The caliper seal must
be in good condition and free of cracks, swelling or distortion. Never
use compressed air to clean the inner caliper.
10 Installation is a reversal of the removal instructions but the following points must be adhered to. When fitting the shims and stop plates,
lubricate them with Delco Brake Lube 5450032 or an equivalent. This
should also be applied to the new stop plates when fitted to the caliper
sliding portion as shown in Fig. 9.15.
    When fitting the linings to the support the wear indicated must be
located to the lower side of the support.

Fig. 9.15. Lubricate the stop plates

12 Disc brake caliper - removal, overhaul and installation

1   Follow instructions 1, 2 and 3 in the previous Section.
2   Wipe clean the flexible hose connections between the caliper and
brake line. Undo the front flexible hose connection and disconnect it
from the brake line. Plug the end of the line to prevent spillage of
fluid and the ingress of dirt.
3   Disconnect the caliper unit from the support and remove the stop
plates from the caliper.
4   Unscrew and remove the flexible hose connection from the caliper.
5   With a small screwdriver, prise the dust seal from the caliper - see
Fig. 9.16.
6   Remove the piston from the caliper by applying compressed air
into the flexible hose connection. Do not catch the piston by hand,
but place a suitable block of wood into the caliper to check it on exit.
7   Detach and discard the piston square ring seal.
8   Clean all components in clean brake fluid and blow dry with
compressed air. Check the cylinder bore and pistons for signs of wear,
corrosion or surface defects such as scoring and renew if necessary.
9   The dust seal and piston seal must always be renewed when the
caliper is dismantled.
10 To reassemble the caliper, lubricate the caliper bore and the piston
square ring seal with Delco Silicone Lube 5459912 or an equivalent
before inserting the piston seal into the bore.

Fig. 9.16. Remove the dust seal

11 Carefully insert the piston into the caliper unit (Fig. 9.17) using only finger pressure.

12 Apply Delco Silicone Lube 5459912 or an equivalent to the piston and then fit the dust seal to the piston and caliper. Insert the seal ring into the dust seal, and then refit the flexible hose to the caliper together with new gaskets.

13 Smear the stop plates and sliding surfaces of the caliper with Delco Brake Lube 5450032 or an equivalent and insert the stop plates into the caliper. Now refit the caliper, stops and new stop pins.

14 Reconnect the flexible brake hose to the brake line, with the identification stripe in a straight line. The hose should be clear of any interference during the full movement of the steering and suspension components.

15 Refit the roadwheel and then bleed the brake system, topping up the master cylinder to replace any loss, as described in Section 5.

13 Brake disc/hub - removal, inspection and installation

1 Remove and suspend the caliper unit as described in Section 11, paragraphs 1 to 4.

2 Prise the hub grease cap free using a screwdriver and withdraw the cotter pin, spindle nut retainer and nut. The hub and disc rotor assembly can now be lifted clear. Take care not to drop the wheel bearings.

3 Clean off the component parts including the dust shield and adaptor. Inspect the disc and hub for signs of wear, cracks or score marks. The hub and disc are replaced as a unit if they are in need of renewal. The dust shield and adaptor must also be renewed if they are damaged. To remove them, unscrew the attachment bolts and detach them from the steering knuckle (Fig. 9.18).

4 Installation of the dust shield and adaptor, and the disc/hub and caliper assemblies is a direct reversal of the removal procedure, but note the following:

   a) Tighten all bolts to the specified torque settings.
   b) When the caliper has been refitted and the brake line reconnected, top up the master cylinder and bleed the brakes as described in Section 5.

14 Rear brake shoes - inspection, removal and installation

1 Raise the rear of the vehicle on a hoist and chock the front wheels. Remove the rear wheels.

2 Slacken off the parking brake equaliser check nuts to release the brake cable tension.

3 Unscrew the brake drum retaining screws and remove the drum/s. If the drums are held by the shoes, detach the rubber hole plugs in the flange plate and retract the brake shoes by inserting a screwdriver and turning the self-adjuster. Mark the drum location to hub, to ensure correct refitting position. Do not press the brake pedal whilst the drums are removed.

Fig. 9.17. Insert the piston using only finger pressure

Fig. 9.18. Method of removing the dust shield and adaptor

Fig. 9.19. The rear brake layout

Fig. 9.20. The front wheel cylinder components

Fig. 9.21. The rear wheel cylinder components

14.5 The pull back springs on anchor pin

14.7 Detach the spring from the adjuster lever

14.16 Locate the cable over the anchor pin and round the guide

Fig. 9.22. The power cylinder component parts

1	Vacuum check valve	14	Silencer
2	Grommet	15	Silencer retainer
3	Seal retainer	16	Bearing retainer
4	Front shell seal	17	Bearing
5	Front shell	18	Rear shell seal
6	Power piston return spring	19	Rear shell
7	Piston rod	20	Washer
8	Reaction disc	21	Lock washer
9	Power piston	22	Nut
10	Diaphragm	23	Air filter
11	Push rod retainer plate	24	Push rod boot
12	Push rod assembly	25	Clevis locknut
13	Silencer	26	Clevis

Fig. 9.23. Using special tool No. J - 9504 to dismantle the power cylinder

4   The brake shoes and associate components can now be wiped clean and inspected as detailed in Section 10, paragraphs 4 and 5. If the shoes are to be removed, proceed as follows.

5   Unhook the brake pull-back springs from the anchor pin (photo) and detach the springs.

6   With a pair of pliers, remove the brake shoe hold down springs. Press in the spring retainer and twist it thru 90° to align the slot with the flanged end of the pin.

7   The self-adjuster cable is removed by detaching the spring from the adjuster lever (photo) and the cable end from the anchor pin.

8   Withdraw the adjuster lever and the hold down wire from the brake shoe pivot. Detach the brake shoes from the wheel cylinder pushrods and then separate the respective brake shoes, the adjuster, return spring and parking brake strut units. If the brake shoes are to be refitted, note and mark their respective locations so that they may be reinstalled into their original locations.

9   The parking brake lever and rear cable can now be disconnected and the parking brake lever detached from the secondary shoe by removing the dip and washer.

10 Having removed the self-adjuster cable check it for damage or elongation and renew it if necessary. Additionally inspect the parking brake cable, lever and strut and if worn or defective renew them.

11 Commence installation by lubricating the parking brake cable with Delco Brake Lube 5450032 or an equivalent.

12 Refit the parking brake lever to the secondary shoe and then connect the parking brake cable to its lever.

13 Locate the brake shoes together and place the adjuster screw into position. The adjuster assembly must be installed with the star wheel closer to the secondary shoe.

14 Refit the parking brake strut with the spring on the primary shoe end and refit the brake shoes to the wheel cylinder pushrods.

15 With a pair of pliers, relocate the brake shoe hold down springs. Press the springs and retainers and twist thru 90° to locate.

16 Fit the guide plate to the anchor pin, and reassemble the self-adjuster lever and lever hold down wire to the pivot pin in the secondary pin. Locate the adjuster cable over the anchor pin (photo) and run the cable round the shoe shield (guide). Attach the spring to the opposing end of the adjuster lever.
17 Using pliers, refit the pull-back springs: Lubricate the brake shoe contact surfaces with Delco Brake Lube 5450032 or an equivalent by prising the shoes from the flange plate.
18 Check that the actuator lever operates correctly by hand operating the self-adjustment.
19 Adjust the brakes as specified in Sections 2 and 4 prior to using the vehicle on the road.

15 Brake wheel cylinders - removal, servicing and installation

1   Raise the vehicle with a hoist and remove the roadwheel and brake drum. Mark the drum location to the hub for refitting.
2   Detach the hydraulic brake line connection from the wheel cylinder. Plug the end of the line to prevent spillage of fluid and the ingress of dirt.
3   Disconnect the brake pull-back springs using a pair of pliers.
4   Remove the wheel cylinder to flange plate retaining screws.
5   Disconnect the brake cylinder pushrod from the shoes and withdraw the cylinder.
6   Detach the boot/s from the ends of the wheel cylinder, and withdraw the piston/s and cup/s.
7   Using clean brake fluid, clean the wheel cylinder components. Do not use gasoline, kerosene or any other type of cleaning solvent, as they are detrimental to rubber.
8   Inspect the components carefully and if the cylinder bore/or piston scored or corroded, they will have to be renewed. The rubber cups and boots must always be renewed irrespective of their condition.
9   Assemble by first lubricating the cylinder bore with clean brake fluid. As each component is assembled they should be lubricated in a similar fashion.

Front wheel cylinders
10 On the front wheel cylinders insert the piston assembly into the cylinder taking great care not to distort or damage the boot.

Rear wheel cylinders
11 On the rear cylinders install the spring expander into the cylinder bore. Fit the new cups with their flat face towards the outer cylinder ends. They must be wiped clean before assembly with a lint free cloth. Insert the new pistons into the cylinder with the flat face to the cylinder center.
12 Fit the rubber boots onto the cylinder.
13 Locate the wheel cylinder to the brake flange plate and secure it with screws tightened to the recommended torque.
14 Refit the pushrods and the pull-back springs. Unplug the hydraulic hose and reconnect it to the cylinder. Tighten to the specified torque wrench figure.
15 Refit the brake pull-back springs, the drum and wheel.
16 Bleed the brake system as described in Section 5. Lower the vehicle and remove the hoist.

16 Power cylinder - removal and installation

1   Remove the master cylinder as described in Section 6 but leave attached to the power cylinder.
2   Slacken the vacuum line damp screw from the check valve, and then unscrew the clip to sender skirt retaining screws. Move the vacuum line out of the way.
3   Detach the brake pedal return spring, and withdraw the cotter pin and washer from the pushrod clevis to brake pedal pin. Extract the pin.
4   Unscrew the power cylinder to dash panel nuts and remove with lockwashers and washers. The master cylinder and power cylinder can now be carefully removed as a unit from the vehicle.
5   Drain off any remaining fluid from the master cylinder reservoirs.
6   The master cylinder to power cylinder retaining nuts and washers can now be removed and the two components detached.
7   Installation is the reverse procedure of removal. On refitting, top up the master cylinder fluid level and bleed the system. Check and adjust the brake pedal travel as described in Section 3.

17 Power cylinder - dismantling, inspection and reassembly

1   Prior to dismantling the power unit, refer to Fig. 9.23 and 9.25, which show the special tool, Spanner Wrench J-9504, which is required to dismantle the unit. If this is available, proceed as follows.
2   Clean the outside of the power unit thoroughly before dismantling. It is of utmost importance that cleanliness be a prime factor during the overhaul.
3   Mark the relative positions of the front and rear shell units for correct alignment on reassembly.
4   Locate the master cylinder flange in a vise but do not overtighten. The power cylinder must be facing upwards.
5   Slacken the pushrod clevis locknut and remove the clevis and locknut.
6   Detach the pushrod boot.
7   Locate the special spanner wrench J-9504 over the rear shell studs and press downwards whilst unscrewing (the rear shell is under spring pressure). Remove the rear shell and also the piston rod, power piston and return spring and retainer, refer to Fig. 9.22.
8   Unscrew and remove the master cylinder to power cylinder retaining nuts/washer. Discard the gasket on separating the two units.
9   Prise the air silencer retainer from the power piston and detach the air silencer and idler.
10 Carefully remove the rubber diaphragm from the piston.
11 Turn the piston so that the pushrod retainer slot position is down, then press the pushrod and let the retainer fall out of the piston. Withdraw the pushrod assembly and the reaction disc. Do not dismantle the pushrod unit. If on inspection it is found to be defective, renew it as a unit.
12 Inspect the rear seal and if defective prise it out of the retainer using a small screwdriver, and then withdraw the spacer and seal assembly.

Fig. 9.24. Set the retainer to the depth shown

Fig. 9.25. Use special gauge J - 24568 to check the piston adjustment

2½"

NO. 16 U.S.S.
GAUGE SHEET
STEEL

2"

.729"
.736"

5/8"   1¼"

Fig. 9.26. If a height gauge is not readily available, it can be made from dimensions shown

BRAKE
MASTER
CYLINDER

CLUTCH AND
BRAKE PEDAL
SUPPORT

CLUTCH
CYLINDER

RETURN
SPRING

BRAKE
PEDAL

CLUTCH
PEDAL

PADS

Fig. 9.27. The clutch and brake pedal layout

PARKING BRAKE
SWITCH BRACKET

HANDLE
ASSEMBLY

EQUALIZER
RETURN SPRING

CABLE
COVER

PULLEY

FRONT
CABLE

CABLE
LEVER

INTERMEDIATE
CABLE

PARKING
BRAKE SWITCH

EQUALIZER
LEVER

EQUALIZER
ADJUSTING BOLT

REAR
CABLE

Fig. 9.28. The parking brake layout

20.7 The equalizer lever and return spring

13 Inspect the front seal and, if defective, similarly prise it out with a small screwdriver and renew it.

14 If defective, the vacuum check valve can be removed by rotating it backwards and forwards. Remove the grommet.

15 All metal, plastic and rubber parts of the power cylinder must be cleaned with a solution of denatured alcohol. Do not use any mineral based cleaning solvents, ie, gasoline, kerosene etc.

16 Blow out the passages and valve holes and air dry. Any rust found on the inside of the shells can be removed using a fine emery or crocus cloth. Clean out all rust and dirt particles.

17 Renew all suspect components - do not attempt to repair them.

18 Reassemble in the reverse order of dismantling but note the following:

19 The front shell seal, if removed, must be smeared with a liberal amount of Delco Silicone number 5459912 lubricant or an equivalent. The lip of the seal faces forwards.

20 Similarly, lubricate the rear shell seal. The seal is fitted with the lip facing rearwards. Set the retainer to the depth specified in Fig. 9.24.

21 A thin coat of Delco Silicone lubricant must also be applied to the piston seal and inner surface lip of the piston housing. Take care when fitting the pushrod piston not to damage the seal. Should it be damaged on assembly, the pushrod assembly must be renewed.

22 On installing the diaphragm, turn it one half of a turn to ensure that it is correctly located. Then, temporarily retain the master cylinder to the front shell with nuts and washers. Locate the flange part of the master cylinder in the vise with the front shell side upwards. Lubricate the piston rod face, the reaction disc and outer rim of the diaphragm with Delco Silicone Lubricant (No. 5459912) and refit the reaction disc in the power piston unit.

23 The rear shell, power piston, piston rod, return spring retainer and spring, and finally the rear shell can now be assembled in order. Locate the front and rear shells using the special spanner wrench used for removal, and align the relative marks. Be certain that the rear shell is locked to the front shell by all of the tabs before releasing the pressure on the special tool.

24 Relocate pushrod boot, and loosely install the pushrod clevis locknut and clevis. Remove the master cylinder from the power cylinder and locate the power cylinder in the vise so that the piston rod is up. Do not overtighten the vise.

25 Locate the special gauge J-24568 over the piston rod with its 'legs' resting on the master cylinder mounting face - see Fig. 9.25. The piston rod must touch the cutaway portion of the gauge. Adjust the piston if required by holding the rod at the serrated portion with a pair of pliers and rotate the thread at one end accordingly. The piston rod must be fully bottomed in the cylinder before adjusting. A height gauge may be made from the dimensions shown in Fig. 9.26.

18 Brake/clutch pedal - removal and installation

1 A common bolt retains both the clutch and brake pedals in the pedal support bracket. Pedal removal is as follows.

2 Detach the ground cable from the battery.

3 Detach the clutch pedal return spring from the instrument panel,

and the brake pedal return spring from the pedal.

4 Withdraw the cotter pins from the clevis pin, and remove the brake and clutch pedal clevis pins and washers.

5 Undo the pivot bolt nut and remove with the lockwasher. Withdraw the pivot bolt, and remove the pedals, bushes and plastic thrust washers.

6 Installation is the reverse procedure of removal but lubricate the bushes with Delco Brake Lube 5450032 or an equivalent before refitting the pedals. Adjust the brake light switch and clutch switch on completion.

19 Parking brake - removal and installation

1 On all Series models, detach the ground cable from the battery.

2 Remove the air cleaner from the carburetor. On Series 1 models only, detach the accelerator control rod from the dash panel.

3 Drain the cooling system and disconnect the heater hoses from the core outlet tubes in the dash panel.

4 Detach the parking brake front cable from the control lever on the right-hand side engine compartment, and then unscrew the right-hand pulley center bolt and remove it.

5 Unscrew and remove the cable cover nuts at the dash panel to remove the cover. Disconnect the windshield wiper switch from the instrument panel, and on Series 1 models the hazard warning light wiring connections from the switch. Remove the switch.

6 Unscrew the lever unit to instrument panel securing screws and detach the parking brake light switch wires from the switch. Remove the lever and front cable.

7 Installation is a direct reversal of removal. Refit the cooling system on completion and check for hose leaks at their connections. Also check the hazard warning light, brake light and parking brake warning lights on reconnecting the ground cable.

20 Parking brake cables - removal and installation

Front parking brake cable

1 Follow the instructions given in paragraphs 1 to 6 in Section 19 and disconnect the lever unit from the instrument panel.

2 Pull the assembly to the rear and lay it on the floor. Slacken the parking brake light switch bracket screw and then turn the switch and bracket thru 90°. Free the ratchet and press the handle fully in.

3 Withdraw the cotter pin and remove with washer pivot pin and pulley, then withdraw the cable.

4 To install the cable, attach it to the handle lower end and pull the handle to the rear several notches.

5 Turn the parking brake light switch and bracket back into position and tighten the retaining screw. Re-insert the pivot pin with washers and fit a new cotter pin to retain. The remaining assembly procedures are the reversal of removal.

Intermediate parking cable

6 Securely raise the vehicle on a hoist and chock the front wheels.

7 Detach the equalizer lever spring from the lever and then slacken the cable guide nut to remove the cable assembly (photo).

8 Refitting is a reversal of the above procedure; but on completion readjust the parking brake as given in Section 4.

Rear parking brake cable

9 Raise the vehicle securely at the rear on a hoist and chock the front wheels. Remove the right- and left-hand rear wheels.

10 Disconnect the rear cable retaining clamps on the right- and left-hand side. Detach the equalizer lever return spring from the lever and disconnect the equalizer adjusting bolt nut. Remove the rear cable from the adjustment bolt.

11 Remove the brake drums and shoes as described in Section 14, and detach the cable from the brake lever.

12 Using a suitable box end wrench, remove the rear cable spring as shown in Fig. 9.29.

13 Remove the cable assembly by withdrawing the cable ends from the right- and left-hand flange plates.

14 Installation is the reversal of the above procedure but on completion check and adjust the parking brake as described in Section 4.

Fig. 9.29. Removing the rear cable spring using a box end wrench

21 Fault diagnosis

Symptom	Reason/s
Pedal travels almost to floor before brakes operate	Brake fluid level too low. Wheel cylinder leaking. Master cylinder leaking (bubbles in master cylinder fluid). Brake flexible hose leaking. Brake line fractured. Brake system unions loose. Shoes linings excessively worn.
Brake pedal feels 'springy'	New linings not yet bedded-in. Brake drums badly worn or cracked. Master cylinder securing nuts loose.
Brake pedal feels 'spongy' and 'soggy'	Wheel cylinder leaking. Master cylinder leaking (bubbles in master cylinder reservoir). Brake pipe line or flexible hose leaking. Unions in brake system loose. Blocked reservoir cap vent hole.
Excessive effort required to brake vehicle	Shoe linings badly worn. New shoes recently fitted - not yet bedded-in. Harder linings fitted than standard resulting in increase in pedal pressure. Linings and brake drums contaminated with oil, grease or hydraulic fluid. Servo unit inoperative or faulty. Scored drums.
Brakes uneven and pulling to one side	Linings and drums contaminated with oil, grease or hydraulic fluid. Tire pressure unequal. Radial ply tires fitted at one end of the vehicle only. Brake shoes fitted incorrectly. Different type of linings fitted at each wheel. Anchorages for front or rear suspension loose. Brake drums badly worn, cracked or distorted. Incorrect front wheel alignment. Incorrectly adjusted front wheel bearings.
Brakes tend to bind, drag or lock-on	Air in hydraulic system. Wheel cylinders seized. Handbrake cables too tight. Weak shoe return springs. Incorrectly set foor pedal or pushrod. Master cylinder seized. Brakes over-adjusted.

Chapter 10 Electrical system

Contents

Air conditioning components 42
Alternator - dismantling, inspection, testing and reassembly ... 9
Alternator - general description, maintenance and precautions ... 6
Alternator - removal and installation 7
Alternator - testing 8
Back-up (reverse) lamps 22
Battery - charging 5
Battery - electrolyte replenishment - 4
Battery - maintenance 3
Battery - removal and installation 2
Blower motor and heater core unit - removal and replacement ... 36
Blower resistor - removal and replacement 43
Dash outlet grille - removal and refitting 41
Direction signal and dimmer switch - removal and installation ... 32
Dome (interior) lamp 23
Fault diagnosis - electrical system 45
Front combination lamps 18
Fuses 15
General description 1
Hazard warning switch - removal and installation 33
Headlamps - adjustment (beam alignment) 17
Headlamps - removal and installation 16
Heater control cable - adjustment 40

Heater controls - removal and refitting 37
Heater unit - removal and refitting 35
Heater water valve - removal and refitting 38
Horn 31
Ignition switch 26
Instrument panel - dismantling and reassembly 25
Instrument panel - removal and installation 24
Licence plate light 20
Radio equipment - removal and installation 34
Rear combination lamps 19
Regulator - description and testing 10
Regulator - removal, adjustment and installation 11
Side marker lights - front and rear 21
Starter motor - dismantling, servicing and reassembly 14
Starter motor - general description 12
Starter motor - removal and installation 13
Thermostatic switch - removal and replacement - 44
Turn signal and dimmer switch - testing 27
Ventilation air inlet valve - removal and refitting 39
Windshield washer 30
Windshield wiper motor - dismantling and inspection 29
Windshield wiper motor - removal and installation 28

Specifications

System type	12 volt, negative ground (earth)

Battery

Model	N50
Capacity	12V - 50AH

Alternator

Make	Hitachi
Drive	V-belt
Model - Series 1 to 3 models	LT 130-83
Voltage output	12V - 30A
Series 4 models	LT 135-26
Voltage output	12V - 35A
Series 5 and 6 models	LT 135-30
Voltage output	12V - 35A
Weight	8.6 lb (3.9 kg)
Rated speed	5000 rpm
Operating speed	1000 - 13500 rpm
Pulley diameter	2.756 in (70 mm)
Pulley ratio	1.96
Brushes	
Standard length	0.57 in (14.5 mm)
Minimum length	0.276 in (7.0 mm)
Brush spring tension	0.66 lb (2.9 n)

Shaft diameter	
Front	0.6 in (15 mm)
Rear	0.47 in (12 mm)
Rotor coil resistance @ 20°C (68°F)	4.3 ohm
Stator single coil resistance @ 20°C (68°F)	0.13 ohm

Regulator

Model	
Series 1 to 3 models	TL 1Z 66
Series 4 to 6 models	TL 1Z 87
Fold relay actuates voltage	5 volts
Regulated voltage	
Series 1 to 3	13.5 to 14.5 volts
Series 4 to 6	13.8 to 14.8 volts
Core gap	0.024 to 0.039 in (0.6 to 1.0 mm)
Point gap	0.012 to 0.016 in (0.3 to 0.4 mm)
Field charge relay	
Voltage coil resistance	31.9 ohms
Core gap	0.032 to 0.039 in (0.8 to 1.0 mm)
Point gap	0.016 to 0.024 in (0.4 to 0.6 mm)

Starter motor

Make	Hitachi
Model	
Series 1 to 3 models	S114 - 118
Series 4 model	S114 - 136
Series 5 and 6 models	S114 - 202
Rating	30 sec
Output	12V - 1.0 HW
Rotation direction	Clockwise from pinion side
Clutch type	Overrunning clutch
Engagement method	Magnetic shifting
Pinion activating voltage	8V or less
No load performance	
Terminal voltage	12V
Current	60A or less
Speed	600 rpm or more
Loaded performance	
Voltage (potential drop characteristics)	12V/OA - 5V/300A
Current	200A or less
Torque	3.6 ft lbs (4.9 Na)
Speed	1,100 rpm or more
Constrained	
Voltage	12V/OA - 5V/300A
Current	330A or less
Torque	5.8 ft lbs (7.8 Na) or more

Fuses

Fuse box location	Inner wing panel of engine compartment
Fuse rating	Marked on fuse box cover

Windshield wiper motor

Operating voltage	10 - 16V
Minimum operating voltage	8V
Wiper operating angle	
Driver side	90°
Passenger side	110°

Windshield washer

Rating	12V - 2.5A
Operating voltage	10 - 15V
Delivery pressure	13 psi (90 kpa)
Nozzle hole diameter	0.03 in (0.8 mm)
Tank capacity	0.4 gall (1.5 liters)

Horn

Rated voltage	12V
Rated current	3A (max)
Sound energy	105 ± 5 dB
Standard frequency	370 ± 20 H2

Bulbs

Headlamp Type 1	12V - 37.5W
Type 2	12V - 37.5/50W

Front combination lamp	12V - 23/8W
Turn signal lamp	12V - 23/8W
Clearance lamp	12V - 23/8W
Interior (dome) lamp	12V - 5W
Stop/tail lamp	12V - 23/8W
Rear turn signal lamps	12V - 23W
Back up (reverse) lamp	12V - 23W
Licence plate lamp	12V - 7.5W
Front side marker lamps	12V - 8W
Rear side marker lamps	12V - 8W
Indicator - headlamp high beam lamp	12V - 3.4W
Oil pressure indicator warning lamp	12V - 3.4W
Seat belt warning lamp	12V - 3.4W
Catalytic converter warning lamp	12V - 3.4W
Turn signal indicator lamp	12V - 3.4W
Instrument panel lamps	12V - 3.4W
Wiper illumination switch lamp	12V - 3.4W
Heater illumination switch lamp	12V - 1.3W
Ash tray lamp	12V - 3.4W
Generator indicator lamp	12V - 3.4W
Brake system warning lamp	12V - 3.4W

Heater blower motor
Series 1 models

Type	Outside and recirculating air
Voltage	12V
Blower speed	
High	3,500 rpm
Low	2,500 rpm
Blower motor loaded current	Below 7 amps (high blower)

Series 2 to 6

Type	Full time outside air
Voltage	12V
Blower speed	
High	3,800 rpm
Medium	3,400 rpm
Low	1,800 rpm
Blower motor loaded current	Below 7 amps (high blower)

1 General description

The electrical system is of 12 volt negative ground (earth) type. The major components comprise the battery, a belt-driven alternator and a pre-engaged starter motor.

The battery supplies a steady current to the ignition system (see Chapter 4), and for the operation of the electrical accessories.

The alternator maintains the charge in the battery, and the voltage regulator adjusts the charging rate according to the system demands. Silicon diodes within the alternator rectify the alternating current produced into direct current. A cut-out prevents the battery discharging when the engine is switched off or when it is running at idle speed.

2 Battery - removal and installation

1 The battery is in a special carrier fitted on the right-hand wing valance of the engine compartment. It should be removed once every three months for cleaning. Disconnect the leads from the battery terminals by slackening the clamp retaining nuts and bolts, or by unscrewing the retaining screws if terminal caps are fitted instead of clamps.

2 Unscrew the clamp bar retaining nuts, then remove the clamp. Carefully lift the battery from its carrier. Hold the battery vertical to ensure that none of the electrolyte is spilled.

3 Installation is a direct reversal of this procedure. **Note:** Install the negative lead before the positive lead and smear the terminals with petroleum jelly to prevent corrosion. **Never** use an ordinary grease as applied to other parts of the car.

3 Battery - maintenance

1 Keep the top of the battery clean by wiping away dirt and moisture.

2 Remove the plugs or lid from the cells and check that the electrolyte level is just above the separator plates. If the level has fallen, add only distilled water until the electrolyte level is just above the separator plates.

3 As well as keeping the terminals clean and covered with petroleum jelly, the top of the battery, and especially the top of the cells, should be kept clean and dry. This helps prevent corrosion and ensures that the battery does not become partially discharged by leakage through dampness and dirt.

4 Once every three months, remove the battery and inspect the battery securing bolts, the battery clamp plate, tray and battery leads for corrosion (white fluffy deposits on the metal which is brittle to touch). If any corrosion is found, clean off the deposits with an ammonia or soda solution and paint over the clean metal with a fine base primer and/or underbody paint.

5 At the same time inspect the battery case for cracks. If a crack is found, clean and plug it with one of the proprietary compounds marketed for this purpose. If leakage through the crack has been excessive then it will be necessary to refill the appropriate cell with fresh electrolyte as detailed later. Cracks are frequently caused to the top of the battery case by pouring in distilled water in the middle of winter *after* instead of *before* a run. This gives the water no chance to mix with the electrolyte and so the former freezes and splits the battery case.

6 If topping-up the battery becomes excessive and the case has been inspected for cracks that could cause leakage, but none are found, the battery is being over-charged and the voltage regulator will have to be checked and reset.

7 With the battery on the bench at the three monthly interval check, measure its specific gravity with a hydrometer to determine the state of charge and condition of the electrolyte. There should be very little variation between the different cells and if a variation in excess of 0.025 is present it will be due to either:

   a) Loss of electrolyte from the battery at some time caused by spillage or a leak, resulting in a drop in the specific gravity of

electrolyte when the deficiency was replaced with distilled water instead of fresh electrolyte.
b) *An internal short circuit caused by buckling of the plates or a similar malady pointing to the likelihood of total battery failure in the near future.*

8   Fully charged, the battery will have a specific gravity reading of approximately 1.270 at an electrolyte temperature of 80°F. For every 10°F above 80°F, add four specific gravity points (0.004) and for every 10°F below 80°F subtract four specific gravity points (-0.004).

4   Battery - electrolyte replenishment

1   If the battery is in a fully charged state and one of the cells maintains a specific gravity reading which is 0.025 or lower than the others, and a check of each cell has been made with a voltage meter to check for short circuits (a four to seven second test should give a steady reading of between 1.2 and 1.8 volts), then it is likely that electrolyte has been lost from the cell with the low reading at some time.
2   Top-up the cell with a solution of 1 part sulphuric acid to 2.5 parts of distilled or de-ionized water. If the cell is already fully topped-up draw some electrolyte out of it with a hydrometer.
3   When mixing the sulphuric acid and water **never add water to sulphuric acid** - always pour the acid slowly onto the water in a glass container. **If water is added to sulphuric acid it will explode.**
4   Continue to top-up the cell with the freshly made electrolyte and so recharge the battery and check the hydrometer readings.

5   Battery - charging

Note: If the battery is to remain in the vehicle when being charged always disconnect the battery leads.
1   In winter time when a heavy demand is placed on the battery, such as when starting from cold, and virtually all of the electrical equipment is continually in use, it is a good idea to occasionally have the battery fully charged from an external source at a rate of approximately 4 amps.
2   Continue to charge the battery at this rate until no further rise in specific gravity is noted over a four hour period.
3   Alternatively, a trickle charger, charging at the rate of 1.5 amps can be safely used overnight.
4   Special rapid 'boost' charges which are claimed to restore the power of the battery in 1 to 2 hours are not recommended unless they are thermostatically controlled as they can cause serious damage to the battery plates through overheating.

6   Alternator - general description, maintenance and precautions

1   Briefly, the alternator comprises a rotor and stator. Current is

generated in the coils of the stator as soon as the rotor revolves. This current is three-phase alternating, which is then rectified by positive and negative silicon diodes; the charging current required to maintain the battery charge is controlled by a regulator unit.
2   Maintenance consists of occasionally wiping away any oil or dirt which may have accumulated on the outside of the unit.
3   No lubrication is required as the bearings are grease-sealed for life.
4   Check the drivebelt tension periodically to ensure that its specified deflection is correctly maintained (see Chapter 2).
5   Take extreme care when making circuit connections to a vehicle fitted with an alternator and observe the following.
   When making connections to the alternator from a battery, always match correct polarity.
   Before using electric-arc welding equipment to repair any part of the vehicle, disconnect the connector from the alternator and disconnect the battery cables.
   Never start the car with the battery charger connected.
   Always disconnect both battery cables before using a mains charger.
   If boosting from another battery, always connect in parallel using heavy cable.

7   Alternator - removal and installation

1   Detach the ground cable from the battery.
2   Remove the air pump as described in Chapter 3, but do not detach the refrigerant feed lines to and from the pump.
3   Detach the alternator wires from the connector and the cable from 'A' terminal.
4   Unscrew and remove the lower alternator mounting bolts and the adjustment bracket bolts (photo).
5   Disconnect the fan belt and remove the alternator.
6   Installation is the reversal of removal but retension the fan belt as given in Chapter 2, Section 7 and the air pump belt as given in Section 41.

8   Alternator - testing

1   Testing and repair of the alternator is a job best left to your GM dealer or local auto-electrician who has the specialized knowledge and equipment necessary to undertake this task. If you have electrical knowledge and test equipment available, proceed as follows.
2   With a resistance tester, measure the rotor coil resistance across terminals 'F' and 'E' as in Fig. 10.1. The normal resistance is 5 ohms.
3   Should the resistance be higher, then there is a poor contact between the brushes and commutator. If there is no continuity between these terminals the problem is an open rotor coil circuit, a sticking brush or a broken lead wire. A lower resistance may indicate a rotor coil layer short or the circuit is being grounded.
4   Test the rectifying diodes to indicate continuity, irrespective of the diode conditions, as follows.

a) *Connect the test negative (-) lead to the alternator 'A' terminal and the positive (+) lead of the tester to the alternator 'N' terminal. If continuity exists, one or more of the three diodes in the positive side are shorting.*
b) *Connect the tester negative (-) lead to the alternator 'N' terminal and the positive (+) lead to the alternator 'E' terminal. If there is continuity one or more of the three diodes in the negative side are shorted.*

9   Alternator - dismantling, inspection, testing and reassembly

Refer to Fig. 10.2
1   Unscrew and remove the pulley locknut and washer and withdraw the pulley and fan.
2   Melt the solder on the brush lead and extract the brush holder assembly and remove the three thru bolts. Taking care, separate the rotor assembly and front cover and ensure that the stator unit is not detached from the rear cover.
3   Remove the diode cover and lift the stator coil lead clip. Melt the

Fig. 10.1. **Measuring the resistance across terminals F and E**

Fig. 10.2. The generator component parts

1	Rotor assembly	7	Brush assembly (F)
2	Spacer	8	Brush assembly (E)
3	Stator assembly	9	Brush holder assembly
4	Rear cover assembly	10	Brush holder
5	Terminal bolt assembly	11	Diode cover
6	Diode assembly	12	Terminal

13	Front cover assembly	19	Through bolt
14	Seal	20	Nut and lockwasher assembly
15	Seal retainer	21	Front ball bearing
16	Bearing retainer	22	Rear ball bearing
17	Pulley assembly w/Fan	23	Screw
18	Through bolt	24	Key

7.4 The generator showing the adjustment bracket bolt

Fig. 10.3. Separate the stator unit from the rear cover

Fig. 10.4. Measure the resistance between the slip rings

Fig. 10.5. Test the stator coil continuity

Fig. 10.6. Check the stator and insulation

solder on the lead and separate the stator unit from the rear cover (Fig. 10.3).

4   Detach the rotor from the front cover by lightly tapping the rotor shaft with a soft faced mallet. Unscrew the cover screws and remove the front bearing.

Testing the rotor

5   To check the rotor for an open circuit, measure the resistance between the slip rings as in Fig. 10.4. Normal resistance is 5 ohms. Check the rotor core and positive (+) side slip ring resistance using a 500 volt megger meter. The standard resistance is 1 megohm or above.

Test the starter coils

6   Refer to Fig. 10.5 and make a continuity test between the stator coil. If the circuit is open there will be no continuity. Refer to Fig. 10.6 and check the stator coil to core resistance with a megger meter. Normal resistance is 1 megohm or above.

Test the diodes

7   Test the resistance between the diode terminals and holder in forward and reverse directions with the tester leads switched. Normal diode resistance is nearly zero ohms in one direction and indefinitely high in the other. Equal resistance or no resistance in both directions indicates that the diode is defective and must be renewed together with the holder.

Brushes and brush holders - inspection

8   Check the brushes for excessive wear or damaged or broken leads. Check the respective brush movement in holders. Renew brush holder unit if wear has reached the limit line on brushes or they are damaged or slack in their holders.

Bearings

9   Clean and inspect the bearings. Renew the bearings if they are worn, noisy or if they are a loose fit in their respective covers, renew the covers.

10 Reassemble the alternator in the reverse order of dismantling. Take care not to damage the insulated parts during assembly and ensure that the terminals to be soldered are secure. Ensure that the insulating tubes washers and plates are clean and carefully installed.

---

10 Regulator - description and testing

---

1   The regulator is located on the right side of the engine compartment, and incorporates a separate voltage regulator and cut-out (photo).

2   The voltage regulator controls the output from the alternator depending upon the state of the battery and the demands of the vehicle electrical equipment, and it ensures that the battery is not overcharged. The cut-out is virtually an automatic switch which

Fig. 10.7. Test the resistance between the diode terminals

completes the charging circuit as soon as the alternator starts to rotate and isolates it when the engine stops so that the battery cannot be discharged through the alternator. One visual indication of the correct functioning of the cut-out is the ignition warning lamp. When the lamp is out, the system is charging.

3 Before testing, check that the alternator drivebelt is not broken or slack, and that all electrical leads are secure. Where possible test the regulator when it is cold, not immediately after driving.

4 Start the engine and run at 2,500 rpm for a few minutes and then check the ammeter reading which should be 5 amps or less. If the reading is higher fit a fully charged battery in place of the existing one and recheck the reading.

5 Run the engine at idle speed and increase gradually to 2,500 rpm and take a voltmeter reading. If normal, the reading should be within 13.8 to 14.8 volts. If the reading deviates from these figures, the regulator is in need of adjustment or defective. If adjustment is made with the regulator in position on the vehicle, disconnect the connecting leads to prevent the battery circuit from being shorted.

---

11 Regulator - removal, adjustment and installation

1 If the regulator is still under guarantee by the manufacturer it should not be disturbed, but must be reset or exchanged by the manufacturer.

2 Detach the battery ground cable from the terminal.

3 Disconnect the regulator leads taking note of their positions.

4 Unscrew the mounting screws and remove the regulator.

5 Detach the regulator cover.

6 Clean the contact points with 500 or 600 grade sand paper.

7 Refer to Fig. 10.8 and check the core gap which should be 0.024 to 0.039 in (0.60 to 0.99 mm). To adjust, loosen the screws

securing the contact set to yoke and move the set up or down as required.

8 Refer to Fig. 10.10 and check the point gap which should be between 0.012 and 0.016 in (0.30 to 0.40 mm). To adjust loosen the upper contact screw and move the contact as required.

9 Always adjust the core gap first followed by the point gap. Yoke gap adjustment is not necessary.

10 To increase the regulator voltage turn the adjustment screw inwards (Fig. 10.9). To decrease the voltage, screw it out. Lock the screw in position by tightening the locknut.

11 Refit the cover and relocate the regulator in position on the vehicle and recheck the voltage.

---

12 Starter motor - general description

1 The starter motor comprises a four-pale, four-brush direct current motor, with an ignition switch which is fitted with a safety lock. The starter motor circuit has a negative ground polarity.

2 The starter motor engagement mechanism is integral. The main switch is fitted into the magnetic switch which actuates the starter pinion. An overrun clutch is fitted to the pinion.

---

13 Starter motor - removal and installation

Series 1 to 4 models

1 Detach the ground cable from the battery.

2 Disconnect the wiring from the starter motor terminals.

3 Unscrew and remove the starter motor securing bolts/nuts and withdraw the starter motor.

Fig. 10.8. Adjusting the regulator core gap

Fig. 10.10. Adjusting the regulator point gap

Fig. 10.9. Adjusting the regulator voltage

10.1 The regulator

Fig. 10.11. The voltage regulator showing the core gap and points gap adjustment points

13.1 The starter motor

Fig. 10.12. The regulator testing circuit

Fig. 10.13. Lifting the brush spring to remove the brush

Fig. 10.14. The principle components of the starter motor

Series 5 and 6 models

4   Detach the ground cable from the battery.
5   Detach the EGR pipe from the EGR valve and exhaust manifold. Remove the EGR pipe.
6   Disconnect the wiring from the starter motor.
7   Unscrew and remove the starter motor retaining bolts, and withdraw the starter motor thru the clearance beneath the inlet manifold.
8   Installation of the starter motor is the reverse of removal.

---

14 Starter motor - dismantling, servicing and reassembly

1   Detach the lead magnetic switch terminal marked 'M'.
2   Unscrew the magnetic switch retaining bolts and remove the switch.
3   Withdraw the torsion spring from the magnetic switch.
4   Remove the dust cover and snap-ring washer.
5   Unscrew the thru bolts and the two rear cover screws and remove the rear cover.
6   Lift the brush spring and withdraw the brush and remove the brush holder assembly.
7   Withdraw the yoke from the gearcase and remove the dust cover. Withdraw the armature and shift lever.
8   Withdraw the pinion stop clip and detach the pinion stop. Remove the pinion unit.
9   Clean the respective parts ready for inspection.
10 Inspect the armature. Check the commutator face for burning or roughness. Reface the commutator with fine sand paper if required - do not use emery cloth as the fine carborundum particles will become embedded in the copper surfaces. If the commutator is very rough or out of round it may be lightly cleaned down on a lathe, but refer to the specifications for the outside diameter limits.
11 Undercut the commutator separators using an old hacksaw blade ground to suit, to a depth of 0.02 to 0.03 in (0.5 to 0.8 mm).
12 If an ohmmeter is available, test the field coil for continuity. To do this, connect one probe of the meter to the field coil positive terminal and the other to the positive brush holder. If no reading is indicated then the field coil circuit has a break in it.
13 Connect one probe of the meter to the field coil positive lead and the other one to the yoke. If there is a low resistance, then the field coil is earthed due to a breakdown in insulation. When this fault is discovered, the field coils should be renewed by an automotive electrician as it is very difficult to remove the field coil securing screws without special equipment. In any event, it will probably be more economical to exchange the complete starter motor for a reconditioned unit.
14 The armature may be tested for insulation breakdown again using the ohmmeter. To do this, place one probe on the armature shaft and the other on each of the commutator segments in turn. If there is a reading indicated at any time during the test then the armature must be renewed.
15 Check the brushes for wear. The standard brush lengths are:

Series 1 to 4 models 0.73 in (18.5 mm) - minimum limit 0.05 (12.70 mm)
Series 5 and 6 models 0.629 (16.0 mm) - minimum limit 0.47 (11.9 mm)

If the brushes are worn beyond this limit they must be renewed.
16 Inspect the drive gear components for wear or damage, particularly the pinion teeth, and renew as required.
17 Reassembly of the starter motor is a reversal of dismantling but note the following:

   a) *Grease the bearings and sliding faces before assembly.*
   b) *When the shift lever is set to the guide on the pinion, do not rotate the armature as the lever may be detached from the guide on the pinion.*
   c) *When installing the yoke align the jointing portion groove with the corresponding projection.*
   d) *Ensure that the brushes are free in their holders and do not bind or stick.*
   e) *Fit the torsion spring with the adjustment plate on the negative switch.*

Locate the shift lever end into the plunger fitting hole in the switch,

and set the torsion spring end into the groove in the intermediate part of the shift lever.

---

15 Fuses

1   A comprehensive fuse box is fitted to the inner wing panel within the engine compartment, and the fuse cover is labelled to denote the particular fuse circuit and fuse valve (photo).
2   In the event of a fuse 'blowing', always establish the cause before installing a replacement. The most likely cause is faulty insulation in the circuit.
3   Always carry a spare fuse for each rating and do not substitute a piece of wire or nail for the fuse as a fire may result or at least, the electrical component ruined.

---

16 Headlamps - removal and installation

1   Detach the headlamp rim (photo).
2   Slacken the three sealed beam unit retaining screws (photo).
3   Turn the sealed beam unit by turning it counterclockwise and withdraw.
4   Detach the wire connector (photo) to remove the sealed beam unit completely.
5   Installation is a reversal of the removal procedure but ensure that the headlamp lens is correctly located with the 'TOP' mark upwards.

---

17 Headlamp - adjustment (beam alignment)

1   Before adjusting the headlights, ensure that the tire pressures are as specified, and that the vehicle is standing on level ground and unladen.
2   Refer to Fig. 10.16 and adjust the respective screws accordingly.

Screw A adjusts the vertical alignment.
Screw B adjusts the horizontal alignment.

3   The most accurate method of checking and setting the beam alignment is by using a special optical tester as used by most garages.
4   If this equipment is not available, the vehicle should be parked approximately 32 feet (10 mm) from a vertical wall and standing level.
5   Measure the height from the ground to the center of the headlight lens and chalk a line at this height horizontally across the wall in line with the vehicle.
6   Measure the distance between the headlight centers and correspondingly mark these on the wall dissecting the horizontal line.
7   Switch the headlights on and adjust each light beam to the corresponding mark on the wall.

Fig. 10.15. The rotor insulator undercut

15.1 The fuse box and cover indicating the various circuits and valves

16.1 Remove the headlamp rim

16.2 Loosen the sealed beam unit retaining screws

16.4 Detach the wire connector

18.1 The front combination lamp with lens removed

19.1 The Series 1 model rear light lens removed

18 Front combination lamps

Bulb renewal
1   Remove the two screws retaining the lamp lens, and remove the lens (photo).
2   Press and turn the bulb to remove it from its socket.
3   Install the new bulb and ensure that it is correctly located.
4   Refit the lens and retaining screws.

Lamp removal and installation
5   Undo and remove the lamp housing to front bumper retaining nuts.
6   Detach the wiring from the connector and remove the lamp unit.
7   Refitting is the reversal of removal.

19 Rear combination lights

Bulb replacement
1   Remove the lens retaining screws and detach the lens, (photo) and Fig. 10.17.
2   Press and turn the bulb to remove.
3   Reinstall the bulb and lens in the reverse order.

Lamp unit removal
4   *Series 1 models:* Unscrew the four retaining nuts securing the lamp housing to the lamp panel and remove the cover. Detach the wiring from the connector and partly pull the socket out. Installation is the reverse of removal.
5   *Series 2 to 6 models:* Remove the rear gate bumper rubber and unscrew the four nuts securing the light housing to the panel. Detach the wiring from the connector and withdraw the light unit. Installation is the reverse of removal.

20 Licence plate light

Bulb - removal and installation
1   On Series 1 models, prise the lens from the body as in photo. On Series 2 to 6, unscrew the lens retaining screws and remove the lens (Fig. 10.18) (photo).
2   Press and turn the bulb to remove. Renew the bulb and install in the reverse order.

Light unit - removal and installation
3   *Series 1 models:* Unscrew the lamp housing to body panel retaining screws and remove the lamp unit. Disconnect the wiring. Install in the reverse order.

21 Side marker lights - front and rear

Bulb renewal
1   Unscrew and remove the lens retaining screws. Remove the lens, press and twist the bulb to remove. Install in the reverse order.

Light unit - removal and installation
2   Unscrew the lens retaining screws and detach the wiring from the connector. Remove the lamp unit. Reverse the removal procedure to install.

22 Back up (reverse) lamps

Bulb renewal
1   Withdraw the grommet on the rear face of the lamp housing and press and twist the bulb to remove. Install in the reverse order.

Fig. 10.16. The headlight adjustment screws

Fig. 10.17. The rear combination light, Series 2 to 6 lens removal

Fig. 10.18. Removing the licence plate lens - Series 2 to 6

20.1 The Series 1 model license plate light
with lens removed from body and light unit

Lamp unit - removal and installation

2   Unscrew the lamp bracket retaining nuts and remove the bracket
and lamp unit. Unscrew the lamp to bracket retaining nuts and remove
the lamp unit. Install in the reverse order.

23 Dome (interior) lamp

1   To renew the bulb, unclip the lamp cover (Fig. 10.19) and withdraw the bulb from the connectors. Fit the new bulb, check that it
works and install the cover.
2   To remove the lamp unit, unclip the cover and unscrew the self-
tapping screws and withdraw the lamp unit. Detach the wiring. Install
in the reverse order.

24 Instrument panel - removal and installation

1   From the rear of the instrument panel detach the speedo cable.
2   Unscrew the instrument panel retaining wing nuts and withdraw
the panel sufficiently to disconnect the harness from the connector.
3   Remove the panel.
4   Installation of the panel is the reversal of removal but take care not
to trap the wiring harness between the fascia panel and the
instrument panel.

25 Instrument panel - dismantling and reassembly

1   With the instrument panel removed, as described in Section 24, the
gauges or lights can be removed for renewal, but special care must be
taken to handle the gauges with great care during removal and
installation. Do not attempt to repair gauges as this must be entrusted
to an instrument specialist or simply renewed. To dismantle the complete
panel proceed as follows.
2   Remove the screws from the rear of the instrument panel and
separate the meter case from the panel (Fig. 10.20).
3   Disconnect and remove the speedometer and lights that are not
print wired.
4   Remove the combination fuel and temperature gauge.
5   Rotate the instrument light and indicator lights counterclockwise
and remove them.
6   Remove the retaining screws and separate the print wiring board
from the case (Fig. 10.21).
7   Reassembly of the instrument panel is the reversal of the removal
sequence.

26 Ignition switch

1   When the ignition switch is in the OFF position, all of the electrical
circuits except the lighting circuit are de-energised.
2   With the ignition switch in the second stop (clockwise) the starter
motor is energized to crank the engine. On releasing the ignition key,
the switch returns to the ON position.
3   In the ON position, lead wires 'B', 'L' and 'BY' are connected.
4   The ACC position is the first stop in the counterclockwise direction

Fig. 10.19. Unclip the lens and hinge up to remove the bulb

from the OFF position, When engaged, lead wire 'L' is connected to 'B'.

5   The ignition switch is a pre-sealed and set unit and therefore cannot be adjusted or repaired. However, continuity of the terminals can be tested using a voltmeter. Continuity must only exist between those indicated on the chart (Fig. 10.23).

27 Turn signal and dimmer switch - testing

1   The turn signal and dimmer switch are an integrated unit, and actuation is by a single lever.
2   Using a tester, the switch terminals may be tested for continuity to determine a possible switch fault. Continuity should only exist between those terminals shown in Fig. 10.25 and Fig. 10.26.
3   The turn signal and dimmer switch is a fully integrated unit and therefore if faulty must be renewed.

28 Windshield wiper motor - removal and installation

1   Detach the wiper blades and arms from the pivots by unscrewing the wiper arm retaining nut (photo).
2   Pull the arm from the pivot shaft to remove (photo).
3   Unscrew and remove the two bolts retaining the pivot.
4   Unscrew the wiper motor mounting bolts and detach the motor unit and linkage. Disconnect the wiring.
5   Installation is a reversal of removal but when fitting the wiper arms and blades, check their position on the pivot before tightening the retaining nut. Also ensure that the wiper motor linkage is not fouling any adjacent parts during the wiping action.

29 Windshield wiper motor - dismantling and inspection

1   Unscrew the cover securing bolts and turn the cover assembly to remove.
2   Withdraw the rotor unit turning in a clockwise direction (Fig. 10.28) taking care not to damage the brushes.
3   Clean the components before inspection. If the commutator segment grooves are blocked, remove the carbon from the grooves between the segments using a small knife blade or other such suitable tool. Lightly reface the commutator with fine sand paper.
4   Inspect the brushes and springs for wear, signs of damage, corrosion or distortion. Renew if required.
5   The self-parking device is faulty if, when the wiper motor switch is turned off, the motor continues to run, or if the motor stops immediately when the switch is de-activated.
6   Renew parts as required and reassemble the motor in the reverse sequence of dismantling.

Fig. 10.20. The instrument cluster and case

Fig. 10.21. The print wiring board and case

Fig. 10.22. The ignition switch positions

28.1 Unscrew the wiper arm retaining nut   .

	Circuit	Battery	Accessories	Ignition	Starter
Switch position	Cable color	B	L	BY	BW
On		◯————◯	◯————◯	◯	
Start		◯			◯
Acc.		◯————◯	◯		

Fig. 10.23. The starter switch connections

LOW BEAM
HIGH BEAM

(1.25 RW) LIGHTING SWITCH
(0.5 GW) FLASHER UNIT
(0.5 GR) HORN
(0.5 GB) TURN SIGNAL L.H.
(0.5 GL) TURN SIGNAL R.H.
(1.25 RY) HEAD LAMP (LOW BEAM)
(1.25 R) HEAD LAMP (HIGH BEAM)

Fig. 10.24. The turn signal and dimmer switch operation diagram

28.2 Remove the arm from the splined pivot

Cable color		GW	GL	GB
S Switch position				
RH		◯————◯		
LH		◯————————◯		

Fig. 10.25. Test for continuity in the turn signal switch terminals

Cable color		RY	RW	R
Switch position				
Low Beam			◯————◯	
High Beam		◯————◯		

Fig. 10.26. Test for continuity in the dimmer switch terminals

Fig. 10.27. The windshield wiper motor and linkage

Fig. 10.28. Remove the rotor

Fig. 10.29. The windshield wiper circuit

30 Windshield washer

1   The windshield washer fluid level must be checked regularly for the fluid level. To protect against freezing use GM Optikleen or an equivalent fluid. This also increases cleaning action.
2   The windshield washer is actuated by the windshield wiper switch and, if the washer unit should fail to operate, check the continuity between the switch terminal and washer motor. Check the fuse.
3   If the above items are in order, the washer motor is defective or the feed pipes/nozzles are blocked.
4   Detach the interconnecting pipes from the washer motor and check that they are clear, and, if this is the case, the motor is defective and must be removed for repair or renewal.

31 Horn

1   If the horn fails to operate when the button is depressed, check the fuse and wiring for good connections.
2   Check that the horn ground wire is connecting properly.
3   To test the horn button, remove it from the steering wheel and short the lower section of the button to the steering shaft. If the horn does not operate, the contact in the combination switch is not connecting with the lower part of the steering wheel. If the horn sounds, the button is defective and must be renewed.
4   To adjust the horn turn the adjustment screw (Fig. 10.31) as required to readjust the horn point gap.

32 Direction signal and dimmer switch - removal and installation

1   Detach the battery ground cable from its terminal.
2   Unscrew and remove the steering column cowling retaining screws.
3   Disconnect the wire connectors from the combination switch to harness.
4   Unscrew the switch clamp to column retaining screws and withdraw the switch.
5   Installation is a direct reversal of the removal procedure and on completion check the switch for correct functioning.

Fig. 10.30. The windshield washer

Fig. 10.31. Adjust the horn

Fig. 10.32. The direction signal and indicator switch

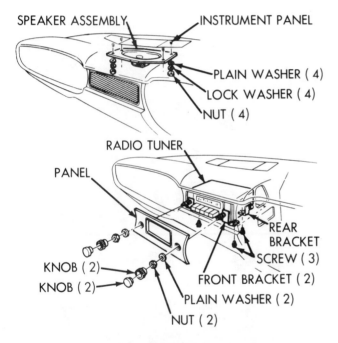

Fig. 10.33. The radio and speaker location

33 Hazard warning switch - removal and installation

1   Detach the ground cable from the battery terminal.
2   Unscrew and remove the steering column cowling screws.
3   Unscrew the hazard warning switch retaining screws, and detach the wires from the connector. Withdraw the switch.
4   Installation is the reversal of removal but check the switch for correct functioning on completion.

34 Radio equipment - removal and installation

Radio
1   Detach the ground cable from the battery.
2   Detach the ash tray and plate.
3   Unscrew and remove the volume control knob and tuner knob together with nuts, washers and face panel (Fig. 10.33).
4   Unscrew the rear and front mounting bracket screws.
5   Detach the electrical connections and the antenna lead from the radio.
6   Withdraw the radio and remove the front mounting brackets.
7   Installation is a direct reversal of removal.

Radio speaker
8   Remove the radio as above.
9   Unscrew the speaker retaining nuts, washers and lockwashers and withdraw the speaker and disconnect the wire connections. Remove the speaker unit.
10 Installation is the reverse of removal.

Antenna and lead
11 Dsiconnect the antenna lead from the radio.
12 Unscrew the antenna retaining cap and remove the antenna carefully pulling the cable thru the body panel grommets.
13 Installation is the reversal of removal but be sure to refit the grommets securely to the body panels.

Radio suppressors
14 If the radio operates but suffers from interference, check the suppressors shown in Fig. 10.36.
15 Disconnect the capacitor cable and remove the capacitor retaining screw. Remove and renew the capacitor.
16 Another possible cause for interference of the radio is an insecure antenna. Check the antenna and cable connections and ensure that they are secure.

35 Heater unit - removal and refitting

Series 1 models
1   Disconnect the ground cable from the battery, and drain the cooling system (see Chapter 2).

Fig. 10.34. The antenna location

Fig. 10.35. The antenna lead connection

Fig. 10.36. The radio interference suppression components

Fig. 10.37. The heater assembly and control levers

Fig. 10.38. The blower unit and core tubes

2   Detach the heater hoses from the heater unit and blank off the connection ends to prevent spillage.

3   Unscrew the two instrument panel to heater control screws via the access holes in the lower flange of the control unit, and lower the control. The blower switch leads can now be disconnected and the heater case to dash panel screws removed.

4   Carefully lower the unit and detach the resistor leads. From the door bell crankarm disconnect the defroster door and air door Bowden cables. Detach the defroster hoses from the floor outlet and remove the unit from the vehicle.

5   Refitting is a reversal of the above procedure. When reconnecting the defroster door and air cables adjust and tighten the clamp screws so that the doors can fully close. Refill the system with coolant and check for leaks.

Series 2

6   Disconnect the ground cable from the battery.

7   Locate a drain pan under the heater core tubes and slacken the hose clamp screws to the tubes. Detach the tubes and blank off the hose and tube ends to prevent further spillage. Position the hoses in a vertical position.

8   Unscrew the five screws retaining the parcel shelf and remove it.

9   Slacken the air diverter and defroster door cable clamps from the heater case and detach the cables.

10 Detach the blower and resistor leads, and then unscrew the control unit to instrument panel retaining screws. Hinge the control to the left being careful not to distort the water valve Bowden cable. Lay the control unit on the floor.

11 Unscrew the heater unit to dash screws and withdraw the heater unit to the rear so that the core tubes clear the dash opening and then move the heater downwards and to the right and remove it.

12 Refitting is the reversal of removal but ensure that the cowl seal is correctly positioned and finally that the control levers can operate. Readjust the cables if required. Check the hose connections for signs of leakage.

Series 3 to 6 models

13 Follow the instructions for Series 2 models in paragraphs 6 and 7 then proceed as follows.

14 Remove the interior of the glove box.

15 Detach the Bowden cables from the heater unit, and remove the ash tray.

16 Disconnect and remove the right dash outlet hose unit.

17 Unscrew the control to instrument panel retaining screws and lower the control. Detach the electric connections and the water valve Bowden cables.

18 Disconnect the defroster hoses.

19 From the right frame lever, disconnect the parking brake cable. Detach the parking brake cable pulley cover in the engine compartment and remove the parking brake to dash and instrument panel attachments. Place out of the way.

20 Disconnect the windshield wiper switch.

21 Unscrew the heater unit to dash panel retaining screws and pull the heater rearwards until the core tubes are clear of the dash opening. Move the heater to the left and downwards and withdraw it.

22 Undo the core tube clamp screw and remove the clamp. The two heater case halves may now be separated and the core removed.

23 Installation is the reversal of removal but ensure that the core seals are repositioned and are intact. Check that the cowl and evaporator unit seals are correctly positioned. Adjust the operating cables as described in Section 39.

36 Blower motor and heater core unit - removal and installation

1   Remove the heater unit as described in Section 23.

2   Undo the six screws retaining the floor outlet unit to the heater case and carefully prise the floor outlet from the case. Unscrew the front/rear case screws to separate the casing.

3   With a pair of pliers, bend the blower motor ground cable tab in half and push it thru the rear case.

4   Remove the blower motor from the rear case by unscrewing the retaining screws. The heater core unit can now be removed from the front case half if necessary.

5   Refitting of the blower motor is a direct reversal of removal, but insert the blower motor ground cable thru the rear casing hole, and then refit the motor to the casing. If the ground cable tab breaks or is too distorted to reconnect, a new one must be soldered to the cable.

37 Heater controls - removal and refitting

1   Disconnect the ground cable from the battery.

2   Remove the ash tray (some models) and remove the side outlet hoses from the control unit.

3   Remove the screws retaining the control to the instrument panel thru the access hole in the control lower flange.

4   Detach the electrical harness from the blower switch and disconnect the Bowden cables from the control levers. Remove the control unit.

5   Refit in the reverse order and adjust the control cables.

38 Heater water valve - removal and installation

1   Drain the cooling system (see Chapter 2), slacken the heater hose to valve clips and remove the hoses from the valve. Position the hose vertically to prevent spillage of coolant.

2   Slacken the water valve Bowden cable clamps and remove the cable from the valve.

3   The valve retaining screw can now be removed and the valve lifted clear.

4   Refit in the reverse order, refill with coolant and check for leaks.

39 Ventilation air inlet valve - removal and refitting

1   Disconnect the ground cable from the battery.

2   Slacken the hose clip screw and detach the hose from the valve.

3   From the inlet, detach the floor outlet operating rod, and then remove the valve extension clamp (lower) from the right-hand side and withdraw the extension.

4   Unscrew the valve to dash panel retaining screws to remove the valve unit.

5   Refitting is a reversal of the above procedure.

40 Heater control cable - adjustment

Vent door

1   If the control unit is already in position loosen the retaining screws to the instrument panel.

2   Position the select lever to the vent position.

3   Retain the vent door in vent position and align the vent cable and loop with the hook on the lever at the side of the heater by moving the panel fore and aft.

4   Tighten the nuts retaining the control to instrument panel and insert the cable onto the vent door lever.

Fig. 10.39. The water valve and heater hoses

Air inlet door cables

5   Position the selector lever on A/C, and connect the A/C cable to the link lever hook on the evaporator unit lower portion.
6   Adjust the cable to give a clearance of 0.3 in (7.6 mm) between the link lever hook end and the link lever bracket as in Fig. 10.42.
7   Tighten the cable clamp screw and close the outside heater air door.
8   Fit the A/C recirculation door cable to the heater outside air door shaft and tighten the cable clamp screw.

Defrost door cable

9   Position the selector lever to DEF.
10 Position the defroster door of the heater unit on the defroster door shaft and tighten the cable clamp.

Water valve cable

11 Position the temperature lever to cold.
12 Position the water valve in the closed position and connect the cable to the lever.

13 The cable is fitted in the clamp to give a clearance of 0.3 in (7.6 mm) between the clamp and the end of the cable sheath. Tighten the clamp and water valve screw.

Thermostatic switch cable

14 Position the temperature cable at cold.
15 Locate the switch in the cold position and insert the switch hook. Tighten the cable clamp.

41 Dash outlet grille - removal and installation

1   Undo the three screws retaining the outlet grille to the instrument panel and withdraw the grille.
2   Slacken the hose clip at the air inlet and remove the outlet unit to instrument panel screws. The outlet and hose are removed as a unit and then separated.
3   Refit in the reverse order, aligning the outlet unit so that the levers will not bind on the grille bars when the grille is refitted.

Fig. 10.40. The air flow system

Fig. 10.41. The dash outlet grille removal

Fig. 10.42. The air inlet cable adjustment

Fig. 10.43. The heater air inlet cable adjustment

Fig. 10.44. The water valve cable adjustment

Fig. 10.45. The thermostatic switch cable adjustment

Fig. 10.46. Check the air pump drive belt adjustment

Fig. 10.47. Thermostatic switch

42 Air conditioning components

1 Should any part of the air conditioning system fail to operate correctly it is not recommended that the 'home mechanic' repair or renew any of the defective components. Specialised tools, equipment and most important, knowledge are required to service and repair items within the system.

2 Do not disconnect any of the air conditioning supply lines during overhaul or repair procedures, see special note in Chapter 1.

Maintenance

3 Ensure that the engine exhaust is suitably ventilated.

4 Check the compressor drivebelt for correct tension and general condition. Renew the belt and retension as shown in Fig. 10.46. by slackening the center bolt and tightening the adjustment screw until 11 lb of force is required to deflect the belt 0.2 to 0.28 in. Retighten the pulley center bolt to 10 lb f ft (1.3 kg f m).

5 Set the controls for system operation and run the engine at 2000 rpm for ten minutes. Check the clutch pulley bolt and ensure that the compressor and clutch pulley are operating at the same speed. A speed variation indicates clutch slippage and the compressor unit will have to be serviced by your GM dealer.

6 Prior to switching off the engine, check the sight glass to ensure that the refrigerant charge is sufficient. The glass is normally clear although during mild weather traces of bubbles may be present. Foam in the charge is indicative of a low charge. No charge is indicated by there being no liquid visible and no temperature difference between

the compressor inlet and outlet lines. If recharging is necessary, have this done by your local GM dealer.

7 Check the refrigerant line connections for secureness.

8 Check the compressor unit for signs of excessive oil leakage. A small leakage from the front seal is permissible but if a serious leak is apparent, get your GM dealer to check it out.

43 Blower resistor - removal and installation

1 Detach the ground cable from the battery.

2 Disconnect the right-hand defroster duct.

3 Detach the wires from the resistor and unscrew the mounting screws. Remove the resistor.

4 Installation is the reversal of removal

44 Thermostatic switch - removal and installation

1 Detach the ground cable from the battery.

2 Remove the interior of the glove box.

3 Detach the thermostatic switch wires and loosen the switch cable clamp and remove the cable from the switch.

4 Unscrew and remove the switch to bracket screws. Remove the bracket and then the switch. The bracket has to be removed as the switch capillary tube is coiled inside the evaporator.

5 Installation is the reversal of removal.

45 Fault diagnosis - electrical system

Symptom	Reason/s
Starter motor fails to turn engine	Battery discharged. Battery defective internally. Battery terminal leads loose or ground lead not securely attached to body. Loose or broken connections in starter motor circuit. Starter motor solenoid switch faulty. Starter motor pinion jammed in mesh with flywheel gear ring. Starter brushes badly worn, sticking or brush wire loose. Commutator dirty, worn or burnt. Starter motor armature faulty. Field coils grounded.
Starter motor turns engine very slowly	Battery in discharged condition. Starter brushes badly worn, sticking or brush wires loose. Loose wires in starter motor circuit.
Starter motor operates without turning engine	Pinion or flywheel gear teeth broken or worn.
Starter motor noisy or engagement excessively rough	Pinion or flywheel teeth broken or worn. Starter motor retaining bolts loose.
Starter motor remains in operation after ignition key released	Faulty ignition switch. Faulty solenoid.
Charging system indicator on with ignition switch off	Faulty alternator diode.
Charging system indicator light on - engine speed above idling	Loose or broken drivebelt. Shorted negative diode. No output from alternator.
Charge indicator light not on when ignition switched on but engine not running	Burnt out bulb. Field circuit open. Lamp circuit open.
Battery will not hold charge for more than a few days	Battery defective internally. Electrolyte level too weak or too low. Battery plates heavily sulphated.
Horn will not operate or operates intermittently	Loose connections. Defective switch. Defective relay. Defective horn.
Horns blow continually	Faulty relay. Relay wiring grounded. Horn button stuck (grounded).
Lights do not come on	If engine not running, battery discharged. Light bulb filament burnt out or bulbs broken. Wire connections loose, disconnected or broken. Light switch shorting or otherwise faulty.
Lights come on but fade out	If engine not running battery discharged. Light bulb filament burnt out, or bulbs or sealed beam units broken. Wire connections loose, disconnected or broken. Light switch shorting or otherwise faulty.
Lights give very poor illumination	Lamp glasses dirty. Lamps badly out of adjustment.
Lights work erratically - flashing on and off, especially over bumps	Battery terminals or ground connection loose. Lights not grounding properly. Contacts in light switch faulty.
Wiper motor fails to work	Blown fuse. Wire connections loose, disconnected, or broken. Brushes badly worn. Armature worn or faulty. Field coils faulty.
Wiper motor works very slowly and takes excessive current	Commutator dirty, greasy or burnt.

Armature bearings dirty or unaligned.
Armature badly worn or faulty.

Wiper motor works slowly and takes little current

Brushes badly worn.
Commutator dirty, greasy or burnt.
Armature badly worn or faulty.

Wiper motor works but wiper blades remain static

Wiper motor gearbox parts badly worn or teeth stripped.

Fig. 10.48. Wiring diagram - Series 1 models

Fig. 10.49. Wiring diagram - Series 2 model

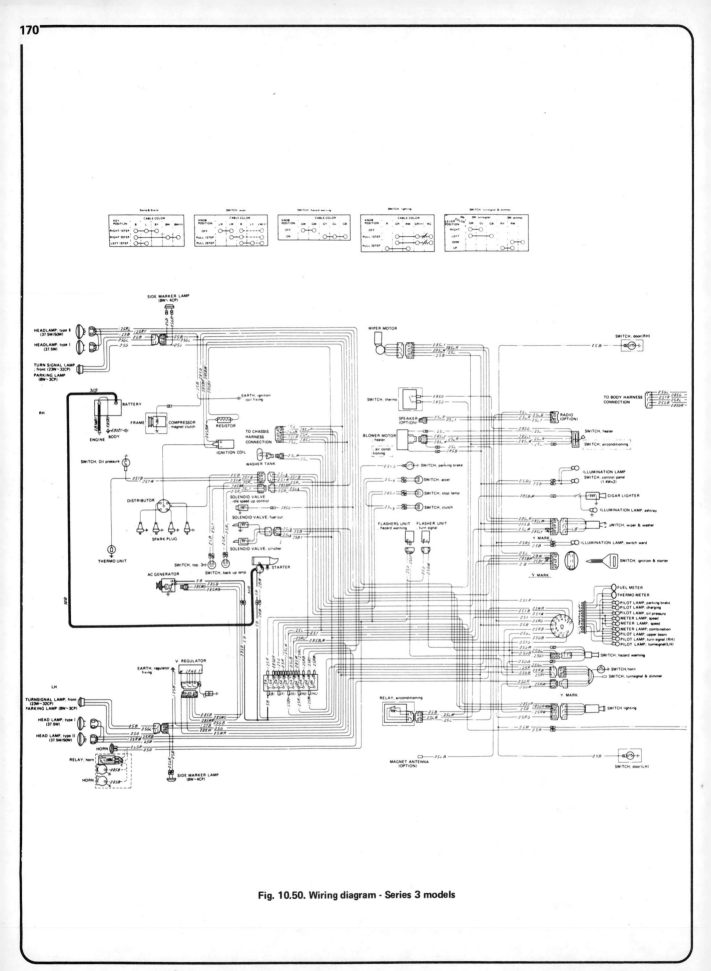

Fig. 10.50. Wiring diagram - Series 3 models

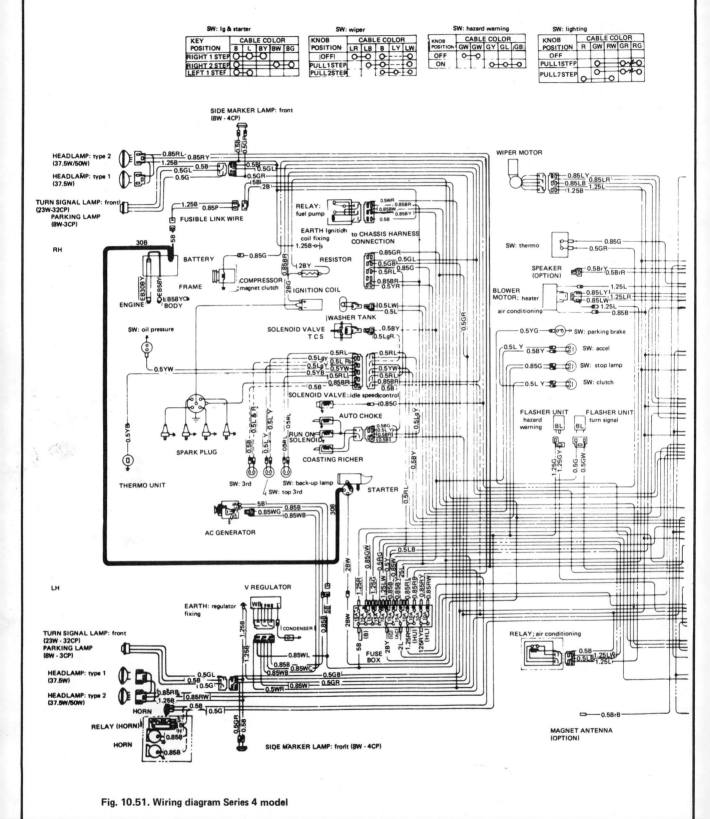

Fig. 10.51. Wiring diagram Series 4 model

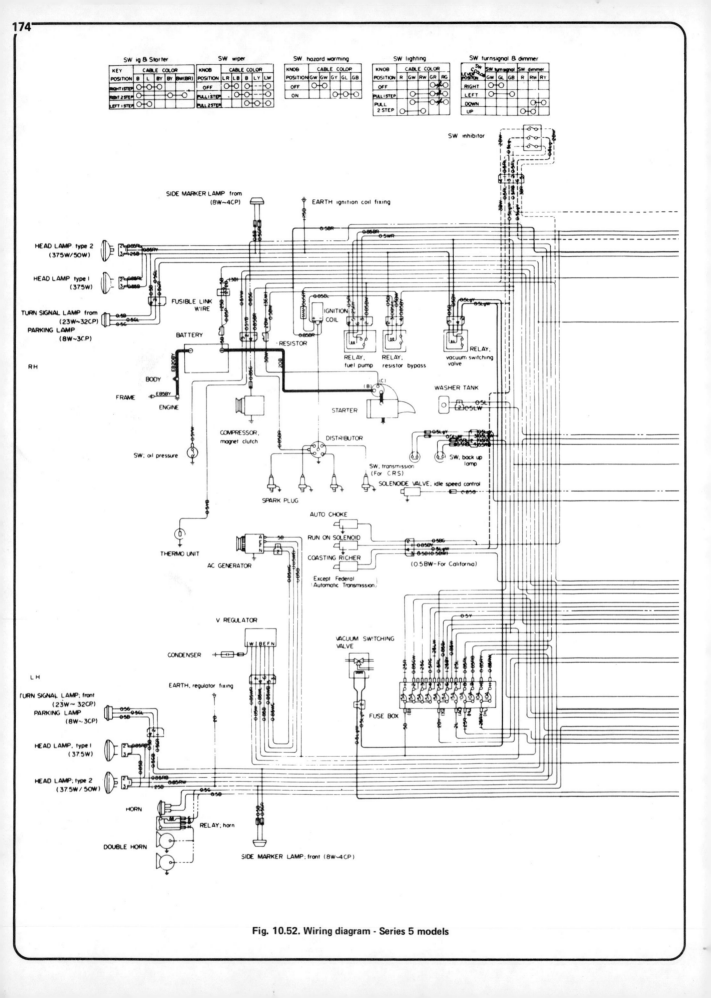

Fig. 10.52. Wiring diagram - Series 5 models

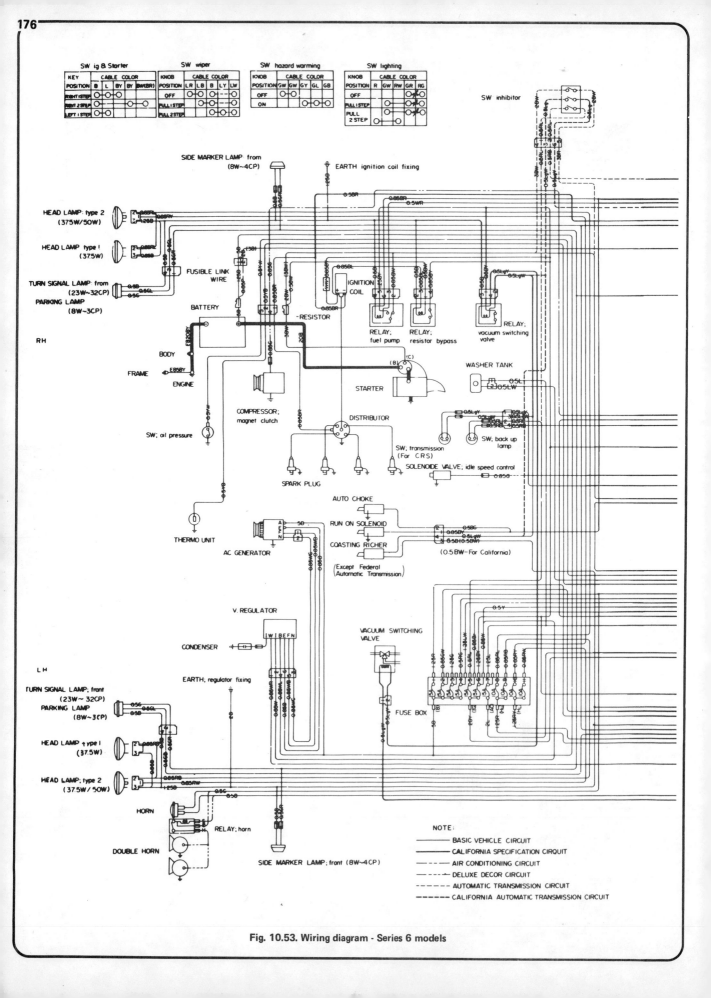

Fig. 10.53. Wiring diagram - Series 6 models

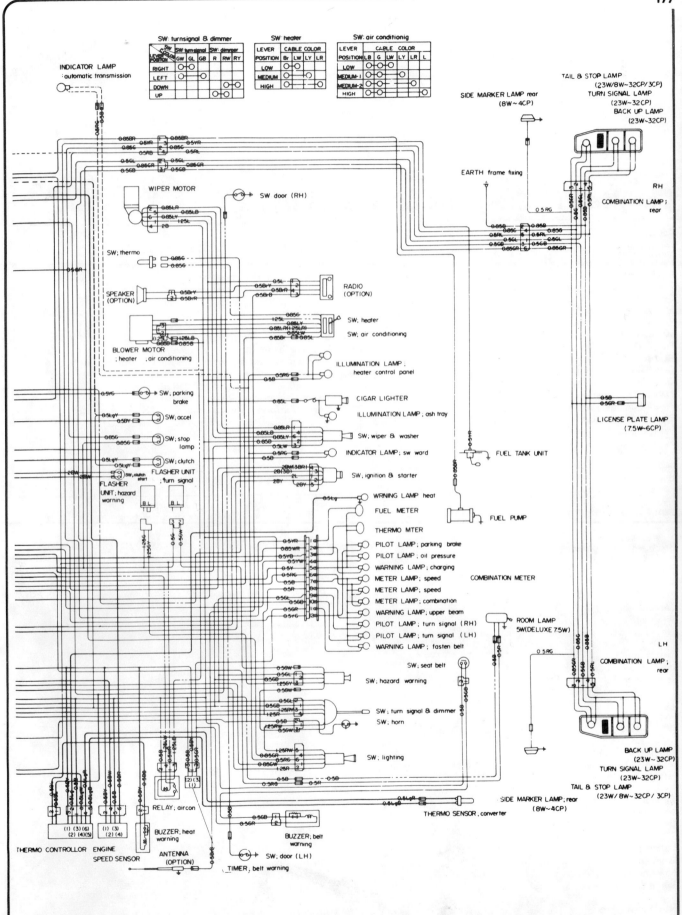

Chapter 11 Suspension and steering

Contents

Fault diagnosis - suspension and steering 27	Steering gear (steering box) - removal and installation 23
Front wheel bearing - adjustment 3	Steering geometry - checking 4
Front wheel hub - removal and installation 2	Steering knuckle - removal and installation 13
General description 1	Steering shaft flexible coupling - removal and installation 22
Idler arm, pivot shaft and/or bracket - removal and installation ... 19	Steering shaft - renewal 21
Lower control arm and ball joint - removal, inspection and	Steering wheel - alignment 15
installation 12	Steering wheel - removal and installation 16
Pitman shaft seal - renewal 25	Strut bar - removal and installation 9
Rear suspension - removal, inspection and installation 26	Tie rod links (steering arms) - removal and installation 17
Ride height - checking 5	Tie rod - removal and installation 18
Shockabsorber - removal, inspection and installation 7	Torsion bar - removal and installation 11
Stabilizer bar - removal and installation 8	Torsion bar springs - adjustment 6
Steering column - removal and installation 20	Upper control arm and ball joint assembly - removal and
Steering gear - adjustment 14	installation 10
Steering gear - dismantling, inspection and reassembly 24	

Specifications

Front suspension type	Independent with torsion bar springs, stabilizer bar and double acting shockabsorbers
Front wheel alignment	
Series 1 to 4 models	52.7 in unloaded - 52.8 in loaded
Series 5 models	53.8 in
Series 6 models	54 in
Camber angle	
Series 1 to 5 models	+ 1° unloaded - + 1° - 25' loaded
Series 6 models	+ 30'
Caster angle	
Series 1 to 5 models	+ 0° 20' unloaded, + 1° - 20' loaded
Series 6 models	− 10'
Toe-in	
Series 1 to 5 models	+ 1/8 in unloaded - + 1/8 in loaded
Series 6 models	0
Kingpin inclination	
Series 1 to 5 models	7° unloaded - 6° - 35' loaded
Series 6 models	7° 30'
Torsion bar spring data	
Series 1 to 4 models	800 lbs
Series 5 and 6 models	830 lbs
Torsion bar spring	
Length x diameter	38.1 in x 0.851 in
Wheel rate/side	96.9 lbs/in
Spring constant	21.7 ft lbs/degree
Shockabsorbers	
Maximum length	14.0 in

Minimum length	8.86 in
Stroke	5.14 in

Damping force

Rebound side	232 lb/11.8 in/sec
Compression side	79.4 lb/11.8 in/sec

Rear suspension type ... ...   Semi-elliptic leaf springs and hydraulic shockabsorbers

Steering

Type	Ball-screw
Gear ratios	
Series 1 to 5	22.4 overall 17.8
Series 6	23.5 to 27.5
Steering wheel diameter	15.7 in
Steering wheel play	0.394 in (outside diameter)
Ball diameter	¼ in
Number of balls x number of ball circuits	
Series 1 to 5	29 x 2
Series 6	26 x 2
Steering angles	
Outer wheel	30º - 15'
Inner wheel	39º
Oil capacity	0.635 US pints, 10 fl oz
Oil type	1051052 GM Soec. GM 4673M - SAE 90 or equivalent
Worm bearing pre-load	
Series 1 to 5	3.0 to 5.6 in lbs
Series 6	2.6 to 5.2 in lbs
Sector lash adjustment	
Series 1 to 5	3.5 to 8.5 in lbs
Series 6	4.3 to 8.7 in lbs
Sector lash locknut	
Series 1	25 ft lbs
Series 2 to 6	20 ft lbs
Total steering gear pre-load	
Series 1	3.5 to 8.5 in lbs
Series 2 to 6	3.5 to 10.5 in lbs

Wheels

Type	Pressed steel
Size	
Series 1 to 4	4J - 14
Series 5 and 6	5J - 14

Tires

Size	
Series 1 to 4	6.00 - 14 - 6 ply
Series 5 and 6	E78 - 14 - 4 ply
Tire inflation pressures	
Front - Series 1 to 4	21 lbs sq in
Rear (loaded)	42 lbs sq in
(unloaded)	25 lbs sq in
Front - Series 5 and 6	20 lbs sq in
Rear (loaded)	32 lbs sq in
(unloaded)	20 lbs sq in

Torque wrench settings	lb f ft	kg f m
Steering and front suspension		
Tie rod ball joint nuts		
Series 1	40	5.5
Series 2	50	6.9
Series 3 to 6	43.5	5.9
Idler arm mounting bolts		
Series 1 models		
Large	70	9.6
Small	30	4.1
Series 2 models		
Large	55	7.6
Small	20	2.7
Series 3 to 6 models		
Large	50.5	6.9
Small	20	2.7

Idler arm/intermediate rod nut

Series 1	40	5.5
Series 2 to 4	50	6.9
Series 5 and 6	43.5	6.0
Idler arm to idler arm pivot shaft	87	12.0

Pitman arm/intermediate rod nut

Series 1	45	6.2
Series 2	50	6.9
Series 3 to 6	43.5	5.9

Intermediate rod locknuts

Series 1	50	6.9
Series 2	90	12.4
Series 3 to 6	87	12.0

Pitman arm to sector shaft nut

Series 1 and 2	165	22.8
Series 3 to 6	160	22.1

Steering gear mounting bolts

Series 1		
Large	70	9.6
Series 2 to 6		
Large	55	7.6
Series 1		
Small	30	4.1
Series 2 to 6		
Small	20	2.7
Steering wheel nut	25	3.4
Coupling bolts	18	2.4
Shaft coupling damper bolts	20	2.7
Lower coupling/wormshaft clamp bolt	20	2.7
Column to cowl panel screws	10	1.3
Combination switch screws	Snug	

Ball joint stud nut

Lower and upper studs		
Series 1	80	11.0
Series 2 to 6	75	10.3
Ball joint to lower arm	45	6.2

Control arm pivot to frame

Upper - Series 1	55	7.6
Series 2 to 6	50	6.9
Lower - Series 1	135	18.6
Series 2 to 6	130	17.9

Upper control arm pivot shaft bushings

Series 1	250	34.5
Series 2	220	30.4

Shockabsorber

Upper - Series 1	100	13.8
Series 2 to 6	18	2.4
Lower - Series 1	35	4.8
Series 2 to 6	45	6.2

Stabilizer bar

Nuts	7	0.9
Locknuts	18	2.4

Lower control arm to crossmember

Series 1	135	18.6
Series 2 to 6	130	17.9

Backing plate to knuckle

Large bolts - Series 1	55	7.6
Series 2 to 4	50	6.9
Small bolts - Series 1 to 4	35	4.8

Adapter and dust shield to knuckle bolts - Series 5 and 6

Large	55	7.6
Small	35	4.8
Wheel stud nuts	65	8.9

Wheel bearing adjustment	...	...	...	...	...	...	...	22	3.0
Strut bar to lower control arm	...	...	...	...	...	...	...	45	6.2

Strut bar to frame

Nut - Series 1	...	...	...	...	...	...	...	...	175 in lbs	24.1 kg cm
Series 2 to 6	...	...	...	...	...	...	...	...	15	2.0
Locknut - Series 1	...	...	...	...	...	...	...	...	55	7.6
Series 2 to 6	...	...	...	...	...	...	...	...	50	6.9

Rear suspension

Axle to 'U' bolts	...	...	...	...	...	...	...	...	40	5.5
Shackle pins - Series 1 to 4	...	...	...	...	...	...	...	130	17.9
Series 5 and 6	...	...	...	...	...	...	...	95	13.1

1 General description

The fully independent front suspension is of the short and long arm type incorporating torsion bar springs.

The control arms are located to the vehicle with bolts and bushes on their inner pivot points and at the outer points to the steering knuckle. The steering knuckle is an integral part of the front wheel spindles. Each control arm has a ball joint to enable the knuckle to pivot for steering.

Each front wheel hub is located on the knuckle spindle by two roller bearings, and the brake drum (Series 1 to 4) or disc rotor (Series 5 and 6) is located to the hub.

Height control is governed by the third crossmember to which the forged ends of the torsion bar links are bolted at the rear and the control arms in front.

Strut bars regulate the fore and aft movement of the front suspension and these are located between the chassis frame and lower control arms. A torsion bar type stabilizer is fitted by shackle rods to the lower control arm.

The steering system consists of the steering gear unit, the steering column and steering linkage.

The steering gear is of the ball-screw type and is connected to the steering column at one end and the steering linkage at the lower end. On the lower end of the steering gear is a worm shaft gear which engages with a ball nut thru a number of recirculating balls. The turning motion of the steering shaft is transferred onto the sector shaft thru the balls. Provision is made for backlash adjustment between the sector gear and rack by means of an adjustment screw which bears upon the tapered sector gear. The steering wheel rotates 3.3 turns from lock to lock.

The energy absorbing steering column is designed to collapse during a frontal collision under pre-determined loads.

Steering linkage consists of a splined Pitman arm which is connected to an intermediate rod and tie rod, which are adjustable. The intermediate rod is also interconnected with the idler arm, which is located to the other tie rod, and an idler arm pivot shaft fastened to the frame via a bracket.

The non-adjustable tie rods are connected to the brake back plates by tie rod links. Lubrication facilities are located on all ball joints and also the idler arm pivot shaft.

The rear suspension consists of semi-elliptic leaf springs and double-acting telescopic shockabsorbers.

2 Front wheel hub - removal and installation

Series 1 to 4
1 Apply the handbrake firmly and raise the roadwheel clear of the ground.
2 Remove the hub cap, wheel nuts and wheel.
3 Prise the hub grease cap from the hub using a suitable screwdriver.
4 Withdraw the cotter pin (photo) and unscrew the spindle nut retainer and nut (photo).
5 The outer bearing can now be extracted from the hub (photo).
6 If the wheel hub is to be removed, then the brake drum must be removed first (see Chapter 9) or alternatively, it can be withdrawn complete with the hub and then separated.
7 Remove the roller bearing cups from the hub using a suitable drift

or puller, and prise out the grease seal using a screwdriver.
8 Clean all of the old grease from the hub and bearing, and also the hub grease cap. Inspect the hub and bearing for signs of excessive wear, scratches, pits or corrosion or any other signs of damage. If necessary they should be renewed as required.
9 Clean the spindle and adjacent components and inspect for signs of wear and damage. Renew as required.
10 Commence assembly by packing the hub with the recommended wheel bearing grease. Lubricate the wheel bearing cups and cones with the same type of grease.
11 Refit the bearing cups to the hub and the new grease seal.
12 Refit the hub to the spindle and install the outer bearing cone, retaining it with the nut and washer.
13 Adjust the hub as described in the following Section.
14 Refit the brake drum and roadwheel.
15 Pad the grease cap with the recommended wheel bearing grease and tap into position. Refit the hub cap and lower the vehicle.

Series 5 and 6
16 Follow the instructions given in paragraphs 1 and 2.
17 Undo the disc brake support unit retaining bolts to the adaptor and withdraw the support and caliper unit.
18 Prise the hub grease cap from the hub with a screwdriver and withdraw the cotter pin. Remove the spindle nut retainer and nut. The rotor and hub units can now be removed.
19 Undo the bolts to separate the rotor from the hub.
20 Clean and inspect the hub/bearing unit as described in paragraphs 7 to 10.
21 Assemble in the reverse sequence and adjust the hub as given in the following Section.

3 Front wheel bearing - adjustment

1 Apply the handbrake and raise the front of the vehicle so that the front wheel is clear of the ground.
2 Remove the hub cap and carefully tap or prise out the hub grease cap.
3 Wipe any excess grease from the end of the spindle and then withdraw the cotter pin and castellated nut retainer.
4 Spin the roadwheel and tighten the hub nut to a torque of 22 lb f ft.
5 Rotate the hub two or three complete turns and loosen the nut sufficiently to allow the hub to be turned with the fingers, and check that there is no free play in the hub. Ensure when rotating the hub that the brake linings are not in contact with the drum.
6 Refit the castellated nut retainer and insert a new cotter pin, then bend over the ends to retain it in position.
7 Check that the wheel rotates freely and then install the grease cap and hub cap. **Note:** If the wheel does not rotate freely, then the bearings are probably due for renewal - see previous Section.

4 Steering geometry - checking

1 In order to obtain satisfactory tire wear and good steering stability, it is essential that the steering geometry is correctly set. This is not really a do-it-yourself job and it is always preferable to have the job undertaken by your vehicle main dealer who will have the correct

Fig. 11.1. The front suspension and wheel hub assembly

2.4a Withdraw the cotter pin ...

2.4b ... remove the retainer, nut and washer

2.5 Extract the bearing

7.5 The upper shock absorber location nut and bushes

alignment gauges. However, if you feel competent to do the job yourself, the basic procedure is given below.

2   Before commencing any checks, the vehicle must be standing on a level floor, the tires must be inflated to the correct pressures (cold), excessive mud must be removed from the vehicle underframe and the fuel tank, engine oil level and coolant level must be correct.

3   In addition to the above, it must be known that the following components are in good condition and correctly tightened and/or adjusted:

- a) Wheel bearings.
- b) Steering shaft coupling and steering box.
- c) Tie rod and steering connections.
- d) Front springs.
- e) Front spring heights and shockabsorbers.
- f) Control arms and stabilizer bar.

Before adjustment is made to the castor angle and camber angle, lift the front bumper and release it to allow the vehicle to return to its normal height.

Camber angle

4   The camber angle is the angle by which the wheel tilts outwards when the weight is on the suspension.

5   To obtain the specified camber angle, change the shims at the front and rear of the upper control arm pivot shaft and frame (Fig. 11.4). Add an equal amount of shims at the front and rear of the pivot shaft to decrease the positive camber.

Caster angle

6   Fit shims front to rear and rear to front. The transfer of one shim to the front bolt from the rear increases the positive caster.

7   Both caster and camber angles can be adjusted in one operation and on completion the toe-in must be checked as follows.

Toe-in

8   Raise the front end of the vehicle so that the wheels are clear of the ground, and in the straight ahead position.

9   Turn each wheel by hand and scribe a chalk line in the centre of the tire tread around its circumference.

10 Measure between the chalk marks at the front and rear of the tire at equal heights from the ground. If the toe-in is correct, the distance between the chalk marks at the rear should be greater than the distance between them at the front by the amount given in the Specification.

11 If adjustment is required, loosen the tie-rod clamp bolts and rotate the tie rod as necessary. Each tie rod is threaded right-hand at one end and left-hand at the other end in order to retain the correct balance of the linkage; the two tie rods must be the same length after any adjustment.

Fig. 11.2. Exploded view of the front suspension component parts

1   Upper control arm
2   Pivot shaft
3   Bushing (2)
4   Cover
5   Grease fitting
6   Upper balljoint
7   Grease fitting
8   Boot
9   Shim
10 Nut, cotter pin
11 Washer
12 Staked nut
13 Bolt, washer
14 Shims
15 Lower control arm
16 Lower control arm link
17 Bolt
18 Nut, lockwasher
19 Bolt
20 Nut, lockwasher
21 Lower balljoint
22 Grease fitting
23 Boot
24 Lockwasher
25 Nut, cotter pin
26 Bolt, nut, lockwasher
27 Knuckle
28 Bearing shoulder piece
29 Tie rod link
30 Bolt
31 Bolt
32 Nut, lockwasher
33 Hub
34 Wheel stud
35 Drum
36 screw
37 Outer wheel bearing
38 Inner wheel bearing
39 Grease seal
40 Washer
41 Nut
42 Nut retainer
43 Cotter pin
44 Dust cap
45 Wheel stud nut
46 Plate

Fig. 11.3. The torsion bar, strut rod and stabilizer components

1	Torsion bar	10	Strut rod assembly	18	Link stud
2	Height control arm	11	Strut rod bushings	19	Link stud bushings
3	Pivot nut	12	Strut rod washer	20	Stabilizer link stud washers
4	Height control seat	13	Strut rod washer	21	Stabilizer link stud washers
5	Height control bolt	14	Nuts and washer	22	Nuts
6	Boot	15	Bolt, washer, nut	23	Stabilizer bar bracket
7	Boot	16	Stabilizer bar	24	Bolt and washer
8	Cotter pin	17	Stabilizer bushings	25	Lower control arm bumper
9	Seal				

26	Bolt, washer
27	Upper control arm bumpers (2)
28	Nut, washer
29	Shock absorber
30	Bushing
31	Retainer
32	Retainer
33	Bolt, lockwasher, nut

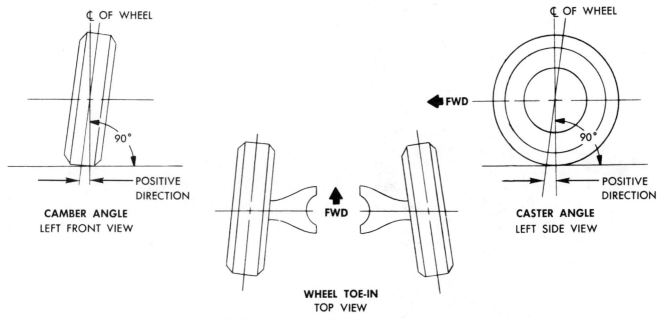

Fig. 11.4. The caster and camber angles and toe in

TRIM HEIGHTS

Fig. 11.5. Trim height points

5 Ride height - checking

1 Park the vehicle on a smooth level surface. Bounce the front end of the vehicle up and down several times then lift at the front and allow to settle to normal height.
2 Refer to Fig. 11.5 and measure the indicated distances.
3 The distances should be as indicated in the Specifications with the vehicle at kerb weight ie. no passengers, full tank of gas and spare tire and jack fitted.
4 The measurements should not differ beyond ½ in for both sides of the vehicle. If adjustment is needed proceed as follows.

6 Torsion bar spring - adjustment

1 The vehicle height is adjusted by means of an adjustment bolt on the height control arms.
2 Follow the instructions given in the preceding Section and ensure that the tire pressures are as specified.
3 Slacken the front end of the strut bar nuts and calculate the buffer clearance between the rubber bumper and lower control arm.
4 Adjust the clearance bolt on the height control arms to set the buffer clearance at 7/8 in (22.2 mm).
5 To increase the height, turn the bolt inwards.
6 Ensure that the trim heights are as specified and tighten the strut bar nuts to the specified torques.

Fig. 11.6. The stabilizer bar link assembly

Fig. 11.7. Strut rod unit component parts and location

Fig. 11.8. Special tool no. J.24258 located between the control arm forks acts as a spacer when tightening the pivot shaft bushing

Fig. 11.9. The height control unit

7   Shockabsorber - removal, inspection and installation

1   Apply the parking brake and jack up the vehicle.
2   To prevent the shockabsorber upper stem from turning when undoing the retaining nut, retain it with an open-ended wrench. Undo and remove the upper stem retaining nut, retainer and rubber grommet (photo).
3   Undo and remove the lower shockabsorber pivot to lower control arm retaining bolt and remove the shockabsorber unit.
4   Clean the shockabsorber outer surface and inspect for signs of oil leakage and/or weak damping tension. Renew the unit if necessary. It is not possible to repair faulty shockabsorbers.
5   If the lower or upper bushes are worn, damaged or defective, they must be renewed.
6   Fully extend the shockabsorber and with the lower retainer and rubber grommet in position over the upper stem, install the shockabsorber upwards thru the control arm and ensure that the upper stem passes thru the frame bracket mounting hole.
7   Fit the upper rubber grommet, retainer and attachment nut over the upper stem of the shockabsorber.
8   Retain the upper stem with an open ended wrench to prevent it turning and tighten the retaining nut.
9   Fit the retainers that attach the lower pivot to the lower control arm, and tighten.
10 Lower the vehicle and remove the jack.

8   Stabilizer bar - removal and installation

1   Apply the parking brake and jack up the front of the vehicle.
2   Remove the stabilizer bar bracket retaining bolts and detach the brackets and bushes.
3   Unscrew and remove the stabilizer bar link bolts, spacers and rubber grommets from the lower control arms.
4   Clean the respective components and renew as required.
5   Note before reassembly that the washers with the center ring must be fitted with the stabilizer bar and lower control arm brackets interposed between the washers.
6   Slide the new frame bushes into position and fit the stabilizer brackets over them. Reconnect them to the frame but do not fully tighten yet.
7   Reconnect the stabilizer ends to the link bolts of the lower control arms.
8   Tighten the bracket bolts and link bolt nuts to the specified torque.

9   Strut bar - removal and installation

1   Apply the parking brake and jack up the vehicle.
2   Unscrew and remove the double nuts, washer and rubber bush from

the front of the strut bar and remove the frame side bracket.
3   Undo the strut bar to lower control arm bolts and remove with the strut bar.
4   Clean and inspect the strut bar and bushings for defects or wear. Renew as required.
5   Fit the washers and bushes to the strut rod and insert thru the frame bracket.
6   Fit the second set of washers and bushes to the strut rod and one nut. Do not tighten the nut at this stage.
7   Fit the strut rod to the lower control arm and tighten the bolts to the specified torque.
8   Lower the vehicle and tighten the first nut, to the specified torque to the frame bracket. Fit and tighten the second nut to the specified torque.

10 Upper control arm and ball joint assembly - removal and installation

1   Apply the parking brake and jack up the front of the vehicle. Place chassis stands or blocks under the lower control arm. Remove the roadwheel.
2   Withdraw the cotter pin from the nut retaining the upper control arm and upper ball joint unit. Detach the upper control arm from the steering knuckle, but support the knuckle unit by tying it with wire or cord and hang it out of the way. Do not allow it to hang from the brake hose!
3   Remove the upper pivot shaft bolts and remove the control arm from the bracket, noting the position and number of camber and caster angle shims.
4   Undo the bush nuts from the pivot shaft, loosening in an alternate manner, and remove the pivot from the control arm.
5   Clean and inspect the components for excessive wear, and for signs of deterioration or damage. Renew any defective parts.
6   Fit the boots to the pivot shaft, and lubricate the inner bushes with molybdenum disulphide grease.
7   Screw the bushings into the pivot shaft, in an alternate manner and avoid getting grease onto the outer face of the bushes.
8   Fit a suitable length bar or, if available, special tool number J.24258 between the control arm forks as a spacer (Fig. 11.8) and I tighten the pivot shaft bushing.
9   Ensure that the bushes are centered correctly and that the control arm rotates with resistance but does not bind on the pivot shaft when tightened to the specified torque.
10 Refit the grease fittings and lubricate.
11 Fit the ball joint stud thru the knuckle and locate the castellated nut which must be tightened to the specified torque and then to the

Fig. 11.10. The steering column and gearbox component parts

1	Coupling	25	Column cowling
2	Flange, upper coupling	26	Cowling screws and washers
3	Flange, lower coupling	27	Bolt, washer
4	Cross strap	28	Steering gear housing
5	Cross strap	29	Sector shaft bushings
6	Thrust washer	30	Wormshaft seal
7	Spring	31	Sector (Pitman) shaft seal
8	Thru bolt	32	Filler plug
9	Lock nut	33	Worm and ball nut assembly
10	Pinch bolt, lockwasher	34	Wormshaft bearing
11	Mast jacket	35	End cover
12	Shaft assembly	36	Top cover
13	Bushing	37	Worm preload shims
14	Grommet	38	Gasket
15	Gasket	39	Bolt, lockwasher
16	Bolt and washers	40	Sector adjuster screw
17	Screw and washer	41	Locknut
18	Wheel assembly	42	Sector shaft
19	Horn shroud seat	43	Adjusting shim
20	Screw	44	Pitman shaft nut
21	Horn shroud	45	Lockwasher
22	Spring	46	Bolt, nut (stopper)
23	Nut	47	Hazard warning switch assembly
24	Shaft nut and washers		

11.4 The torsion bar location to the lower control arm

STEERING GEAR CROSS SECTION

STEERING COLUMN ASSEMBLY

INTERMEDIATE ROD ASSEMBLY

TIE ROD

TIE ROD

TIE ROD LINK (STEERING ARM)

IDLER ARM

PITMAN ARM

IDLER ARM PIVOT SHAFT

STEERING GEAR

IDLER ARM PIVOT SHAFT BRACKET

Fig. 11.11. The steering column, gear and connecting rod layout nearest hole alignment for the cotter pin. Install the new cotter pin and bend over the ends to retain it.

12 Locate the upper control arm into position in the chassis frame and insert the camber and caster angle shims to their respective locations as removed.

13 Tighten the pivot shaft to the specified torque. For good shaft to frame clamping force and retention, tighten the thin shim pack bolt first.

11 Torsion bar - removal and installation

1 Apply the handbrake and jack up the front of the vehicle. Support the front of the vehicle with chassis stands or blocks.

2 Unscrew and remove the height control arm adjustment bolt. Mark its relative location and remove the height control arm from the torsion bar and third crossmember.

3 Mark the torsion bar's relative location and withdraw it from the lower control arm (photo).

4 Clean the torsion bars and inspect for distortion or damage. Renew, if required.

5 Smear some grease to the torsion bars serrated ends, and then, locating the rubber bumpers in contact with the lower control arm (with the front of the vehicle jacked up under the lower control arm), insert the front of the torsion bar into the arm.

6 Fit the height control arm into position with, and contacting, the adjustment bolt. Grease the part of the height control arm which fits within the chassis frame.

7 Insert a new cotter pin and bend over to retain.

8 The adjustment bolt is now tightened to its original location which was marked before removal.

9 Check and adjust the vehicle ride height as in Section 5.

12 Lower control arm and ball joint - removal, inspection and installation

Refer to Fig. 11.2

1 Apply the parking brake and jack up the vehicle at the front. Make secure by placing chassis stands under the frame.

2 Remove the wheel.

3 Detach the strut bar and withdraw the stabilizer from the rod - see Section 9.

4 Remove the torsion bar - see Section 11.

5 Unscrew and remove the shockabsorber to lower control arm retaining nut.

6 Undo and remove the two lower balljoint bolts and detach from the control arm.

7 Remove the lower control arm.

8 Remove the ball joint to steering knuckle retaining nut and cotter pin. Separate the knuckle and ball stud.

9 Unscrew and remove the lower balljoint to strut rod bolts and remove the ball joint.

10 Clean the respective components and inspect for signs of wear and damage. The ball joints must have no visible play when checked, the maximum play allowable being 0.06 in (1.5 mm). Renew any defective parts.

11 Fit the lower ball joint to the lower control arm and tighten the retaining bolts to the specified torque.

12 Locate the ball joint stud into the steering knuckle, fit the castellated nut and tighten to the specified torque, plus a sufficient amount to align the cotter pin holes. Insert the pin and bend it over to retain.

13 Locate the lower control arm to the chassis and drive the bolt carefully into position. Use a soft drift to drive the bolt home in order not to damage the serrated bolt head. Fit the nut and tighten to the specified torque.

14 Refit the torsion bar (see Section 11).

15 Remove the chassis stands/blocks and lower the jack. 'Bounce' the front of the vehicle up and down and then lift at the front, and allow the vehicle to settle at normal height. The strut bars can now be refitted but do not tighten the strut bar to frame nuts until the vehicle ride height has been checked (Section 5).

16 Ensure that the lower control arm side nuts are tightened to the specified torque.

13 Steering knuckle - removal and installation

1 Apply the parking brake and jack up the front of the vehicle to raise the wheels clear of the ground, and support with chassis stands or blocks.

2 Remove the roadwheel.

3 Detach the flexible brake hose from the wheel cylinder - see Chapter 9.

4 Remove the wheel hub - see Section 2 - and brake drum/rotor.

5 Unscrew and remove the tie rod end retaining bolts and detach the rod.

6 Remove the remaining backing plate bolts and detach the backing plate.

7 Withdraw the cotter pins and remove the upper and lower ball joint retaining nuts.

8 Detach the knuckle from the ball joints and remove the knuckle.

9 Clean the respective components and inspect for wear or damage and renew if defective.

10 Reassembly is a direct reversal of removal but note the following.

   a) On reassembly of the wheel hub, adjust the wheel bearing as described in Section 2.

   b) On reconnecting the brake hose, the brakes will require bleeding as described in Chapter 9.

   c) Tighten the respective bolts and nuts to the specified torque and always fit new cotter pins on reassembly.

14 Steering gear - adjustment

1 Adjustment of the steering gear should only be made when items such as the wheel alignment and suspension geometry are known to be correct. The shockabsorbers must be in good condition and the tire pressures as specified. The wheels must be correctly balanced.

2 Detach the ground cable from the battery.

3 Apply the parking brake and jack up the front of the vehicle.

4 Unscrew the retaining nut and remove with washer from the Pitman (idler) arm. Mark the Pitman arm in relation to the shaft and detach it. If special tool no. J-5504-1 is available the arm should be detached by the method shown in Fig. 11.12.

5 Detach the horn shroud and spring.

6 Slowly turn the steering wheel in one direction until it stops and then turn it back halfway. Do not force the steering wheel against the stops when the linkage is detached as the ball guides may be seriously damaged.

7 Using a torque wrench with a maximum torque reading of 50 in lbs, measure the bearing drag when rotating the steering wheel nut thru 90°. Note the torque reading.

Fig. 11.12. Using special tool J.5504 to remove the Pitman arm

Fig. 11.13. Adjust the sector to ballnut backlash

**Fig. 11.14. Separating the ball stud from the link using special tool
J.21687-1**

Fig. 11.15. The idler arm fitting dimension

8　To adjust the over center pre-load, turn the steering wheel from lock to lock and then turn it back to exactly halfway to centralize it.
9　Slacken the locknut and turn the sector (lash) adjuster screw clockwise to eliminate the ball nut to Pitman shaft sector teeth lash. Tighten the locknut.
10 Check the steering wheel rotational torque and note the highest reading in the over center position. Compare this reading with that given in the Specifications and if necessary, readjust the lash adjustment screw to acquire the correct torque reading.
11 Refit the Pitman arm to the shaft with the relative marks in alignment. Fit the nut and tighten to the specified torque.
12 Refit the horn spring and shroud. Remove the jack and reconnect the battery ground cable.

15 Steering wheel - alignment

1　Set the front roadwheels in the straight ahead position and check that the spot mark on the wormshaft which designates the steering high point, is on the top side of the shaft in the 12 o'clock position.
2　If it is not, loosen the left- and right-hand intermediate rod locknuts, and detach the rod ends. Refit turning both ends equally in the same direction to bring the gear back to the high point position.
3　Check and adjust the toe-in as given in Section 4.
4　Now check the steering wheel alignment and if the spokes are not as specified, remove the wheel and center it - see following Section.

16 Steering wheel - removal and installation

1　Detach the ground cable from the battery.
2　Push the horn shroud and turn it counterclockwise. Withdraw the shroud and spring. Disconnect the horn contact ring and wire.
3　Unscrew and remove the steering wheel retaining nut, washer and lockwasher.
4　Mark the relative position of the steering wheel and steering shaft.
5　Remove the four steering column cowling retaining screws and detach the cowling.
6　Using a suitable steering wheel puller, remove the steering wheel.
7　Installation of the steering wheel is the reversal of the above procedure but ensure that the wheel to shaft alignment marks are correct and check the horn operation when the battery is reconnected. Torque the steering wheel nut to that given in the Specifications.

17 Tie rod links (steering arms) - removal and installation

1　Apply the parking brake and jack up the front of the vehicle.
2　Remove the roadwheel.
3　Remove the rotor and hub (Series 5 and 6 models) or brake drum and hub (Series 1 to 4 models) - See Section 2.
4　Unscrew and remove the tie rod link to brake backing plate (Series 1 to 4) or steering knuckle (Series 5 and 6).
5　Withdraw the tie rod ball stud cotter pin and undo the nut.
6　Separate the ball stud from the link - use special tool no. J-21687-01 if available - and detach the tie rod link (Fig. 11.14).
7　Installation is the reverse of removal but note the following.

　　a) Ensure that the tie rod threads are clean before assembly.
　　b) Lubricate the tie rod and ball joint before assembling.
　　c) Fit new cotter pins and tighten the respective nuts to the specified torques.
　　d) Readjust the wheel bearings and bleed the brakes.

18 Tie rod - removal and installation

1　Apply the parking brake and jack up the front of the vehicle.
2　Withdraw the cotter pins from the ball stud retaining nuts. Undo the nuts and separate the ball studs.
3　Install in the reverse order and note the following.

　　a) Ensure that the ball stud threads are clean before refitting.
　　b) Lubricate the ball studs.
　　c) Tie rods are fitted with the lubrication fittings to the front.
　　d) Tighten the ball stud nuts to the torque specified.

19 Idler arm, pivot shaft and/or bracket - removal and installation

1   Apply the parking brake and jack up the vehicle.
2   Unscrew the idler arm to pivot shaft retaining nut and remove with washer.
3   Detach the idler arm from the pivot shaft - if available use special tool no. J-5825.
4   Withdraw the cotter pin and unscrew the nut that retains the intermediate rod and the tie rod to the idler arm. Detach the idler arm.
5   To remove the idler arm pivot shaft and/or bracket, follow the above instructions nos. 1 to 3 and then proceed as follows.
6   Detach the pivot shaft by unscrewing it from the bracket. The bracket is removed by unscrewing the three bolts, nuts and washers from the bracket to frame.
7   Installation is a direct reversal of the removal procedure, but tighten all nuts/bolts to the specified torque. When fitting the idler arm to the bracket and shaft unit, align the lower ends and tighten the nut to the specified torque, and check that the fitting dimensions are as shown in Fig. 11.15.

20 Steering column - removal and installation

1   Detach the ground cable from the battery terminal.
2   Press the horn shroud inwards, twist it counterclockwise and remove the shroud and spring.
3   Detach the steering column cowling and hazard warning switch.
4   Remove the clamp screws and withdraw the direction signal and dimmer switch.
5   Unscrew the steering wheel retaining nut, and withdraw the steering wheel from the shaft using a suitable puller or, if available, special tool no. J-24292. Do not attempt to hammer the wheel from the shaft.
6   Jack up the front of the vehicle and raise the wheels clear of the ground.
7   Slacken the steering shaft flexible coupling clamp bolts, working from the engine compartment, and spread the clamps to allow for the removal of the shaft.
8   Detach the heater hose from its clip on the column. Bend the clip flush to the column.
9   Remove the mast jacket bracket to cowl retaining screws, and the two steering column to instrument panel bolts.
10 Separate the flexible coupling from the shaft and then carefully withdraw the steering column towards the cab.
11 To install, fit the column thru the cowl and locate in position. Insert the steering shaft end into the flexible coupling clamp and install the coupling to gear sector shaft.
12 Fit and tighten the pinch bolts to the specified torque.

13 Fit the column to instrument panel bolts/nuts, but do not tighten yet.
14 Lower the vehicle and remove the jack.
15 Fit the steering column to cowl screws and tighten.
16 Tighten the steering column to instrument panel bolts. It should be noted that the instrument panel must not be removed or installed with the vehicle jacked up.
17 Re-locate the heater hose and retain with the clamp. Refit the direction indicator and dimmer switch to the column.
18 Fit the steering column cowling and locate the hazard warning switch wiring thru the cowling and tighten the setscrews.
19 Refit the steering wheel, washers and nut which must be tightened to the specified torque. Refit the horn shroud and spring, and reconnect the battery ground cable.
20 Check that the horn, combination light switch and hazard warning switch are in operation.
21 Check the interference between the steering column cowling and steering wheel, and also between the column cowling and combination switch.
22 Check the steering wheel free play which should be approximately 0.4 in (10.1 mm) measured at the outside diameter of the steering wheel.

21 Steering shaft - renewal

1   Refer to the previous Section and remove the steering column.
2   Remove the retaining wire from the rubber cup seal and separate the shaft from the mast jacket.
3   Check the ground wire connection on the new shaft and reassemble in the reverse order, and install the column.

22 Steering shaft flexible coupling - removal and installation

1   Apply the parking brake and jack up the front of the vehicle so that the wheels are just clear of the ground.
2   Disconnect and remove the coupling thru bolts (photo). Only two bolts can be removed.
3   Loosen the two pinch bolts to give the necessary clearance and remove the coupling unit.
4   If the coupling clamps are to be removed the steering column must be loosened, so therefore remove the column to cowl mounting screws (photo).
5   Lower the jack and remove the instrument mounting bolts. Slide the column back 1 inch and support it at the steering wheel.
6   Withdraw the column flexible coupling clamps.
7   Reassembly is a reversal of the removal sequence but note the following.

20.2 The flexible coupling

Fig. 11.16. Press and twist the horn shroud to remove

a) Tighten the pinch bolts and other securing bolts/nuts to the specified torques.
b) When reinstalling the instrument panel, ensure that the vehicle is not raised on the jack.

23 Steering gear (steering box) - removal and installation

1 Apply the parking brake and raise the front of the vehicle.
2 Remove the nut and washer securing the Pitman arm to the shaft. Mark the relative positions of the arm and shaft and remove the arm.
3 Detach the engine stone shield.
4 Disconnect the lower clamp to flexible coupling bolts and then the steering gear to frame bolts (photo). Withdraw the steering gear.
5 Installation is a direct reversal of removal but note the following.
   a) Ensure that the Pitman shaft and arm are refitted in the marked positions.
   b) Tighten all securing bolts/nuts to the specified torques.

24 Steering gear - dismantling, inspection and reassembly

1 Remove the steering gear as detailed in Section 22.
2 Clean off the outside of the steering gearbox and drain the lubricant thru the oil filler hole, by removing the plug.
3 Remove the coupling from the worm shaft by withdrawing the pinch bolts.
4 Position the steering shaft in the straight ahead position and remove the top cover bolts, and the adjustment screw locknut.
5 Turn the adjustment screw clockwise and remove the top cover, but hold the sector shaft in the straight ahead position during removal.
6 Remove the adjuster screw and withdraw the sector shaft. Do not remove the shaft by driving out with a hammer or similar harsh methods.
7 Remove the end cover bolts and detach the cover and shims (Fig. 11.20).
8 Extract the worm and ball nut from the gearbox and remove the lower bearing. Retain the worm and ball nut in the horizontal position and do not hold it vertically or the ball nut will fall onto the worm gear end and damage the ball tubes.
9 Clean the respective components for inspection, but do not disturb the clamp plate on the ball tube which is sealed with white paint.
10 Check the following items for wear, distortion, pitting or damage.
   a) Steering shaft
   b) Ball nut teeth
   c) Bearing
   d) Gear casing

11 If, on inspection, the worm shaft components are found to be faulty, then the worm and ball nut unit must be renewed, as they are a matched pair. Oil seals must always be renewed on assembly and bearings, seals, gearbox and covers can be individually renewed as required.
12 To check the ball nut, position the worm and nut vertically and check that the ball nut lowers in a smooth twisting motion. If the motion is not smooth or the ball nut is noisy when lowering, the complete steering shaft unit must be renewed.
13 Check that the sector shaft teeth and serrated portion are not worn or damaged. Measure the reduction in the outside diameter of the shaft. The standard diameter is 1.181 in and the wear limit is 0.001 in. Renew the sector shaft if necessary.
14 Commence reassembly by installing the lower bearing into position in the gearbox.
15 Insert the worm shaft unit and ensure that the lower end of the worm shaft is fitted correctly into the lower bearing.
16 Locate the upper bearing into position on the worm shaft and fit the adjustment shims (Fig. 11.23) between the gearbox and end cover. Smear the end cover and gearbox joint faces with a liquid gasket solution when fitting. Shim adjustment is as follows.
17 Position the gear case in a vice as shown in Fig. 11.24, but do not overtighten the jaws. Locate a pull scale to the flange to coupling bolt and measure the starting torque required. The normal reading should be 3.0 to 5.6 in lbs (2.6 to 5.2 in lbs Series 6) when the coupling starts to turn. Shims are added or subtracted to obtain this reading.

Fig. 11.17. Turn the adjustment screw clockwise

Fig. 11.18. Top cover removed showing gear

22.4 The steering gearbox, showing the column coupling, mounting bolts and adjustment screw. The oil filter is located above the adjustment screw

Fig. 11.19. Withdraw the sector shaft

Fig. 11.20. Remove the end cover

Fig. 11.21. Remove the worm and ball nut

Fig. 11.22. Insert the worm and ball nut

Fig. 11.23. Fit the end cover with shims

Fig. 11.24. Using a pull scale to calculate the starting torque for shim adjustment to the end cover

Fig. 11.25. Install the sector shaft

Fig. 11.26. Fít the sector lash adjuster

Fig. 11.27. Locate the top cover while turning the adjustment screw counterclockwise

Fig. 11.28. Check the total gear preload

Shims are available in thicknesses of 0.002, 0.003, 0.004 and 0.008 inch.

18 Locate the ball nut to the center part of the worm and install the sector shaft. Engage the ball nut, rock with the sector shaft taper gear (Fig. 11.25). The center teeth of the rack and shaft must be engaged in alignment.

19 Fit the adjustment screw into the sector shaft 'T' slot so that there is no clearance between the adjuster screw head and sector shaft. The adjuster screw must slide freely in the slot (Fig. 11.26). If the adjustment screw to sector shaft clearance exceeds 0.001 inch, adjustment can be made by shims available in thickness of 0.059 in.

20 Locate the top cover and gasket smeared with sealant into position while turning the adjustment screw counterclockwise as in Fig. 11.27.

21 Ensure that the ball nut is correctly located with the sector shaft, then fit and tighten the cover retaining bolts.

22 Locate the relative parts in the straight ahead position and pull the flange to coupling bolt with a pull scale as shown in Fig. 11.28. The starting torque required must be 3.5 (4.3 Series 6) to 10.5 in lbs, to rotate the coupling. Adjustment to this torque can be made by turning the adjuster screw accordingly.

23 Fit the adjustment screw locknut and tighten whilst retaining the screw in the set position (Fig. 11.13).

24 Reconnect the sector shaft with the Pitman arm and align the relative marks. Tighten the retaining nut to the specified torque of 160 lb f ft (22.1 kg fm).

25 Align the worm shaft keyway with the key hole in the coupling flange and fit the pinch bolt. Tighten the pinch bolt to 20 lb f ft (2.7 kg fm).

26 Refill the gearbox to the specified level with clean oil of the correct type given in the Specifications.

25 Pitman shaft seal - renewal

1 Apply the parking brake and raise the vehicle.

2 Unscrew the Pitman arm to shaft nut and remove with washer.

3 Mark the arm to shaft relative positions and disconnect the arm.

4 Wipe the seal and surrounding area clean and prise it out using a screwdriver. Clean out the seal recess.

5 If the oil in the steering gear is contaminated, the steering gear should be removed as described in Section 22 and dismantled for inspection as in Section 23 and repaired as required.

6 Smear the new seal with clean steering gear lubricant and locate in the Pitman shaft bore. Tap it carefully into position using a suitable size pipe or socket.

7 Refit the Pitman arm aligning the relative mark to the shaft. Locate the washer and nut and tighten to the specified torque.

8 Lower the vehicle and then check the steering gearbox lubricant level and top up as required, but do not overfill.

Fig. 11.29. The rear suspension component parts

1	Spring pin	18	Shock absorber
2	Bushing	19	Bushing
3	Spring pin	20	Washer
4	Nut	21	Washer
5	Washer	22	Washer
6	Bolt	23	Nut
7	Washer	24	Spring assembly
8	U-bolt	25	Leaf No. 1
9	Plate	26	Leaf No. 2
10	Plate	27	Leaf No. 3
11	Washer	28	Leaf No. 4
12	Nut	29	Leaf No. 5
13	Seat	30	Bolt
14	Rubber	31	Bushing
15	Bolt	32	Nut
16	Washer	33	Bolt
17	Washer	34	Nut

VIEW A

Fig. 11.30. Remove the 'U' bolt nuts

Fig. 11.31. Undo the spring shackle pin bolts

26 Rear suspension - removal, inspection and installation

1 Place blocks under the front wheels to prevent vehicle movement and then jack up the rear axle. Place chassis stands or suitable blocks under the frame near to the rear spring brackets.
2 Undo the shockabsorber retaining nuts and remove the shock-absorbers.
3 Detach the parking brake cable clips.
4 Unscrew the retaining nuts from the leaf spring to axle 'U' bolts. Clean the threaded part of the 'U' bolts and lubricate with penetrating oil to ease removal of the nuts. Remove the 'U' bolts and location plates.
5 Jack up the rear axle sufficiently to separate the leaf spring units.
6 Undo and remove the spring shackle pin retaining nuts from the front and rear. Use a soft drift and hammer out the rear shackle pin and lower the leaf spring.
7 Drift out the front shackle pin and withdraw the leaf spring assembly to the rear.
8 Undo the retaining nut and drift out the shackle pin from the rear bracket and remove the shackle.
9 Clean off the respective components and inspect for wear, and defects.
10 Check the shackles for distortion and the shackle pins for wear, and renew them if necessary.
11 Inspect the leaf springs for signs of cracks, wear or distortion and check the bushes. Renew if required.
12 If the 'U' bolts are distorted, worn or damaged they must be renewed.
13 Check that the jounce bumper is in good condition and firmly seated.
14 The shockabsorbers show signs of oil leakage which indicates that the piston rod seal is being lubricated. If, however, excessive amounts of oil are apparent then the shockabsorber is in need of renewal. It is essential that the shockabsorbers have good compression, tension and make no abnormal noises when operated.
15 Installation is a reversal of removal but be sure to tighten all retaining nuts and bolts to the specified torques. Loosely assemble all parts before tightening.

27 Fault diagnosis - suspension and steering

Symptom	Reason/s
Steering feels vague, car wanders and floats at speed	Tire pressures uneven. Shockabsorbers worn. Spring broken. Steering gear balljoints badly worn. Suspension geometry incorrect. Steering mechanism free play excessive. Front suspension and rear axle pick-up points out of alignment.
Stiff and heavy steering	Tire pressures too low. No grease in steering joints. Front wheel toe-in incorrect. Suspension geometry incorrect. Steering gear incorrectly adjusted too tightly. Steering column badly misaligned.
Wheel wobble and vibration	Wheel nuts loose. Front wheels and tires out of balance. Steering knuckle badly worn. Hub bearings badly worn. Steering gear free play excessive.

Chapter 12 Bodywork and fittings

Contents

Door glass - removal and installation 15	Front fender - removal and installation 21
Door lock - removal and installation 12	General description 1
Door lock cylinder - removal and installation 13	Maintenance - bodywork and underframe 2
Doors - rattles and their rectification 7	Maintenance - hinges and locks 6
Doors - removal and installation 8	Maintenance - upholstery and carpets 3
Door striker - adjustment, removal and installation 14	Major body damage - repair 5
Door trim - removal and installation 9	Minor bodywork damage - repair 4
Door ventilator - removal and installation 10	Rear view mirrors - removal and installation 18
Door ventilator seal and inner frame - removal and installation ... 11	Seat - removal and installation 19
Engine hood/latch/control cable - removal and installation ... 20	Window regulator - removal and installation 16
Front and rear bumpers - removal and installation 22	Windshield/rear window - removal and installation 17

Specifications

Overall length	173.4 ins
Overall width	63.0 ins
Overall height	60.8 ins
Minimum road clearance	8.1 ins
Inside bed length	73.0 ins
Inside bed width	57.5 ins
Inside height of bed	15.6 ins
Width between wheel housings	39.4 ins
Tailgate opening width	53.7 ins
Bed load height	27.2 ins
Bed capacity (approx.)	38 cu ft
Shipping capacity	380 cu ft
Vehicle weight (gross)	3950 lbs
Curb weight	2450 lbs
Payload - less passengers	1100 lbs
Gross axle weight rating	
Front	1600 lbs
Rear	2650 lbs

1 General description

The integral all steel cab and pick up body are mounted on a steel box section frame having six crossmembers. The engine compartment head, the cab doors and rear tailgate are fitted with removable hinges which incorporate provision for adjustment.

The release catch for the engine compartment hood is located beneath the dash panel. The cab doors have over-riding door locks so that when locked, the latch mechanism becomes inoperative. This is a safety device to prevent accidental opening of the door by movement of the inside handle. The doors can be locked from the outside using either the ignition key or by pressing the lock button and pulling the outside handle whilst shutting the door. The doors are locked from inside the cab by pushing down the lock button and unlocked by lifting it.

The seat unit is adjustable by pushing the adjustment lever sideways, which is located on the left side at the front of the seat. To the rear of the hinged backrest there is a small stowage area.

A heater and ventilator system are fitted as standard equipment and are fully adjustable from the dash mounted control panel.

The spare tire is located under the 'cargo box' and when required can be lowered from its stowed position by means of a chain and winch system operated by a crank handle inserted at the rear of the body.

2 Maintenance - bodywork and underframe

1 The general condition of a vehicle's bodywork is the one thing that significantly affects its value. Maintenance is easy but needs to be regular and particular. Neglect, particularly after minor damage, can lead quickly to further deterioration and costly repair bills. It is important also to keep watch on those parts of the vehicle not immediately visible, for instance the underside, inside all the wheel arches and the lower part of the engine compartment.
2 The basic maintenance routine for the bodywork is washing - preferably with a lot of water, from a hose. This will remove all the loose solids which may have stuck to the vehicle. It is important to flush these off in such a way as to prevent grit from scratching the finish.

The wheel arches and underbody need washing in the same way to remove any accumulated mud which will retain moisture and tend to encourage rust. Paradoxically enough, the best time to clean the underbody and wheel arches is in wet weather when the mud is thoroughly wet and soft. In very wet weather the underbody is usually cleaned of large accumulations automatically and this is a good time for inspection.
3 Periodically it is a good idea to have the whole of the underside of the vehicle steam cleaned, engine compartment included, so that a thorough inspection can be carried out to see what minor repairs and renovations are necessary. Steam cleaning is available at many garages and is necessary for removal of accumulation of oily grime which sometimes is allowed to cake thick in certain areas near the engine, gearbox and back axle. If steam facilities are not available, grease solvents are available which can be brush applied. The dirt can then be simply hosed off.
4 After washing the paintwork, wipe off with a chamois leather to give an unspotted clear finish. A coat of clear protective wax polish will give added protection against chemical pollutants in the air. If the paintwork sheen has dulled or oxidised, use a cleaner/polisher combination to restore the brilliance of the shine. This requires a little effort, but is usually caused because regular washing has been neglected. Always check that the door and ventilator opening drain holes and pipes are completely clear so that water can drain out. Bright work should be treated the same way as paintwork. Windscreen and windows can be kept clear of the smeary film which often appears, if a little ammonia is added to the water. If they are scratched, a good rub with a proprietary metal polish will often clear them. Never use any form of wax or other body or chromium polish on glass.

3 Maintenance - upholstery and carpets

1 Mats and carpets should be brushed or vacuum cleaned regularly to keep them free of grit. If they are badly stained removed them from the vehicle for scrubbing or sponging and make quite sure they are dry before refitting Seats and interior trim panels can be kept clean by a wipe over with a damp cloth. If they do become stained (which can be more apparent on light colored upholstery) use a little liquid detergent and a soft nail brush to scour the grime out of the grain of the material. Do not forget to keep the head lining clean in the same way as the upholstery. When using liquid cleaners inside the car do not over-wet the surfaces being cleaned. Excessive damp could get into the seams and padded interior causing stains, offensive odours or even rot. If the inside of the vehicle gets wet accidentally it is worthwhile taking some trouble to dry it out properly particularly where carpets are involved. **Do not** leave oil or electric heaters inside the cab for this purpose.

4 Minor bodywork damage - repair

The photographic sequence on pages 206 and 207 illustrates the operations detailed in the following sub-Sections.

Repair of minor scratches in the vehicle's bodywork

If the scratch is very superficial and does not penetrate the metal of the bodywork, repair is very simple. Lightly rub the area of the scratch with a paintwork renovator, or a very fine cutting paste, to remove loose paint from the scratch and to clear the surrounding bodywork of wax polish. Rinse the area with clean water.

Apply touch-up paint to the scratch using a thin paintbrush, continue to apply thin layers of paint until the surface of the paint in the scratch is level with the surrounding paintwork. Allow the new paint at least two weeks to harden; then, blend it into the surrounding paintwork by rubbing the paintwork, in the scratch area with a paintwork renovator, or a very fine cutting paste. Finally apply wax polish.

Where the scratch has penetrated right through to the metal of the bodywork, causing the metal to rust, a different repair technique is required. Remove any loose rust from the bottom of the scratch with a penknife, then apply rust inhibiting paint to prevent the formation of rust in the future. Using a rubber nylon applicator fill the scratch with bodystopper paste. If required, this paste can be mixed with cellulose thinners to provide a very thin paste which is ideal for filling narrow scratches. Before the stopper paste in the scratch hardens, wrap a piece of smooth cotton rag around the top of a finger. Dip the finger in cellulose thinners and then quickly sweep it across the surface of the stopper paste in the scratch; this will ensure that the surface of the stopper paste is slightly hollowed. The scratch can now be painted over as described earlier in this Section.

Repair of dents in the vehicle's bodywork

When deep denting of the vehicle's bodywork has taken place, the first task is to pull the dent out, until the affected bodywork almost attains its original shape. There is little point in trying to restore the original shape completely, as the metal in the damaged area will have stretched on impact and cannot be reshaped fully to its original contour. It is better to bring the level of the dent up to a point which is about 1/8 inch (3 mm) below the level of the surrounding bodywork. In cases where the dent is very shallow anyway, it is not worth trying to pull it out at all.

If the underside of the dent is accessible, it can be hammered out gently from behind, using a mallet with a wooden or plastic head. Whilst doing this, hold a suitable block of wood firmly against the impact from the hammer blows and thus prevent a large area of bodywork from being 'belled-out'.

Should the dent be in a section of the bodywork which has a double skin or some other factor making it inaccessible from behind, a different technique is called for. Drill several small holes through the metal inside the dent area - particularly in the deeper sections. Then screw long self-tapping screws into the holes just sufficiently for them to gain a good purchase in the metal. Now the dent can be pulled out by pulling on the protruding heads of the screws with a pair of pliers.

The next stage of the repair is the removal of the paint from the damaged area, and from an inch or so of the surrounding 'sound' bodywork. This is accomplished most easily by using a wire brush or abrasive pad on a power drill, although it can be done just as effectively by hand using sheets of abrasive paper. To complete the preparations for filling, score the surface of the bare metal with a screwdriver or the tang of a file, or alternatively, drill small holes in the affected area. This will provide a really good 'key' for the filler paste.

To complete the repair see the Section on filling and respraying.

Repair of rust holes or gashes in the vehicle's bodywork

Remove all paint from the affected area and from an inch or so of the surrounding 'sound' bodywork, using an abrasive pad or a wire brush on a power drill. If these are not available a few sheets of abrasive paper will do the job just as effectively. With the paint removed you will be able to gauge the severity of the corrosion and therefore decide whether to replace the whole panel (if this is possible) or to repair the affected area. Replacement body panels are not as expensive as most people think and it is often quicker and more satisfactory to fit a new panel than to attempt to repair large areas of corrosion.

Remove all fittings from the affected area except those which will act as a guide to the original shape of the damaged bodywork (eg; headlamp shells etc.) Then, using tin snips or a hacksaw blade, remove all loose metal and any other metal badly affected by corrosion. Hammer the edges of the hole inwards in order to create a slight depression for the filler paste.

Wire brush the affected area to remove the powdery rust from the surface of the remaining metal. Paint the affected area with rust inhibiting paint, if the back of the rusted area is accessible treat this also.

Before filling can take place it will be necessary to block the hole in some way. This can be achieved by the use of one of the following materials: Zinc gauze, Aluminum tape or Polyurethane foam.

Zinc gauze is probably the best material to use for a large hole. Cut a piece to the approximate size and shape of the hole to be filled, then position it in the hole so that its edges are below the level of the surrounding bodywork. It can be retained in position by several blobs of filler paste around its periphery.

Aluminum tape should be used for small or very narrow holes. Pull a piece off the roll and trim it to the approximate size and shape required, then pull off the backing paper (if used) and stick the tape over the hole; it can be overlapped if the thickness of one piece is insufficient. Burnish down the edges of the tape with the handle of a screwdriver or similar, to ensure that the tape is securely attached to the metal underneath.

Polyurethane foam is best used where the hole is situated in a section of bodywork of complex shape, backed by a small box section (eg; where the sill panel meets the rear wheel arch - most vehicles). The unusual mixing procedure for this foam is as follows: Put equal amounts of fluid from each of the two cans provided in the kit, into one container. Stir until the mixture begins to thicken, then quickly pour this mixture into the hole, and hold a piece of cardboard over the larger apertures. Almost immediately the polyurethane will begin to expand, gushing frantically out of any small holes left unblocked. When the foam hardens it can be cut back to just below the level of the surrounding bodywork with a hacksaw blade.

Bodywork repairs - filling and re-spraying

Before using this Section, see the Sections on dent, deep scratch, rust hole and gash repairs.

Many types of bodyfiller are available, but generally speaking those proprietary kits which contain a tin of filler paste and a tube of resin hardener are best for this type of repair. A wide, flexible plastic or nylon applicator will be found invaluable for imparting a smooth and well contoured finish to the surface of the filler.

Mix up a little filler on a clean piece of card or board - use the hardener sparingly (follow the maker's instructions on the packet) otherwise the filler will set very rapidly.

Using the applicator, apply the filler paste to the prepared area; draw the applicator across the surface of the filler to achieve the correct contour and to level the filler surface. As soon as a contour that approximates the correct one is achieved, stop working the paste - if you carry on too long the paste will become sticky and begin to 'pick-up' on the applicator. Continue to add thin layers of filler paste at twenty-minute intervals until the level of the filler is just 'proud' of the surrounding bodywork.

Once the filler has hardened, excess can be removed using a Surform plane or Dreadnought file. From then on, progessively finer grades of abrasive paper should be used, starting with a 40 grade production paper and finishing with 400 grade 'wet-and-dry' paper. Always wrap the abrasive paper around a flat rubber, cork, or wooden block - otherwise the surface of the filler will not be completely flat. During the smoothing of the filler surface the 'wet-and-dry' paper should be periodically rinsed in water. This will ensure that a very

smooth finish is imparted to the filler at the final stage.

At this stage the 'dent' should be surrounded by a ring of bare metal, which in turn should be encircled by the finely 'feathered' edge of the good paintwork. Rinse the repair area with clean water, until all of the dust produced by the rubbing-down operation is gone.

Spray the whole repair area with a light coat of grey primer - this will show up any imperfections in the surface of the filler. Repair these imperfections with fresh filler paste or bodystopper, and once more smooth the surface with abrasive paper. If bodystopper is used, it can be mixed with cellulose thinners to form a really thin paste which is ideal for filling small holes. Repeat this spray and repair procedure until you are satisfied that the surface of the filler, and the feathered edge of the paintwork are perfect. Clean the repair area with clean water and allow to dry fully.

The repair area is now ready for spraying. Paint spraying must be carried out in a warm, dry, windless and dust free atmosphere. This condition can be created artificially if you have access to a large indoor working area, but if you are forced to work in the open, you will have to pick your day very carefully. If you are working indoors, dousing the floor in the work area with water will 'lay' the dust which would otherwise be in the atmosphere. If the repair area is confined to one body panel, mask off the surrounding panels; this will help to minimise the effects of a slight mis-match in paint colors. Bodywork fitting (eg; chrome strips, door handles etc), will also need to be masked off. Use genuine masking tape and several thicknesses of news-paper for the masking operation.

Before commencing to spray, agitate the aerosol can thoroughly, then spray a test area (an old tin, or similar) until the technique is mastered. Cover the repair area with a thick coat of primer; the thick-ness should be built up using several thin layers of paint rather than one thick one. Using 400 grade 'wet-and-dry' paper, rub down the surface of the primer until it is really smooth. While doing this, the work area should be thoroughly doused with water, and the 'wet-and-dry' paper periodically rinsed in water. Allow to dry before spraying on more paint.

Spray on the top coat, again building up the thickness by using several thin layers of paint. Start spraying in the center of the repair area and then, using a circular motion, work outwards until the whole repair area and about 2 inches of the surrounding original paintwork is covered. Remove all masking material 10 to 15 minutes after spraying on the final coat of paint.

Allow the new paint at least 2 weeks to harden fully; then, using a paintwork renovator or a very fine cutting paste, blend the edges of the new paint into the existing paintwork. Finally, apply wax polish.

5 Major body damage - repair

Where serious damage has occurred or large areas need renewal due to neglect, it means certainly that completely new sections or panels will need welding in and this is best left to professionals. If the damage is due to impact it will also be necessary to completely check the alignment of the bodyshell structure. Due to the principle of con-struction the strength and shape of the whole can be affected by damage to a part. In such instances the services of the official agent with specialist checking jigs are essential. If a body is left misaligned it is first of all dangerous as the car will not handle properly and secondly, uneven stresses will be imposed on the steering, engine and transmission, causing abnormal wear or complete failure. Tire wear may also be excessive.

6 Maintenance - hinges and locks

1 Periodically lubricate the hinges of the doors, hood and tailgate with a few drops of light oil.
2 Similarly lubricate the door catches, hood release mechanism and the release mechanism of the spare wheel.
3 Apply a smear of general purpose grease to the lock strikers, and striker plates.

7 Doors - rattles and their rectification

1 Check first that the door is not loose at the hinges and that the

UPPER HINGE

LOWER HINGE

Fig. 12.1. The component parts of the upper and lower door hinges

latch is holding the door firmly in position. Check also that the door lines up with the aperture in the body.

2   If the hinges are loose, or the door is out of alignment, it will be necessary to reset the hinge positions. This is a straightforward matter after slackening the hinge retaining screws slightly, following which the door can be repositioned in/out or up/down.

3   If the latch is holding the door properly it should hold the door tightly when fully latched and the door should line up with the body. If adjustment is required, slacken the striker plate screws slightly and reposition the plate in/out or up/down as necessary. Fore and aft adjustment of the striker plate is effected by the use of shims.

4   Other rattles from the door could be caused by wear or looseness in the window winder, or the glass channels, seal strips and interior lock mechanism.

8   Doors - removal and installation

1   To remove a door, open and support it with a jack or preferably get an assistant to support it.

2   To aid refitting, mark around the hinge with a soft lead pencil and then unscrew the hinge retaining bolts, and lift the door clear.

3   If a replacement door is being fitted, remove the door trim panel, lock assembly, the window and its regulator assemblies (Sections 9 to 16) and fit them to the new door.

4   Installation of the door is a direct reversal of removal but adjustment will probably be necessary as described in Section 14.

9   Door trim - removal and installation

1   Press the door trim around the window regulator and withdraw the regulator handle retaining clip, then detach the handle (photo).

Fig. 12.2. The component parts of the door assembly

1	Window	4	Lock cylinder	7	Window regulator	10	Inner lever
2	Outside handle	5	Lock assembly	8	Inner lever to lock link	11	Window regulator
3	Lock rod	6	Support bracket	9	Glass stopper		

9.1 Remove the regulator handle

Fig. 12.3. The door trim and associate parts

2   Raise the latch lever and withdraw the escutcheon (photo). Undo the latch lever retaining screws to remove the latch lever.
3   Remove the armrest which is retained by two screws, and then carefully prise away the trim panel from the door. The trim is retained by nine nylon 'bullet type' fasteners.
4   Installation is the reversal of the removal procedure.

10 Door ventilation - removal and installation

1   Remove the inner door trim panel as described in Section 9.
2   Peel back the waterproof sheet from the check hole, and the glass stopper which is retained by a crosshead screw. Lower the door glass, withdraw it from the regulator channel and remove it from the door.
3   Remove the door inner weatherstrip and seal unit.
4   The door ventilation division bar is now detached from the support bracket, then undo the door ventilator to door frame retaining screw and withdraw the ventilator assembly from the door.
5   Installation is the reversal of removal but note the following:

   a) *When installing the waterproof sheet to the check hole, ensure that there is a continuous even bead of adhesive round the opening and stretch the vinyl to avoid wrinkles. A firm finger pressure is sufficient to ensure good adhesion.*
   b) *Having installed the division bar and door frame, the upper clearance should be fitted with cemedine sealer or a similar sealant.*

9.2 Remove the latch lever escutcheon

11 Door ventilator seal and inner frame - removal and installation

1   First remove the pivot by filing (Fig. 12.4).
2   Unscrew the nut and remove with the spring from the lower frame.
3   Detach the inner frame and the seal can then be removed.
4   Refit in the reverse order but note the following:

   a) *When inserting the pin into position from the upper face, caulk it with a suitable drift.*
   b) *Ensure that the inner frame and vent seal are in good contact.*
   c) *Take care when installing the vent seal to avoid damaging it - soapy water will ease fitting.*
   d) *Ensure that the stop washer is correctly located.*

12 Door lock - removal and installation

9.3 The inner door panel with trim removed

1   Remove the inner trim panel from the door as described in Section 9.

Fig. 12.5. The door lock cylinder

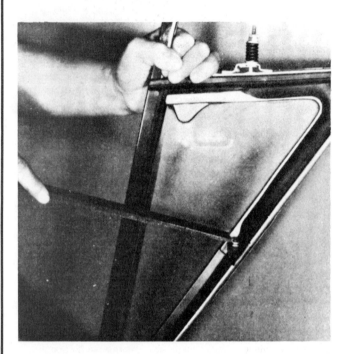

Fig. 12.4. File the pivot to remove

Fig. 12.6. The striker and adjustment sheet

Fig. 12.7. The door glass and channel showing the correct relative position

2   Peel back the water deflectors from the check holes and extract the retaining clip from the lock side of the inner lever assembly.

3   Detach the cylinder link from the lock arm nylon fastener and remove the glass rim channel.

4   The relay lever bracket is now removed from the door lock side, and the door lock button from the lock rod.

5   Disconnect the outer link from the handle link (outside) and the retaining screws from the door lock unit. Withdraw the lock from the door.

6   To install the door lock assembly, first grease the respective linkages, then locate the lock into position, and the door lock knob and reconnect the outside handle to the lock link. Refit the securing bolts, but do not tighten.

7   Adjust the linkage so that the maximum handle free play is ¼ inch, and then tighten the adjustment nut with an open ended wrench. The securing bolts can now be tightened.

8   Reconnect the lock link to the cylinder and relocate the glass run channel and support bracket.

9   Fit the inner lever unit into position reconnecting it to the lock link. Check the lock action and if satisfactory, refit the trim panel and handles. The water deflectors must be refitted using a suitable adhesive.

Fig. 12.8. The external door handle and door lock

13 Door lock cylinder - removal and installation

1   Remove the inner trim panel from the door as described in Section 9 and partially peel back the water deflector panel. With the window in the raised position, disconnect the door lock link.

2   Remove the lock cylinder retaining clip using a screwdriver to prise it with and withdraw the cylinder from the door.

3   Installation is a reversal of the above procedure.

AREA A
APPLY SEALER BETWEEN
BODY AND WEATHERSTRIP

AREA B
APPLY SEALER BETWEEN
GLASS AND WEATHERSTRIP

Fig. 12.9. The windshield upper and lower sealant points 'A' and 'B' together with the upper and lower weatherstrip fitting (insets)

A MAN INSIDE THE CAB PULLS THE ENDS OF CORD IN SEQUENCE AS SHOWN

ASSISTANT PUSHES FROM OUTSIDE

PULL

THE CORD SHOULD BE PULLED IN TOWARD CENTER OF THE WINDOW GLASS.

END OF CORD OVERLAP BY AT LEAST 12 INCHES.

FREE ENDS OF CORD FITTED INTO PINCHED CAVITY OF WEATHERSTRIP SHOULD BE LONGER THAN 8 INCHES.

Fig. 12.10. The rear glass installation diagram

14 Door striker - adjustment, removal and installation

1   Slacken the striker plate screw and adjust it so that the bottom face of the dovetail is parallel to the striker. Tap the striker with a wooden drift and hammer.
2   To adjust the engagement of the striker with the door latch, adjustment sheets are available as required (see Fig. 12.7). Two to three sheets are normally required to get the correct adjustment.
3   If the striker plate is to be removed, first mark its location with a pencil. Unscrew the retaining screws and remove the striker noting the nuber of adjustment sheets.
4   Refit in the reverse order and if necessary adjust as described in paragraph 1.

15 Door glass - removal and installation

1   Remove the inner door trim panel as described in Section 9 and peel back the water deflectors.
2   Unscrew the glass stopper retaining screw and remove the stopper. With the window lowered, extract the window from the regulator and disconnect the inside lever unit.
3   Withdraw the glass run channel and then carefully extract the glass lowering it to its limit and tilting its side upwards. The bottom channel may be removed from the glass by tapping the lower channel lightly with a wooden hammer.
4   Installation is a reversal of the removal sequence but if the glass has been removed from the bottom channel, ensure that the glazing rubber located in the channel is in good condition and located correctly before reinserting the glass. See Fig. 12.8 for the correct bottom channel location to the glass.

16 Window regulator - removal and installation

Series 1 to 5 models
1   Remove the door trim panel and peel the water deflector sheets from the inner door.
2   Unscrew the retaining screw and remove the glass stopper.
3   With the glass lowered disconnect the regulator arm rollers from the bottom window channel.
4   Undo the retaining screw from the window regulator and extract the regulator thru the check hole.
5   Installation is the reversal of removal but apply some grease to the regulator arm rollers before assembly, and check the action of the window before refitting the inner panel and water deflectors.

Series 6 models
6   Follow instruction 1 above.
7   Support the glass by hand and unscrew the regulator securing screws.
8   Remove the regulator arm rollers from the bottom channel and lower the glass. The window regulator can now be withdrawn thru the check hole.
9   Installation is the reversal of removal but apply some grease to the regulator arm rollers prior to assembly, and check the window action before refitting the inner panel and water deflectors.

17 Windshield/rear window - removal and installation

1   If the windshield or rear window glass is in need of renewal due to breakage or the sealing rubber is to be renewed, it is recommended that the job be entrusted to a properly equipped repair shop. Special

skills and tools are required to correctly refit the windshield and rear window glass and in the hands of a novice there is always the danger of breaking the new glass. However in the event of no local workshop having the required facilities the task may be very carefully undertaken as follows. The procedure is identical for the windshield and rear window (with the exception of paragraph 2 for the rear window).

2   Remove the windshield wipers, rear view mirror and sun visor.

3   Insert a flat blade tool between the inner face and flange of the rubber channel and separate the weatherstrip from the body taking great care. Do not use a sharp implement and avoid damaging the rubber strip if possible. The upper and lower corners of the windshield are filled with a sealer solution which is applied between the rubber channel and body flange.

4   If possible wear a pair of gloves and with the aid of an assistant, push on a corner of the windshield and gradually remove it from the body opening. Remove the weatherstrip and clean off all traces of old sealant from the glass and/or weatherstrip and body.

5   Commence installation by locating the weatherstrip round the windshield. Soapy water applied to the weatherstrip will ease fitting.

6   Locate a length of strong cord into and around the outer channel of the weatherstrip and overlap it in the middle at the lower edge by a minimum of 12 inches. Temporarily retain the cord in position by tapping the ends to the inner surface of the glass.

7   The upper and lower corners of the rubber channel should be smeared with a suitable water repellent sealer as shown in positions 'A' and 'B' in Fig. 12.9.

8   With the aid of an assistant, locate the windshield into position from the outside. Whilst the assistant applies pressure to the outside of the glass, carefully pull the ends of the cord inwards so that the inner lip of the rubber channel seats over the body flange, as in Fig. 12.10 (inset).

9   With the glass fully located, remove the cord. Refit the windshield

wipers, interior mirrors and sun visor. Wipe away any surplus sealant that may have smeared onto the glass.

18 Rear view mirrors - removal and installation

Interior mirror

1   The rear view mirror is retained by a bracket which also supports the sun visor.

2   To remove the mirror, press it in the direction shown in Fig. 12.11.

3   To install the mirror, locate the lower part of the mirror assembly clip into the bracket and tap portion 'B' with a soft faced hammer to drive it into position.

External mirror

4   The external mirror is retained by two self-tapping screws which are simply unscrewed to remove the mirror complete with gasket.

5   When refitting, renew the gasket if the old one has perished or worn, align the screw holes and tighten the screws.

19 Seat - removal and installation

1   Hinge forward the driver and passenger seat back and disconnect the seat belts by removing their retaining bolts and spring washers.

2   With the belts removed, undo the four nuts with spring and plain washers which secure the seat adjusters (Fig. 12.12) to the floor. The nuts are located under the floor, and when all are unscrewed the seat can be removed.

3   To install the seat, reverse the removal instructions but tighten the seat belt retaining bolts to a torque of 50 lb f ft (6.9 kg f m).

Fig. 12.11. The interior mirror removal and installation

Fig. 12.12. The seat runner location nuts and washers

Fig. 12.13. The hood latch and control cable

Fig. 12.14. The fender retaining bolt positions

This sequence of photographs deals with the repair of the dent and scratch (above rear lamp) shown in this photo. The procedure will be similar for the repair of a hole. It should be noted that the procedures given here are simplified - more explicit instructions will be found in the text

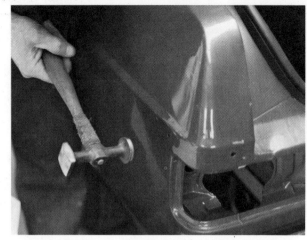

In the case of a dent the first job - after removing surrounding trim - is to hammer out the dent where access is possible. This will minimise filling. Here, the large dent having been hammered out, the damaged area is being made slightly concave

Now all paint must be removed from the damaged area, by rubbing with coarse abrasive paper. Alternatively, a wire brush or abrasive pad can be used in a power drill. Where the repair area meets good paintwork, the edge pf the paintwork should be 'feathered', using a finer grade of abrasive paper

In the case of a hole caused by rusting, all damaged sheet-metal should be cut away before proceeding to this stage. Here, the damaged area is being treated with rust remover and inhibitor before being filled

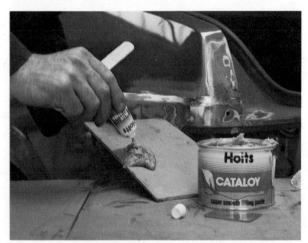

Mix the body filler according to its manufacturer's instructions. In the case of corrosion damage, it will be necessary to block off any large holes before filling - this can be done with zinc gauze or aluminium tape. Make sure the area is absolutely clean before ...

... applying the filler. Filler should be applied with a flexible applicator, as shown, for best results: the wooden spatula being used for confined areas. Apply thin layers of filler at 20-minute intervals, until the surface of the filler is slightly proud of the surrounding bodywork

Initial shaping can be done with a Surform plane or Dreadnought file. Then, using progressively finer grades of wet-and-dry paper, wrapped around a sanding block, and copious amounts of clean water, rub-down the filler until really smooth and flat. Again, feather the edges of adjoining paintwork

The whole repair area can now be sprayed or brush-painted with primer. If spraying, ensure adjoining areas are protected from over-spray. Note that at least one-inch of the surrounding sound paintwork should be coated with primer. Primer has a 'thick' consistency, so will fill small imperfections

Again, using plenty of water, rub down the primer with a fine grade of wet-and-dry paper (400 grade is probably best) until it is really smooth and well blended into the surrounding paintwork. Any remaining imperfections can now be filled by carefully applied knifing stopper paste

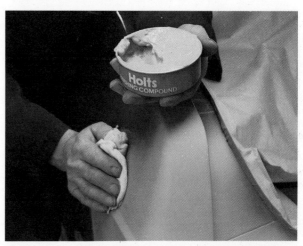

When the stopper has hardened, rub-down the repair area again before applying the final coat of primer. Before rubbing-down this last coat of primer, ensure the repair area is blemish-free - use more stopper if necessary. To ensure that the surface of the primer is really smooth use some finishing compound

The top coat can now be applied. When working out of doors, pick a dry, warm and wind-free day. Ensure surrounding areas are protected from over-spray. Agitate the aerosol thoroughly, then spray the centre of the repair area, working outwards with a circular motion. Apply the paint as several thin coats.

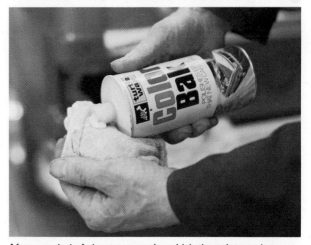

After a period of about two-weeks, which the paint needs to harden fully, the surface of the repaired area can be 'cut' with a mild cutting compound prior to wax polishing. When carrying out bodywork repairs, remember that the quality of the finished job is proportional to the time and effort expended

20.3 The hood latch showing return spring and control cable

20 Engine hood/latch/control cable - removal and installation

Engine hood

1   Raise the hood, and support. Undo the hinge retaining bolts and with the aid of an assistant, carefully lift the hood clear.
2   Installation is the reverse of removal, but to adjust the hood, position it correctly by adjustment of the hinge position to the body for vertical adjustment and hinge to hood for horizontal adjustment.

Hood latch

3   Disconnect the return spring and hood control cable and then remove the latch. Refit in the reverse order.

Hood control cable

4   Unscrew the cable clip retaining screw on the release lever side and disconnect the cable. Then remove the cable from the dashpanel clip.
5   Disconnect the cable from the latch and withdraw the cable thru the engine compartment.
6   To install, reverse the above procedure, inserting the cable end into the latch side clip, and then hinge the latch striker lever to position 'A' in Fig. 12.13. Locate the end of the cable 'C' into hole 'B' and tighten the cable retaining clip.

21 Front fender - removal and installation

1   The front fenders are retained by means of screws and bolts as shown in Fig. 12.14. Remove as follows.
2   Disconnect the windshield wiper arms and the grille.
3   Detach the headlight assembly and the side marker light (see Chapter 10).
4   Detach the front bumper.
5   Unscrew the fender retaining bolts/screws from these positions shown in Fig. 12.14 and remove the fender.
6   To install the fender, reverse the above procedure and check for alignment before fully tightening the fender retaining screws/bolts.

22 Front and rear bumpers - removal and installation

1   The front and rear bumpers may be removed with or without their brackets by unscrewing the bumper to bracket bolts, two on each side, or alternatively by unscrewing the respective bracket retaining bolts.
2   Installation is a direct reversal of the above procedure.

Metric conversion tables

Inches	Decimals	Millimetres	Millimetres to Inches		Inches to Millimetres	
			mm	Inches	Inches	mm
1/64	0.015625	0.3969	0.01	0.00039	0.001	0.0254
1/32	0.03125	0.7937	0.02	0.00079	0.002	0.0508
3/64	0.046875	1.1906	0.03	0.00118	0.003	0.0762
1/16	0.0625	1.5875	0.04	0.00157	0.004	0.1016
5/64	0.078125	1.9844	0.05	0.00197	0.005	0.1270
3/32	0.09375	2.3812	0.06	0.00236	0.006	0.1524
7/64	0.109375	2.7781	0.07	0.00276	0.007	0.1778
1/8	0.125	3.1750	0.08	0.00315	0.008	0.2032
9/64	0.140625	3.5719	0.09	0.00354	0.009	0.2286
5/32	0.15625	3.9687	0.1	0.00394	0.01	0.254
11/64	0.171875	4.3656	0.2	0.00787	0.02	0.508
3/16	0.1875	4.7625	0.3	0.1181	0.03	0.762
13/64	0.203125	5.1594	0.4	0.01575	0.04	1.016
7/32	0.21875	5.5562	0.5	0.01969	0.05	1.270
15/64	0.234275	5.9531	0.6	0.02362	0.06	1.524
1/4	0.25	6.3500	0.7	0.02756	0.07	1.778
17/64	0.265625	6.7469	0.8	0.3150	0.08	2.032
9/32	0.28125	7.1437	0.9	0.03543	0.09	2.286
19/64	0.296875	7.5406	1	0.03937	0.1	2.54
5/16	0.3125	7.9375	2	0.07874	0.2	5.08
21/64	0.328125	8.3344	3	0.11811	0.3	7.62
11/32	0.34375	8.7312	4	0.15748	0.4	10.16
23/64	0.359375	9.1281	5	0.19685	0.5	12.70
3/8	0.375	9.5250	6	0.23622	0.6	15.24
25/64	0.390625	9.9219	7	0.27559	0.7	17.78
13/32	0.40625	10.3187	8	0.31496	0.8	20.32
27/64	0.421875	10.7156	9	0.35433	0.9	22.86
7/16	0.4375	11.1125	10	0.39270	1	25.4
29/64	0.453125	11.5094	11	0.43307	2	50.8
15/32	0.46875	11.9062	12	0.47244	3	76.2
31/64	0.484375	12.3031	13	0.51181	4	101.6
1/2	0.5	12.7000	14	0.55118	5	127.0
33/64	0.515625	13.0969	15	0.59055	6	152.4
17/32	0.53125	13.4937	16	0.62992	7	177.8
35/64	0.546875	13.8906	17	0.66929	8	203.2
9/16	0.5625	14.2875	18	0.70866	9	228.6
37/64	0.578125	14.6844	19	0.74803	10	254.0
19/32	0.59375	15.0812	20	0.78740	11	279.4
39/64	0.609375	15.4781	21	0.82677	12	304.8
5/8	0.625	15.8750	22	0.86614	13	330.2
41/64	0.640625	16.2719	23	0.90551	14	355.6
21/32	0.65625	16.6687	24	0.94488	15	381.0
43/64	0.671875	17.0656	25	0.98425	16	406.4
11/16	0.6875	17.4625	26	1.02362	17	431.8
45/64	0.703125	17.8594	27	1.06299	18	457.2
23/32	0.71875	18.2562	28	1.10236	19	482.6
47/64	0.734375	18.6531	29	1.14173	20	508.0
3/4	0.75	19.0500	30	1.18110	21	533.4
49/64	0.765625	19.4469	31	1.22047	22	558.8
25/32	0.78125	19.8437	32	1.25984	23	584.2
51/64	0.796875	20.2406	33	1.29921	24	609.6
13/16	0.8125	20.6375	34	1.33858	25	635.0
53/64	0.828125	21.0344	35	1.37795	26	660.4
27/32	0.84375	21.4312	36	1.41732	27	685.8
55/64	0.859375	21.8281	37	1.4567	28	711.2
7/8	0.875	22.2250	38	1.4961	29	736.6
57/64	0.890625	22.6219	39	1.5354	30	762.0
29/32	0.90625	23.0187	40	1.5748	31	787.4
59/64	0.921875	23.4156	41	1.6142	32	812.8
15/16	0.9375	23.8125	42	1.6535	33	838.2
61/64	0.953125	24.2094	43	1.6929	34	863.6
31/32	0.96875	24.6062	44	1.7323	35	889.0
63/64	0.984375	25.0031	45	1.7717	36	914.4

1   Imperial gallon = 8 Imp pints = 1.16 US gallons = 277.42 cu in = 4.5459 litres

1   US gallon = 4 US quarts = 0.862 Imp gallon = 231 cu in = 3.785 litres

1   Litre = 0.2199 Imp gallon = 0.2642 US gallon = 61.0253 cu in = 1000 cc

Miles to Kilometres		Kilometres to Miles	
1	1.61	1	0.62
2	3.22	2	1.24
3	4.83	3	1.86
4	6.44	4	2.49
5	8.05	5	3.11
6	9.66	6	3.73
7	11.27	7	4.35
8	12.88	8	4.97
9	14.48	9	5.59
10	16.09	10	6.21
20	32.19	20	12.43
30	48.28	30	18.64
40	64.37	40	24.85
50	80.47	50	31.07
60	96.56	60	37.28
70	112.65	70	43.50
80	128.75	80	49.71
90	144.84	90	55.92
100	160.93	100	62.14

lb f ft to Kg f m		Kg f m to lb f ft		lb f/in^2 : Kg f/cm^2		Kg f/cm^2 : lb f/in^2	
1	0.138	1	7.233	1	0.07	1	14.22
2	0.276	2	14.466	2	0.14	2	28.50
3	0.414	3	21.699	3	0.21	3	42.67
4	0.553	4	28.932	4	0.28	4	56.89
5	0.691	5	36.165	5	0.35	5	71.12
6	0.829	6	43.398	6	0.42	6	85.34
7	0.967	7	50.631	7	0.49	7	99.56
8	1.106	8	57.864	8	0.56	8	113.79
9	1.244	9	65.097	9	0.63	9	128.00
10	1.382	10	62.330	10	0.70	10	142.23
20	2.765	20	144.660	20	1.41	20	284.47
30	4.147	30	216.990	30	2.11	30	426.70

Index

A

Accelerator - 76
Air cleaners - 59
Air conditioning - 165
Air injection system - 73
Alternator - 150
Alternator regulator - 153
Anti-roll bar - 203
Automatic temperature - 60
Automatic transmission
    extension housing seal - 124
    fault diagnosis - 124
    fluid level - 121
    general description - 121
    inhibitor switch - 123
    kick-down switch - 123
    maintenance - 121
    rear oil seal - 124
    removal and installation - 124
    selector linkage - 122
    shift lever - 124
    starter inhibitor - 123
Axle shaft - 125, 127

B

Battery
    charging - 150
    electrolyte replenishment - 150
    maintenance and inspection 149
    removal and installation - 149
Big-end (connecting rod bearings) - 27, 45
Bodywork and fittings
    air conditioning - 165
    bumpers - 208
    doors - 199, 201
    doors - locks - 201
    door glass - 204
    fresh air outlet - 163
    heater - 161 - 163
    hood - 208
    maintenance - 198, 199
    rear mirrors - 205
    repairs
        major damage - 199
        minor damage - 198
    windshield/rear window - 204
Braking system
    bleeding hydraulic system - 136
    brake adjustment - 134
    brake disc/hub - 141
    brake hoses - 138
    brake pedal - 134, 145
    brake hoses - 138
    brake shoes - 138 , 141
    caliper - 140
    disc pads - 140
    fault diagnosis - 146
    general description - 134
    master cylinder - single - 136
    master cylinder - tandem - 134
    parking brake (handbrake) - 136, 145
    power cylinder - 143
    wheel cylinder front - 143
Bulbs - 148
Buying spare parts - 4

C

Cables
    accelerator - 76
    caliper brake - 140
    hood - 208
    parking brake - 136, 145
Camshaft - removal - 24, 27, 45
Carburetors
    air cleaners - 59
    choke - automatic - 69
    emission controls - 73
    exhaust system - 83
    fast idle - 60
    fault diagnosis - 83
    float level - 67
    fuel pump - 69, 70
    overhaul - 60, 64, 65
    series 1 and 2 models - 60
    series 3 models - 64
    series 4 to 6 models - 65
Clutch
    adjustment - 98
    bleeding - 98
    fault diagnosis - 102
    general description - 98
    inspection and renovation - 101
    installation - 102
    judder - 102
    master cylinder - 99
    operating cylinder - 100
    pedal - removal and installation - 98
    release bearing - 102
    removal - 100
    shift fork - 98
    slip - 102
    spin - 102
Coil - 95
Condenser - 88
Connecting rods - 27, 45
Contact breaker points - 88
Cooling system
    antifreeze - 53
    draining - 53
    fan belt adjustment - 54
    fault diagnosis - 55
    filling and flushing - 53

radiator - 54
   thermostat - 54
   water pump - 55
Crankcase emission control - 81, 83
Crankshaft and main bearings - 25, 27. 45
Cylinder head - 23, 34, 42

D

Decarbonisation - 29
Diagrams - wiring - 168, 177
Differential - 131
Disc pads - 140
Distributor
   adjusting points - 89
   timing - stroboscope lamp - 94
Doors - 199, 201
Driveshaft (rear axle) - 125
   balance - 127
   dismantling and reassembly - 125
   removal and installation - 125

E

Electrical system
   alternator - 150
   battery - 150
   coil - 95
   fault diagnosis - 166
   horns - 160
   instrument panel meters and gauges - 157
   lamps - 155, 156
   speedometer - 157
   starter motor - 153, 155
   switches - 157
   voltage regulator - 152
   windscreen washer - 160
   windscreen wiper - 158
   wiring diagrams - 168, 177
Engine (Series 1 to 4)
   ancillary components - 25, 21
   big-end bearings - 27
   camshaft - 24, 27
   connecting rods - 27
   crankshaft removal - 25, 27
   cylinder head - 23, 34
   decarbonising - 29
   dismantling - general - 21
   fault diagnosis - 49
   flywheel - 29, 40
   installation - 37
   oil pan - 23, 34
   oil filter - 34
   oil pump - 23, 30, 33
   pistons and rings - 24, 31
   removal - general - 19
   rocker assembly - 29
   tappets - 37
   timing chain, gear and tensioner - 23, 30
   valve clearances and adjustments - 37
   valves and seats - 29
Engine (Series 5 and 6)
   ancillary components - 42
   big-end bearings - 45
   camshaft - 45
   connecting rods - 45
   crankshaft removal - 45
   cylinder head - 42
   decarbonising - 29
   dismantling - general - 42
   fault diagnosis - 49
   flywheel - 40, 46
   installation - 43
   oil pan - 43
   oil pump - 46
   pistons and rings - 45
   removal - general - 42
   rocker assembly - 43

   tappets - 37
   timing gear, chain and tensioner - 45
   valve clearances and adjustments - 49
   valves and seats - 49
Evaporative emission control - 83
Exhaust gas recirculation - 77
Exhaust systems - 83

F

Fan belt adjustment - 54
Fault diagnosis
   automatic transmission - 124
   braking system - 146
   clutch - 102
   cooling system - 55
   electrical system - 166
   engine - 49
   fuel system - 83, 84
   ignition - 95
   manual gearbox - 124
   rear axle - 132
   suspension and steering - 196
Filters
   air - 59
   fuel - 73
   oil - 34
Flexible coupling - 191
Flywheel - 29, 40, 46
Fuel and exhaust systems
   accelerator cable - 76
   air cleaner - 59
   air injection system - 73
   carburetors - 60, 64, 65
   choke - 69
   exhaust systems - 83
   fault diagnosis - 83, 84
   fuel evaporative emission control system - 83
   fuel tank - 70
   fuel pump - 69, 70
Fuses and fusible link - 155

G

Gearbox - manual
   dismantling - 105, 108, 111
   fault diagnosis - 124
   removal - 105
   reassembly - 114, 117, 119
   steering column linkage - 191
Glass
   door - 204
   ventilator window - 204
   windshield - 204, 205
Glossary - 7
Gudgeon (piston) pin - removal - 25, 31, 45

H

Halfshafts - 125, 127
Handbrake - 136
Hazard warning switch - 161
Headlamp units - 155
Heater - 161 - 163
   controls - 163
   control cable - 163
Hood (bonnet) - 208
Horn - 160
Hydraulic systems
   bleeding brakes - 136
   bleeding clutch - 98

I

Identification numbers - 4
Ignition system
   coil - 95
   condenser - 88
   contact breaker - 88

distributor - 89
dwell angle - checking - 93
fault diaghosis - 95
general description - 86
igniter - 95
routine maintenance - 86
spark plugs and HT leads - 95
switch - 157
timing (mechanical type) - 94
Instrument panel - 157

J

Jacking and towing points - 12

K

Kickdown switch - 123

L

Leads HT - 95
Lighting system
bulb renewal - 156, 157
headlamps - 155, 156
switches - 157
Locks - door - 201
Lubrication chart - 8
Lubrication system - 25, 45

M

Main bearings - 27, 45
Mainshaft dismantling - 110
Maintenance - routine - 9
Major operations - engine in vehicle - 21
Manifolds - 43
Manual transmission - 104
Master cylinder - brake - 136, 137
Master cylinder - clutch - 99
Metric conversion tables - 209, 210

O

Oil filter - 34
Oil pan - 23, 34, 43
Oil pump - 23, 30, 33, 46
Ordering spare parts - 4

P

Parking brake - 136, 145
Piston and rings - 24, 31, 45
Propeller shafts
removal and installation - 125
universal joint - 125
Pump
air - 73
fuel - 69, 70
oil - 23, 30, 33, 46
water - 55

R

Radiator
anti-freeze - 53
draining - filling - flushing - 53
removal - 53
Radio installation - 161
Rear axle
axle shaft - 129
differential - 131
fault diagnosis - 132
general description - 129
housing - removal and installation - 131
removal and installation - 129
Rings - piston - 24, 31, 45
Routine maintenance - 9

S

Shock absorbers - 186
Spark plugs and HT leads - 95

Specifications technical
automatic transmission - 120
bodywork and fittings - 197
braking system - 133, 134
carburation, fuel and emission control system - 56, 57
clutch - 97, 98
cooling system - 52
driveshaft - 125
electrical system - 147, 148, 149
engine - 16, 39
gearbox
automatic - 121
manual - 104
ignition system - 85, 86
manual transmission - 103, 104
rear axle - 128
suspension and steering - 178, 179, 180
starter motor - 153
Speedometer cables - 157
Steering and suspension
balljoints - 187, 189
fault diagnosis - 196
front hubs - 181
front wheel alignment - 216
front wheel bearings - 181
idler arm - 191
pitman shaft seal - 194
rear spring - 196
road wheels and tyres - 216
shock absorbers - 186
stabilizer bar - 186
steering angles - 181, 183
steering gear - 189, 192
steering linkage - 190
steering shaft - 191
steering wheel - 190
torsion bar spring - 185, 189
Strust bar - 186, 187
Sump - see oil pan
Switches - 157

T

Technical specifications - See Specifications
Thermostat - 165
Timing - ignition - 85
Tools and working facilities -14
Transmission
Series 1 to 6 - removal - 105
cleaning and inspection - 113

U

Universal joints - 125
Upholstery - 198

V

Valve
clearances - 37, 49
grinding - 37
seats - 37
Voltage regulator - 152

W

Water pump - 55
Wheel bearings
front - 181
rear - 130
Windshield
glass - 204, 205
wiper blades and arms - 160
wiper motor - 160
washer - 160
Wiring diagrams - 168, 177